AF614811

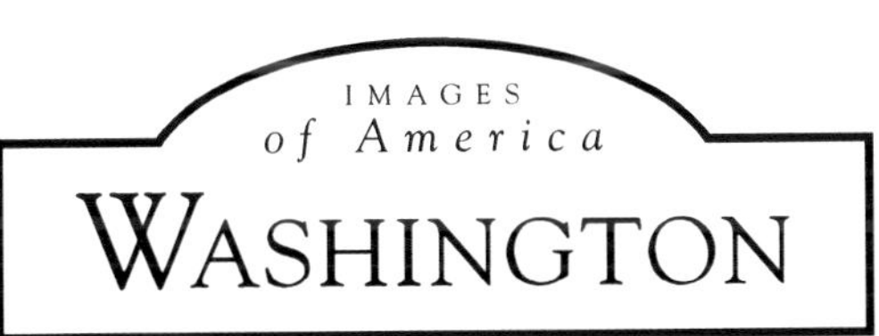
IMAGES
of America
WASHINGTON

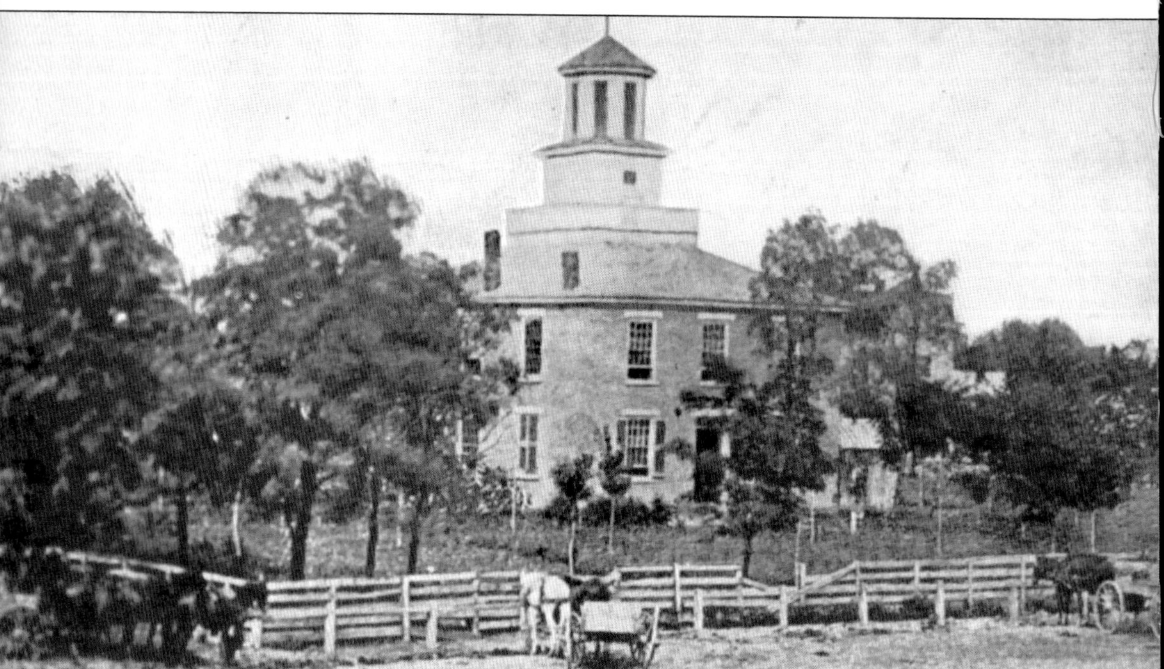

On July 8, 1839, the City of Washington became the county seat of the newly formed Washington County, Iowa. The first courthouse, completed in July 1841, was erected on the southwest corner of the square. Offices occupied the first floor and the courtroom on the second. The second courthouse, pictured here, was located in the middle of what is now Central Park. It was completed in 1847 and remained in use until 1869. This photograph predates the 1866 removal of the cupola. In addition to housing the county offices and courtroom, the building served as a church, school, and public meeting hall.

On the Cover: This image conveys the Troop F, 113th Cavalry Regiment moving along the north side of the square during a Fourth of July parade in Washington.

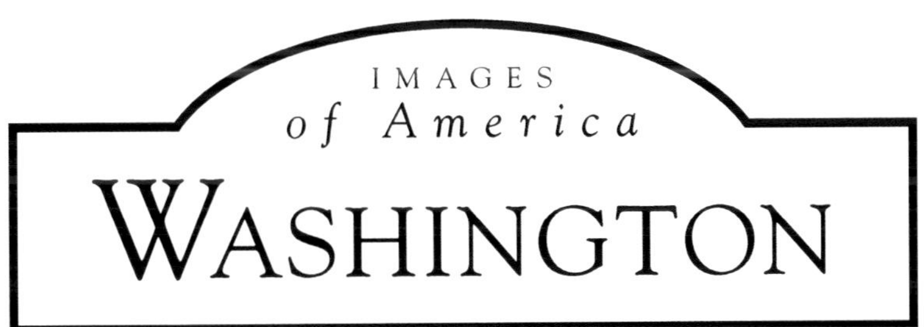

Michael Kramme

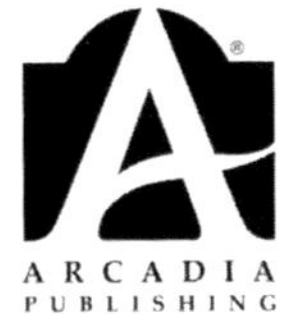

ISBN 978-1-4671-1002-0

Published by Arcadia Publishing
Charleston, South Carolina

Printed in the United States of America

Library of Congress Control Number: 2012955605

For all general information, please contact Arcadia Publishing:
Telephone 843-853-2070
Fax 843-853-0044
E-mail sales@arcadiapublishing.com
For customer service and orders:
Toll-Free 1-888-313-2665

Visit us on the Internet at www.arcadiapublishing.com

To Washington historians Howard Burrell, Edna Jones,
Chuck Hotle, Kathy Fisher, and Mike Zahs

Contents

Acknowledgments

I wish to thank my fellow society board members—Mary Levy, Carlton Mangold, Ferd Marie, Terry O'Neill, Shirley Pfieffer, and Mike Zahs—for allowing the use of the images. Additional images were provided by Lori Bauer, Jeff Batterson, Tom Dawson, Mary Levy, Jim Logan, Mary Patterson, and Mike Zahs.

I also wish to thank Terry O'Neill, for help preparing the images, and Winnie Rodgers and Katie Toussaint, my editors at Arcadia Publishing.

Unless otherwise noted, the images in this book appear courtesy of the Washington County Historical Society.

INTRODUCTION

The Office of the State Archeologist records 473 prehistoric sites in Washington County. Artifacts have been found in the county that date to between 7000 and 3000 BC. In more recent history, the area is known to have been inhabited by Native American tribes that include the Ioway, their close relatives the Oto and the Missouria, the Sauk, and the Meskwaki.

The land that now makes up Iowa was part of the 1803 Louisiana Purchase. It was ceded to the United States under four Indian treaties, the first of which was signed on September 1, 1832. From 1834 to 1836, it was attached to the Michigan Territory, and from 1836 to 1838 it was part of the Wisconsin Territory. It became part of the Iowa Territory in 1838. White settlement began in 1835, and the land was surveyed in 1837.

Washington County was first named Slaughter County for William B. Slaughter, who was named secretary of Wisconsin Territory by Pres. Andrew Jackson. The county's first settler of European descent was Adam Richey, who first arrived in 1835 but soon returned to his home in Illinois. He came back to settle permanently in Iowa in 1836, and others soon followed.

On January 25, 1839, the county's name was changed to Washington, and its boundaries were set. The first court was held on May 7, 1839, in the small village of Astoria, south of present-day Ainsworth. In June 1839, the town of Washington became the county seat. By 1838, the town's population grew to 282, and by 1840 the county's population was 1,594.

The first courthouse, located on the southwest corner of the square, opened on July 8, 1841. It also served as a church, school, and public meeting hall. The second courthouse, located in the center of the public square, opened on July 4, 1847. In 1887, the courtroom and offices moved temporarily to the Masonic Lodge in the old Everson's Opera House while the third, and present, courthouse was built. The second courthouse was demolished in November 1869.

The first known newspaper was the handwritten *Domestic Quarterly Review*. The only surviving issue is from April 1, 1844. The first regular newspaper, the *Argus*, began publication in 1854, and on April 9, 1856, the first issue of the *Washington Weekly Press* appeared. Later, other newspapers emerged, including the first daily paper, *The Daily Hustler*, which would evolve into the present-day *Washington Evening Journal*.

The May 20, 1857, issue of the *Washington Weekly Press* listed the population as 2,000. Town businesses included nine dry-goods stores, two clothing shops, one millinery, two hardware stores, two drugstores, one bookstore, two boot-and-shoe stores, seven groceries, and three furniture stores. There were also five churches, four taverns, a bakery, a sash-and-door shop, three cabinet shops, a boiler factory with a foundry and machine shop, a mitten factory, three stove and tinwork shops, a flour mill, and a carding and fulling mill (that prepared wool for fabric-making purposes). Professionals in town included four blacksmiths, two tailors, 8 to 10 ministers, six or seven lawyers, and eight doctors.

A major celebration was held to welcome the first railroad to Washington. The Mississippi & Missouri Railroad, later absorbed by the Rock Island Railroad, arrived on September 1, 1858. The town's population increased rapidly for the 12 years because it was the Mississippi & Missouri terminus. During this time, the town was so busy that stores were open 24 hours, seven days a week. The Muscatine & Western Railroad arrived in 1873, and the Burlington & Western followed in 1880.

The first Washington Academy came into being in 1854 and only lasted one year. It was replaced by Washington College, which began classes in 1855 and continued until 1864, when it was merged with Monmouth College. The second Washington Academy was incorporated in 1872.

During the Civil War, Washington County furnished 23 staff and field officers, 32 captains, and 84 lieutenants. Over 400 local men and boys died in battle or of wounds and disease.

Washington has had a variety of factories, producing goods that have included cigars, corncob pipes, banana crates, organs, greeting cards, bridge score pads, jigsaw puzzles, mittens, and buggies. The American Pearl Button factory began operation in 1908 and employed over 230 people by 1936. Hugh McCleery started his calendar factory in 1903, and at its peak in the 1970s it employed over 350 workers. Several other industries located to the town, including Northrup King (now Syngenta), the largest processor of farm seed in the nation.

In 1912, Washington opened the first tax-supported rural hospital building. The structure was in the National Register of Historic Places until its demolition in 2006. The YMCA building opened in 1924, making Washington one of the nation's smallest communities to have its own Y.

Washington's population in the 2010 census was 7,266. It has been listed several times in *The 100 Best Small Towns in America*, and in 2008 it was designated an Iowa Main Street town.

One

The Early Years

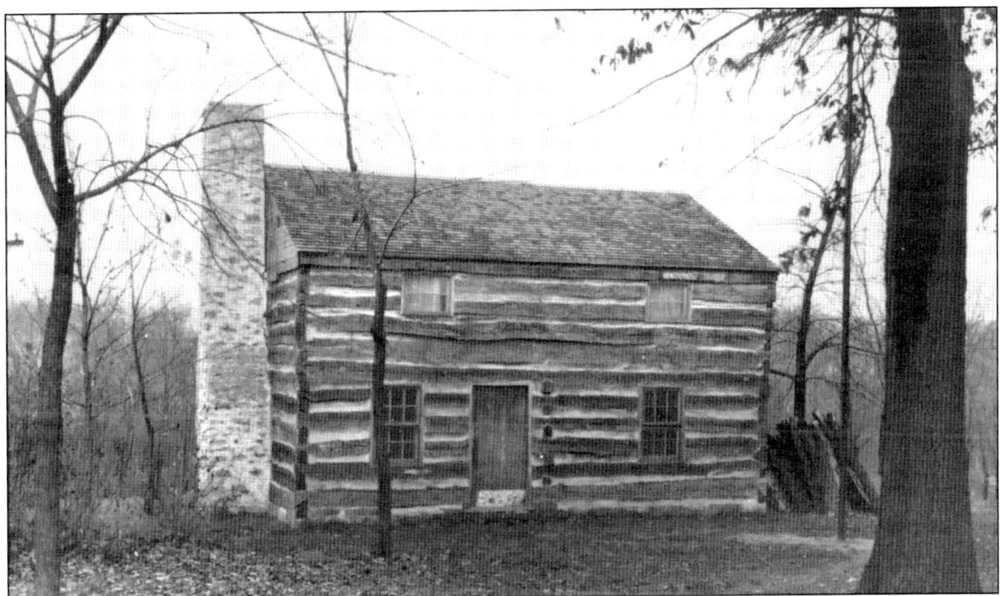

Alexander Young served in the War of 1812. A native of Pennsylvania, he moved from Rush County, Indiana, to Washington County in 1839. He built a log house on land he had settled in Cedar Township. The building is 26 feet by 20 feet and one and a half stories, and its one-room first floor served as a combination living room, dining room, and kitchen. One room on the upper story served as the sleeping area. *Washington Democrat* editor Alex Miller headed a fundraising drive to relocate the structure to its present location in Sunset Park. The move took place in 1912, and the building, now maintained by the Washington chapter of the Daughters of the American Revolution, is open to visitors on Sunday afternoons during the summer as well as by appointment.

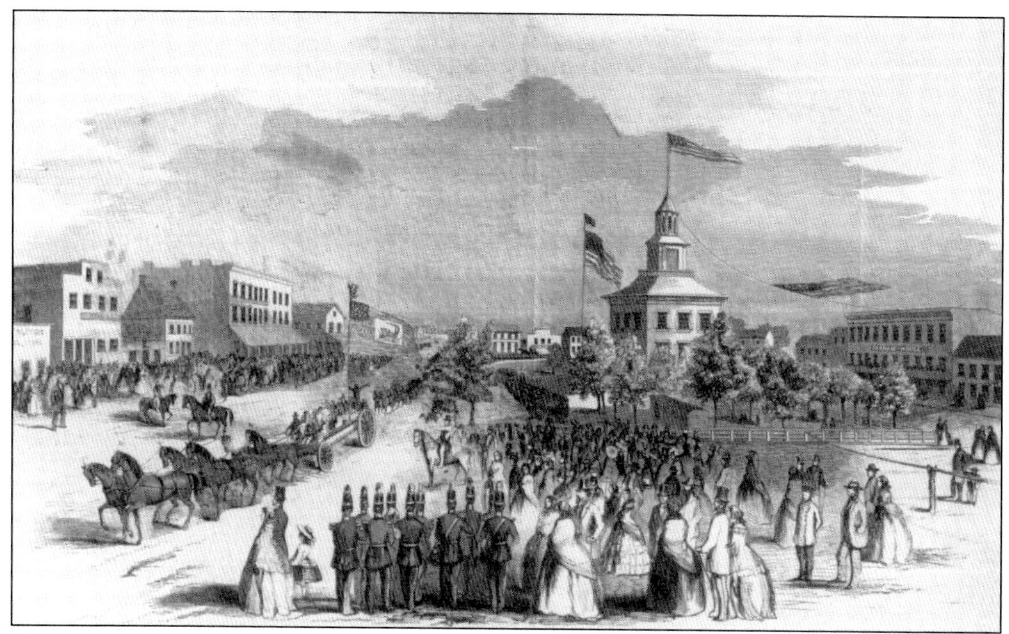

Plans to connect every county seat in the state by railroad began in the early 1850s; however, the first tracks were not laid in Washington County until 1858. This engraving, which appeared in the November 13, 1858, issue of *Frank Leslie's Illustrated Newspaper*, shows the celebration for the arrival of the Mississippi & Missouri Railroad on September 1, 1858.

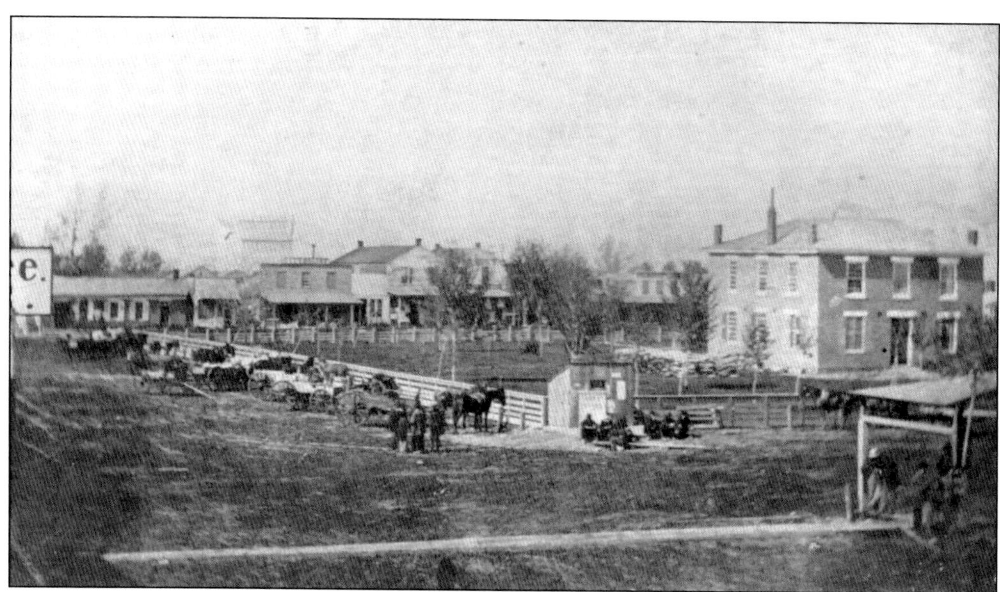

This photograph of the second courthouse was taken sometime between 1866, when the cupola was removed, and 1869, when the building was demolished. In the background is the north side of the square. None of the buildings pictured still exist.

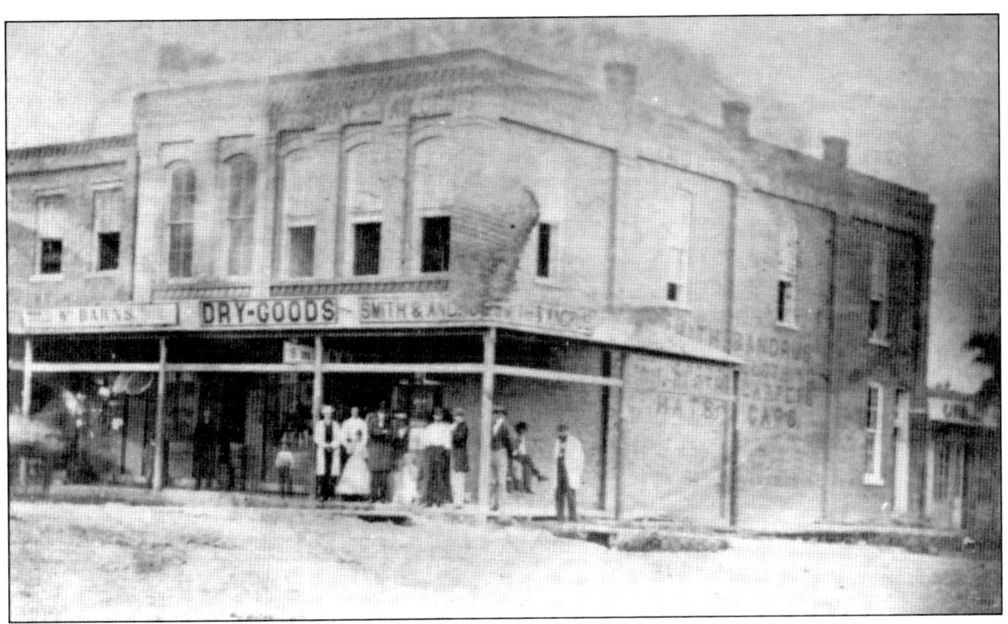

This building is one of the oldest on the square, standing on its southwest corner. For many years, citizens referred to it as "Yellow Brick." The Smith & Andrus Dry Goods store occupied the main floor at the time of this photograph.

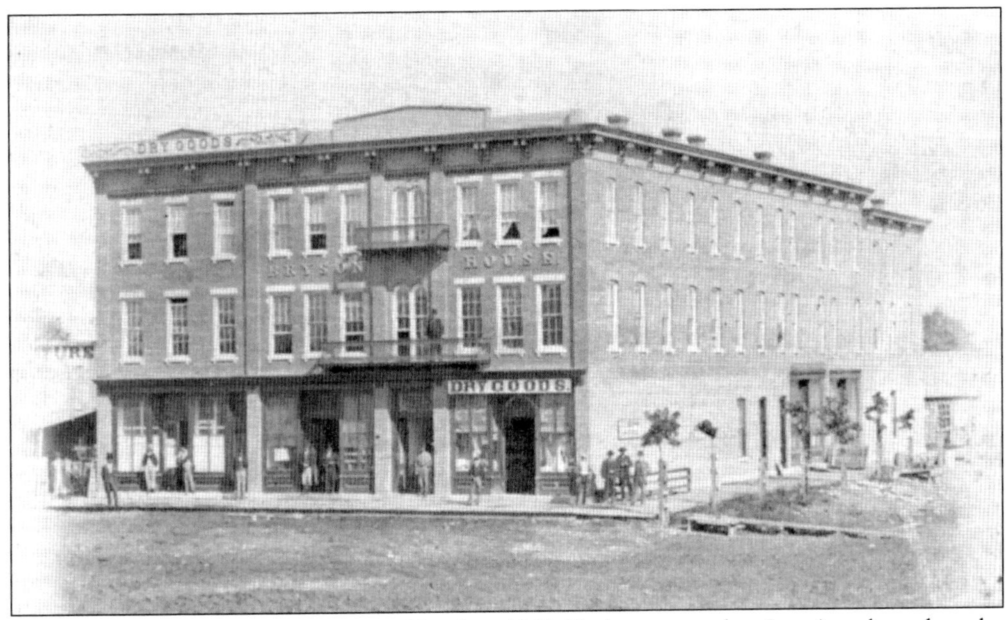

John Bryson built the Bryson House Hotel in 1867. He later moved to Los Angeles, where he served as mayor. The hotel, renamed Hotel Allen by 1891 and the Colenso Hotel around 1900, is one of the oldest buildings remaining in the business district. Its upper floors were closed in 1938, although the lower floor continues to house businesses.

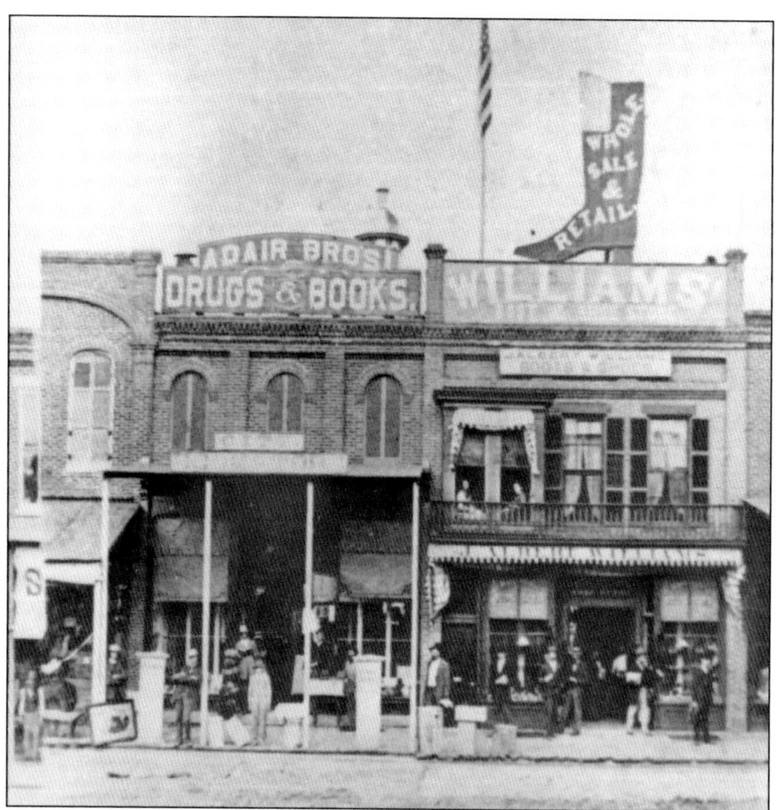

This copy of a stereopticon slide shows part of the east side of the square in the 1870s. The building on the left housed Adair Brothers Drugs & Books. The building on the right, with the large boot sign, housed J. Albert Williams Boot & Shoe Store and is the current location of Brown's Shoe Fit Company. The building has housed a shoe store continuously for over 150 years.

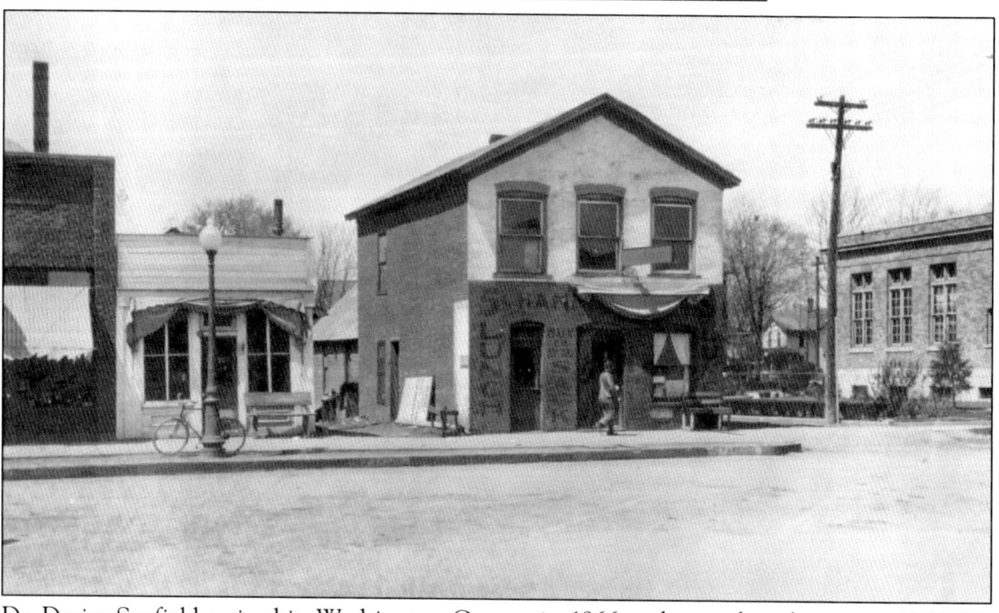

Dr. Darius Scofield arrived in Washington County in 1866 and moved to the city in 1869. He practiced medicine there from 1869 until the 1890s. His office building, seen on the right, later housed a bakery and a restaurant; it is pictured advertising 5¢ hamburgers. For many years, the small structure to the left housed Mott's Barbershop. Both buildings were razed in 1932 for the construction of the *Washington Evening Journal* building.

Norman Everson (1815–1896) was a pioneer Washington businessman. He began his career as a lawyer but soon transitioned into banking. In 1857, he established Washington's first bank. He also built and operated the city's first gas and electric works and built Everson's Opera House. He served as mayor and as a two-term state senator.

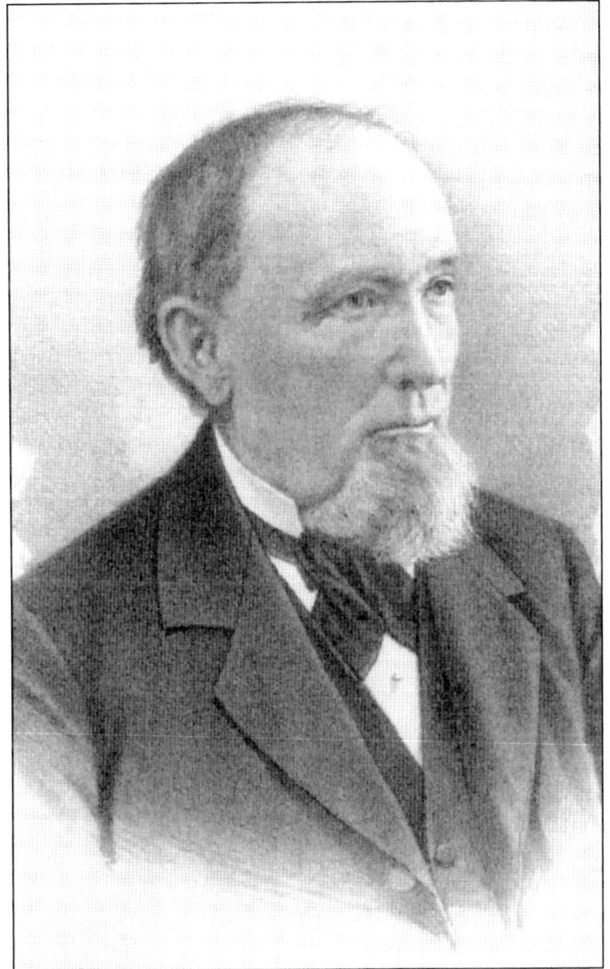

Everson's Opera House, built in 1868, was on the west end of the north side of the square, where the Masonic Lodge is now located. It had stores on the first floor, offices on the second, and the opera house on the third. It housed court offices from 1869 until 1887 while the current courthouse was being built. In 1896, the building became home to the Washington Masonic Lodge. It was destroyed by fire on January 19, 1930.

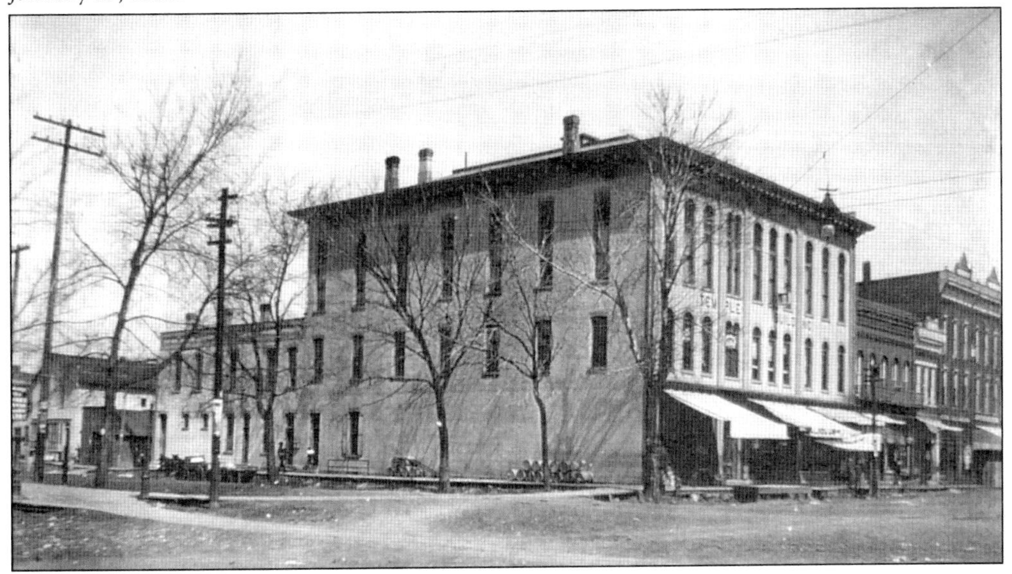

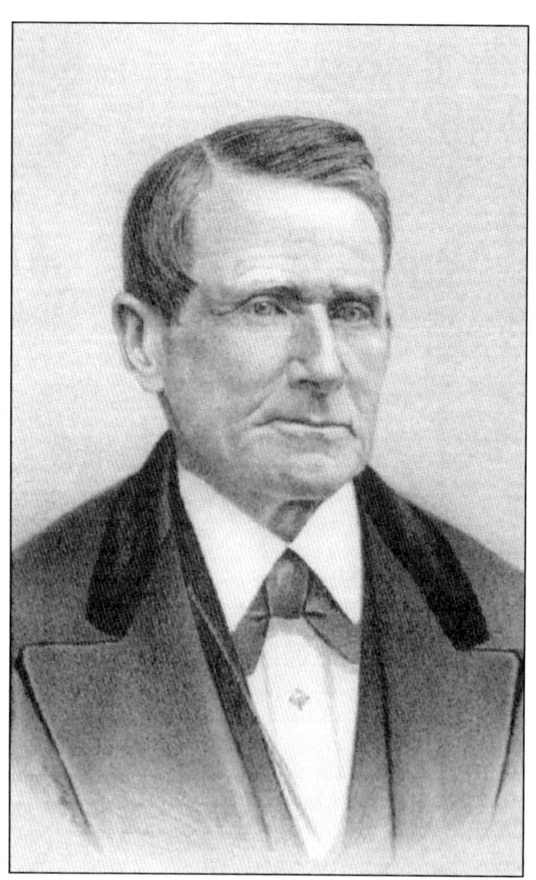

John Graham, the county's first millionaire, arrived in Washington in 1839. He bought 400 acres of land near Brighton in 1839 and at one time owned over 15,000 acres in and around Washington County. He built the first Graham Opera House in 1886 and was a major contributor to the second Graham Opera House—now the State Theater—which was built in 1893.

The first Graham Opera House, built in 1886, was destroyed by a fire in 1892. It was on the southeast corner of the square and housed stores on the first floor and the opera house on the second and third floors. (Courtesy of Tom Dawson.)

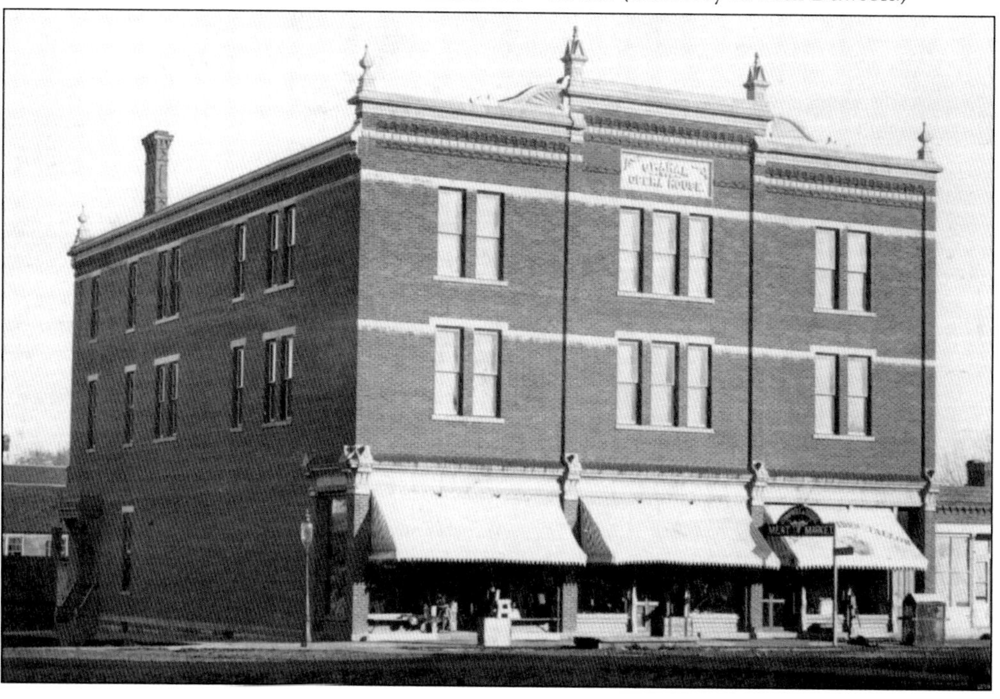

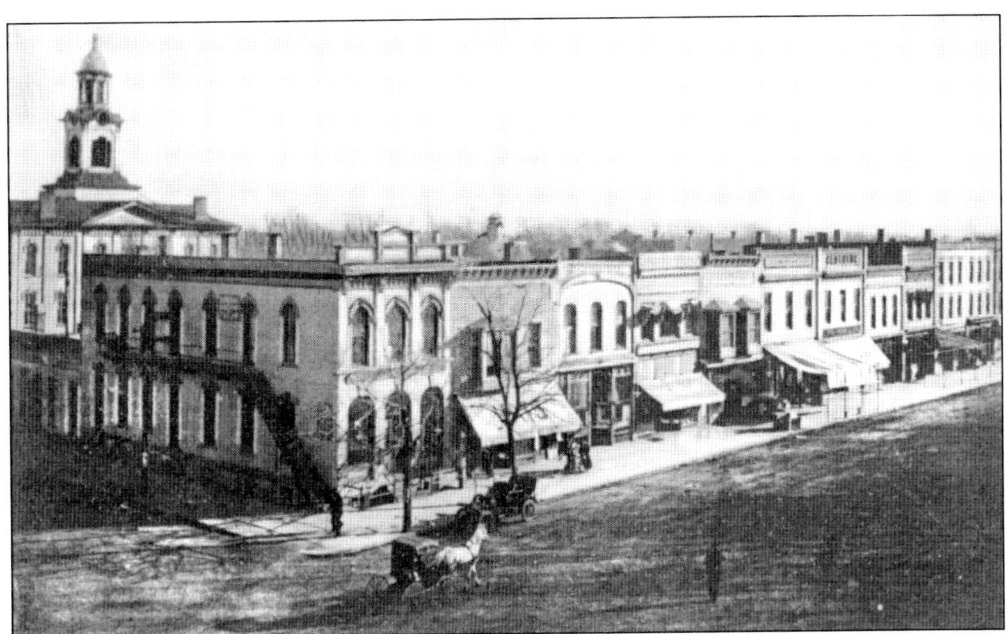

This view of the east side of the square dates to around 1900. The cupola of the Washington Academy can be seen on the left. (Courtesy of Tom Dawson.)

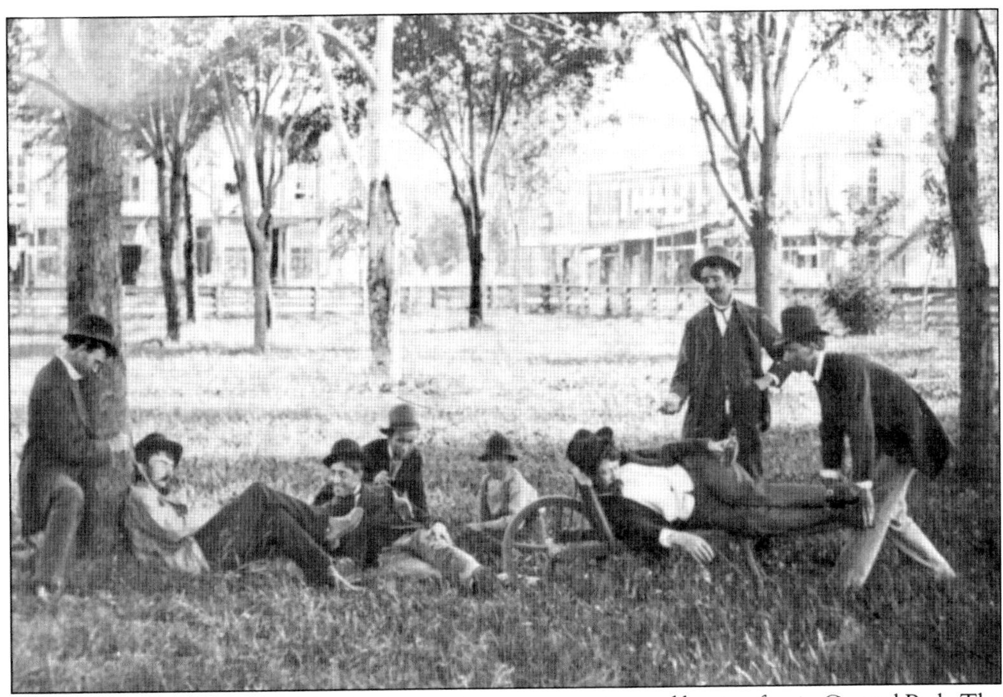

Copied from a stereopticon slide, this image shows men resting and having fun in Central Park. The wood fence surrounding the grounds kept horses and other livestock from grazing in the park.

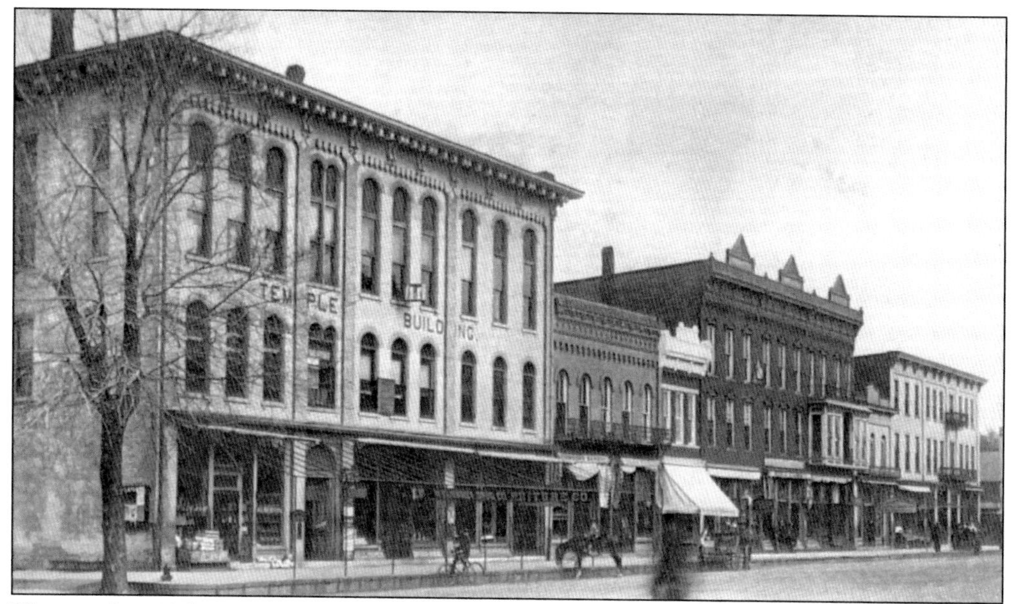

This is a late-19th-century view of the north side of the square. Everson's Opera House (later named the Masonic Building) dominates the western side, and the Bryson House (later the Colenso Hotel) dominates the eastern side. All of the buildings, with the exception of Everson's, remain today.

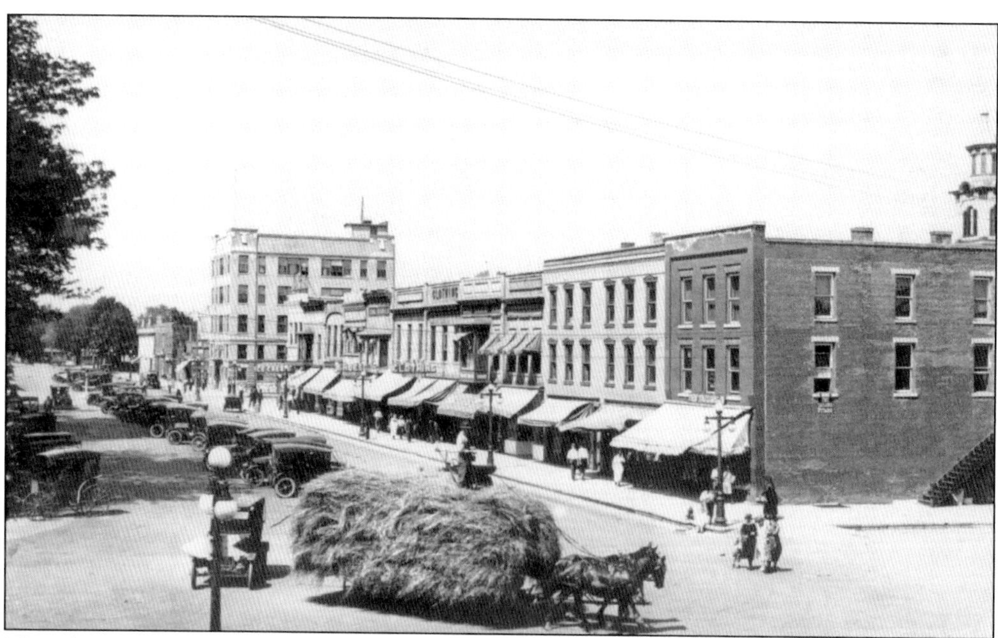

This photograph of the east side of the square is from 1919. The tallest building in the county—the Farmers & Merchants Bank building, also known as the Bailey Building—is visible on the far left, and the cupola of the Washington Academy can be seen on the far right. All of the buildings on the east side remain today.

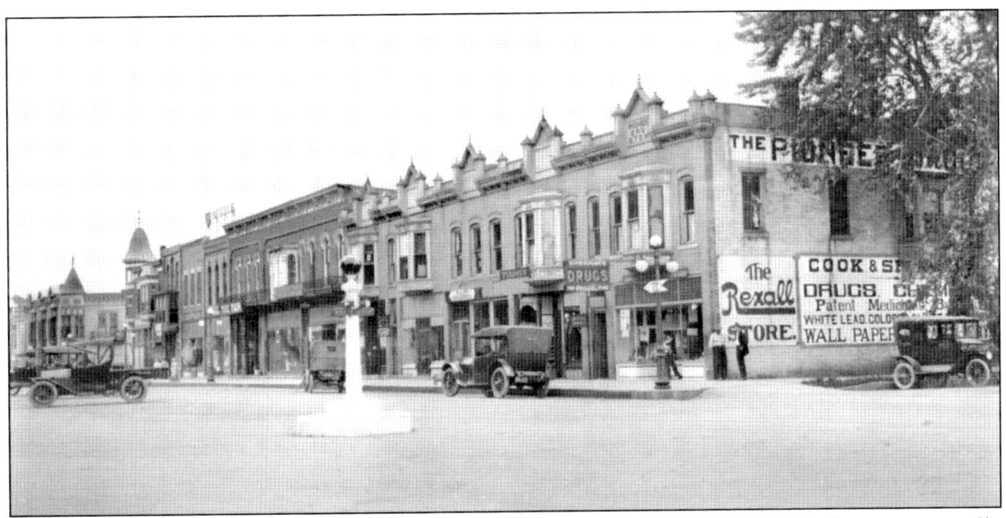

This is the south side of the square as it appeared in 1919. The building on the right was originally the Pioneer Drug Store, as can be seen on the signage at the top center and side. At the time this photograph was taken, the Cook & Sherman Drug Store occupied the space. The building at the east end housed Klein Klothing Ko. for many years.

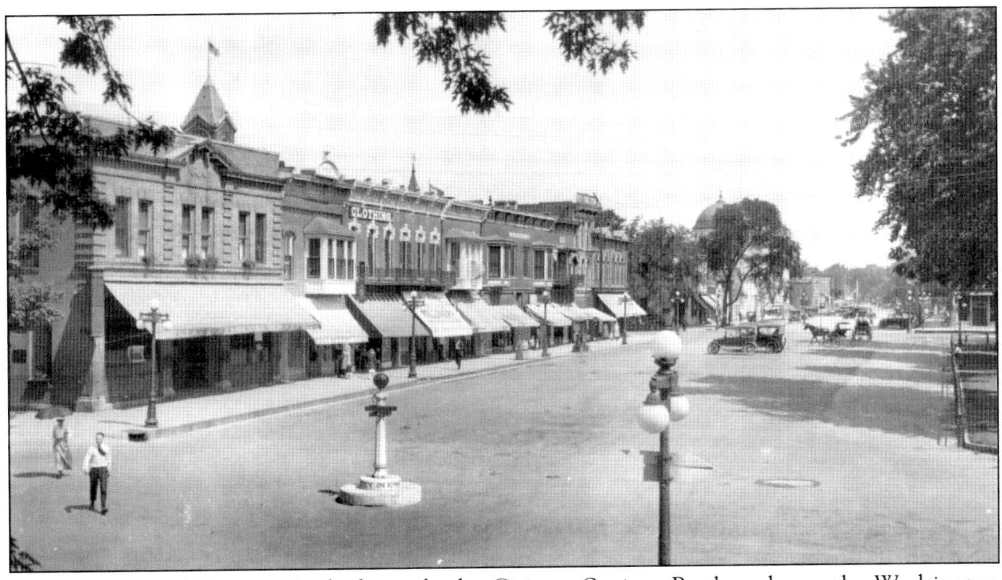

The Commercial Savings Bank, formerly the Citizens Savings Bank and now the Washington State Bank, is at the south end of west side of the square in this 1919 photograph. The original building has been greatly remodeled. At the north end is J.B. Crail's dry-goods store, which later housed J.C. Penney for many years. Behind the buildings are the courthouse clock tower (left), the top of the old city hall (center), and the Methodist church (right).

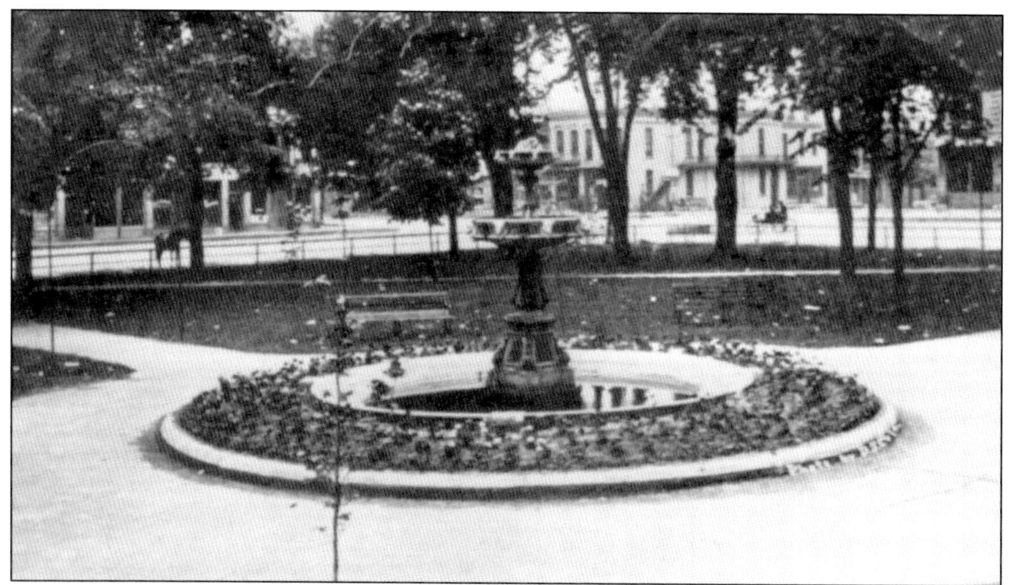

This fountain is the first, or perhaps the second, to be erected in Central Park. Made of iron, it was installed in 1895 and was replaced by the Centennial Fountain in 1939. In this southwestern view, the earlier wooden fence that had been erected to keep livestock out of the park has been replaced by iron hitching rail for horses.

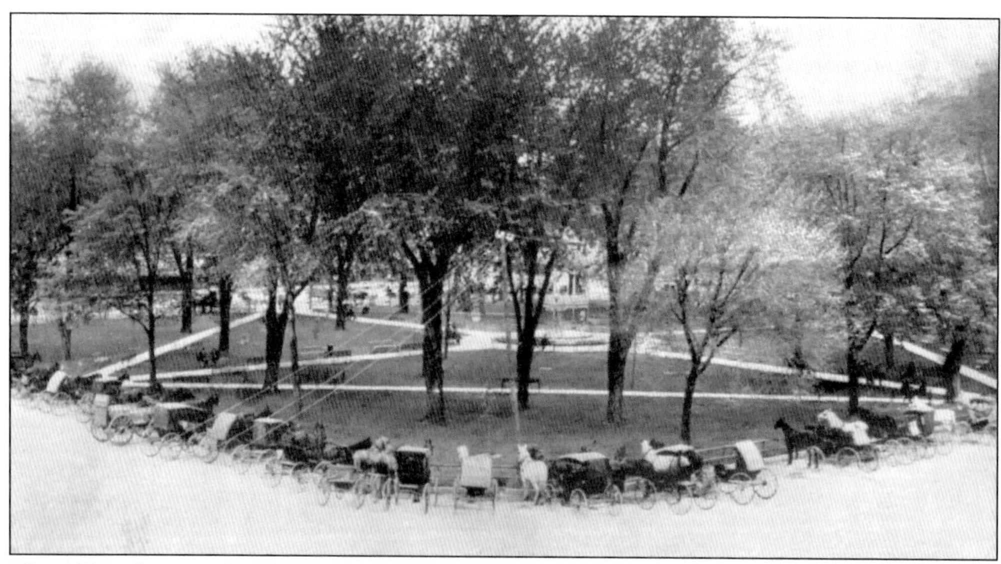

This 1890s photograph of horses and buggies in Central Park is looking to the north. In the center of the square is the 1895 fountain, and beyond it is the first bandstand. An early telephone pole and wires are in the lower center.

Two

Business and Industry

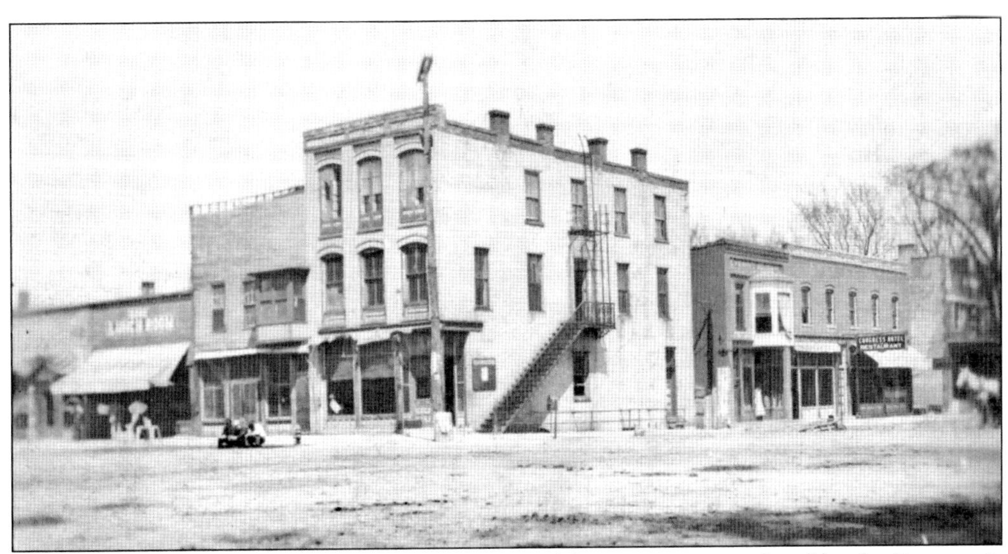

The Civic Hotel, located on the northeast corner of the square, was replaced by the Farmers & Merchants Bank building in 1912. It is currently the site of Federation Bank.

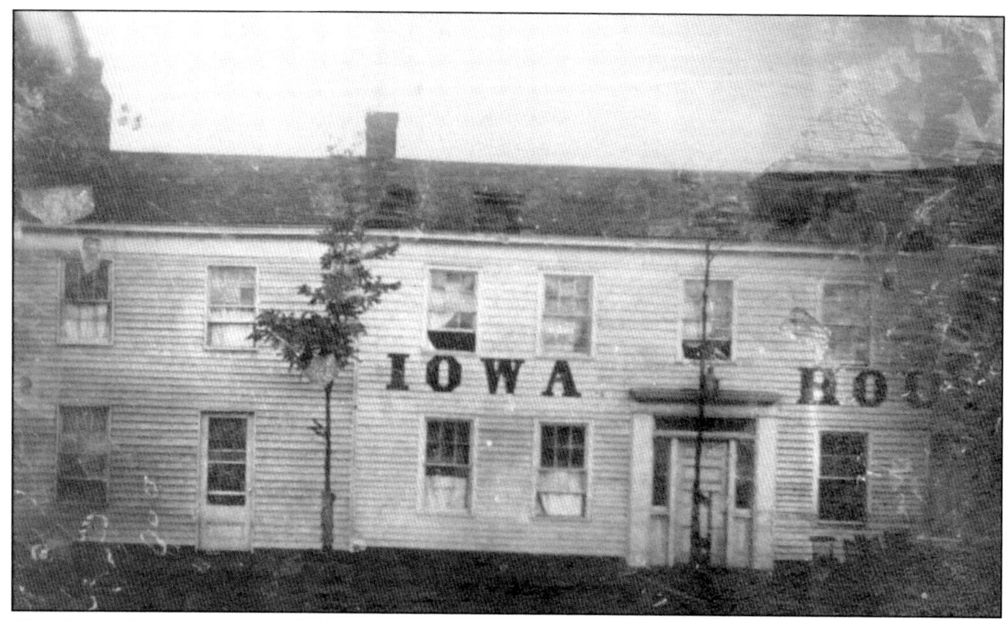

The Iowa House was one of the city's first hotels. Located on the north end of the west side of the square, it was moved to the corner of West Third Street and North Avenue B in 1876 and later became a private residence.

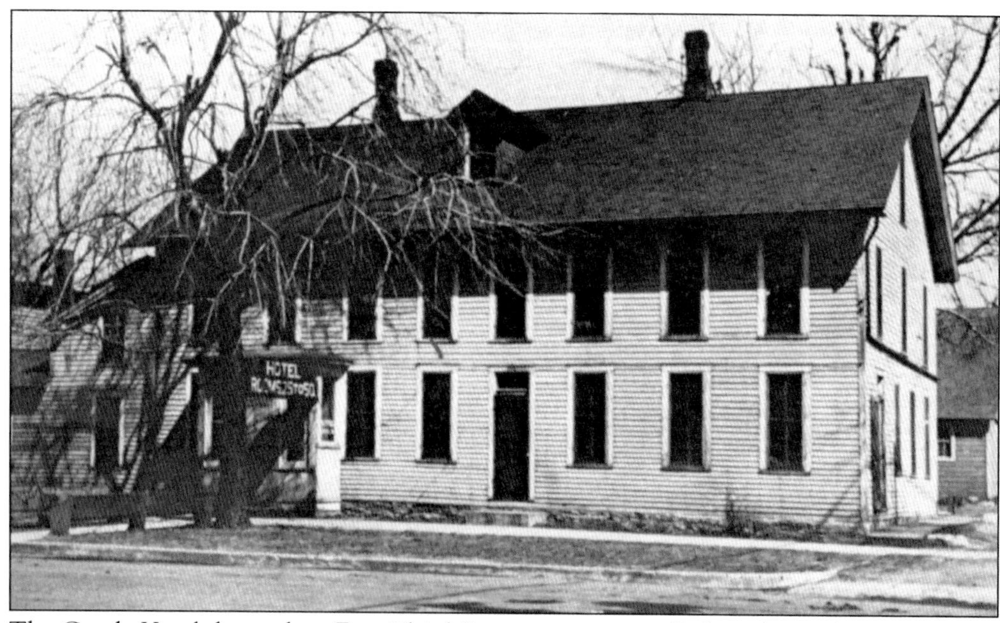

The Goode Hotel, located on East Third Street, may originally have been the Washington House. The Washington House advertised in local papers from 1856 until 1862. The building is believed to have been moved to the site on East Third from an original location at the northeast corner of the square.

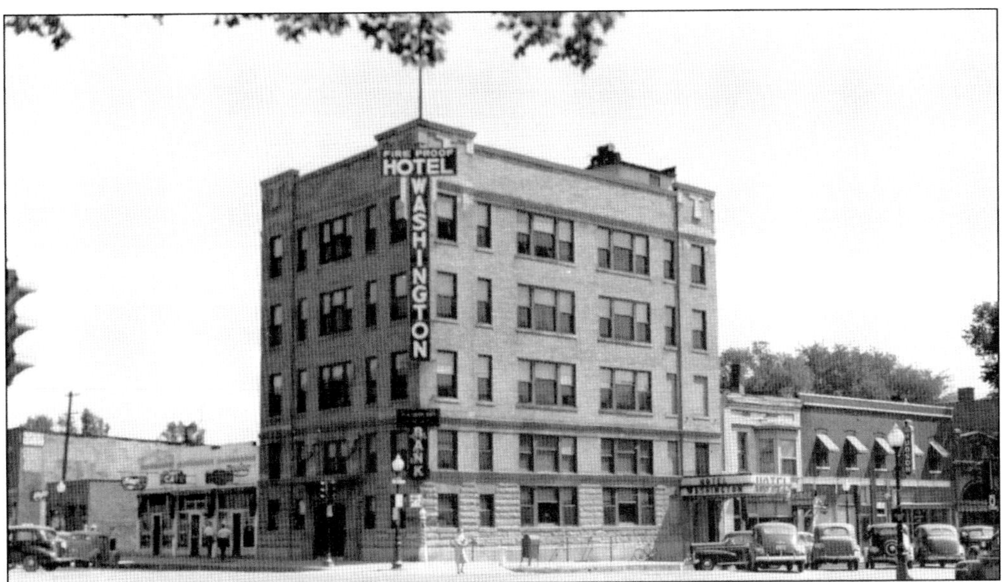

The Hotel Washington was located in the upper floors of the Farmers & Merchants Bank on the northeast corner of the square. Before it was remodeled into a hotel, the space originally housed offices. In 2009, it was converted back into offices.

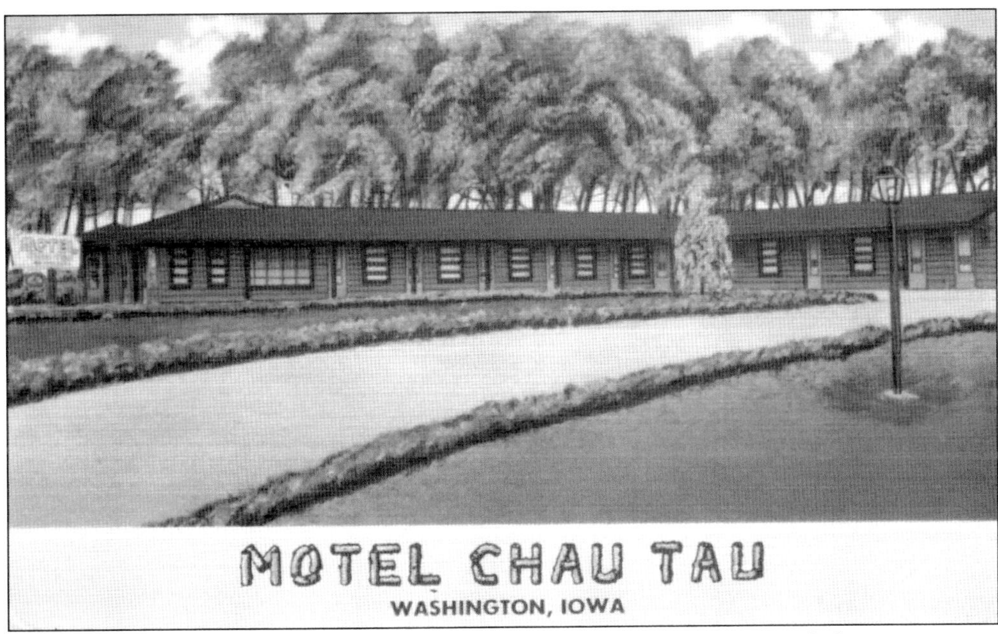

The Chau Tau Motel was on land just to the west of the Chautauqua grounds, hence its name. The Chautauqua grounds are now the site of the Washington County Fairgrounds. The Chau Tau was one of the city's first motels. (Courtesy of Tom Dawson.)

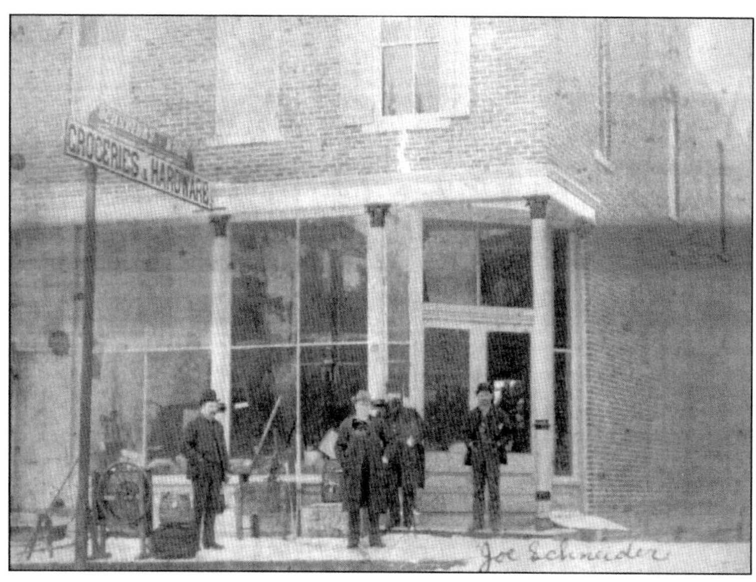

The Schneider brothers owned a grocery and hardware store at 109 East Washington Street in the 1890s. George Schneider is on the left, and Joe Schneider is on the right. At the time of this photograph, Washington still had board sidewalks, and Dr. Eiskamp had an office upstairs in the building.

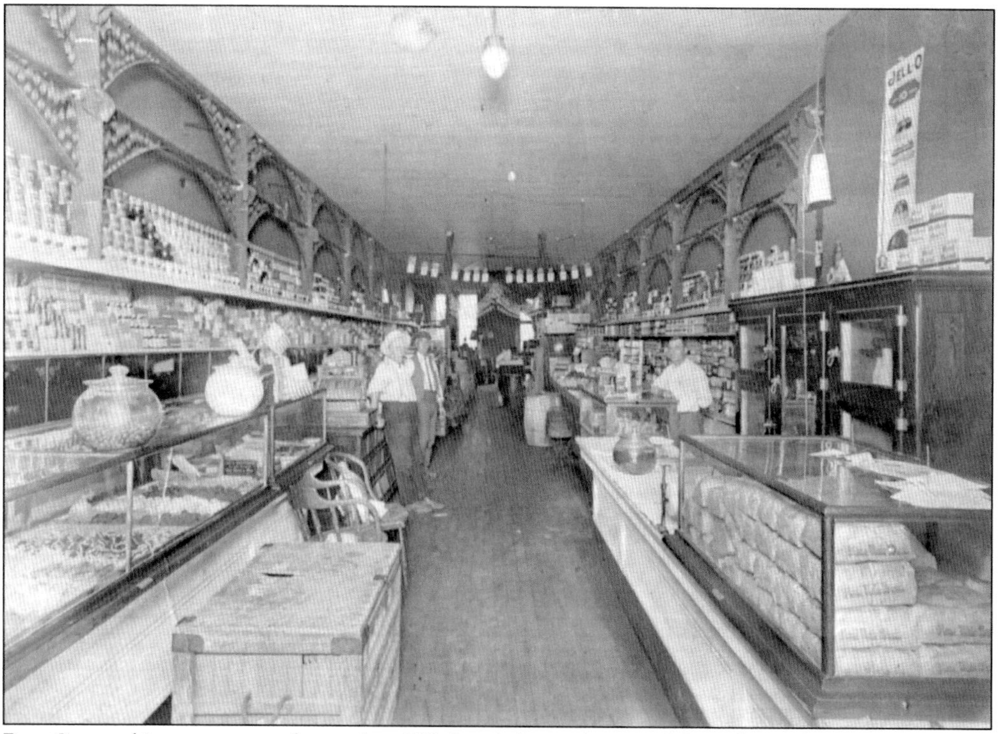

Ben Coppock's grocery was located at 202 South Iowa Avenue. Note the iceboxes on the right and the electrical ceiling fixtures. The photograph was taken after 1891, when electricity became available via the Washington Illuminating Company. (Courtesy of Mary Patterson.)

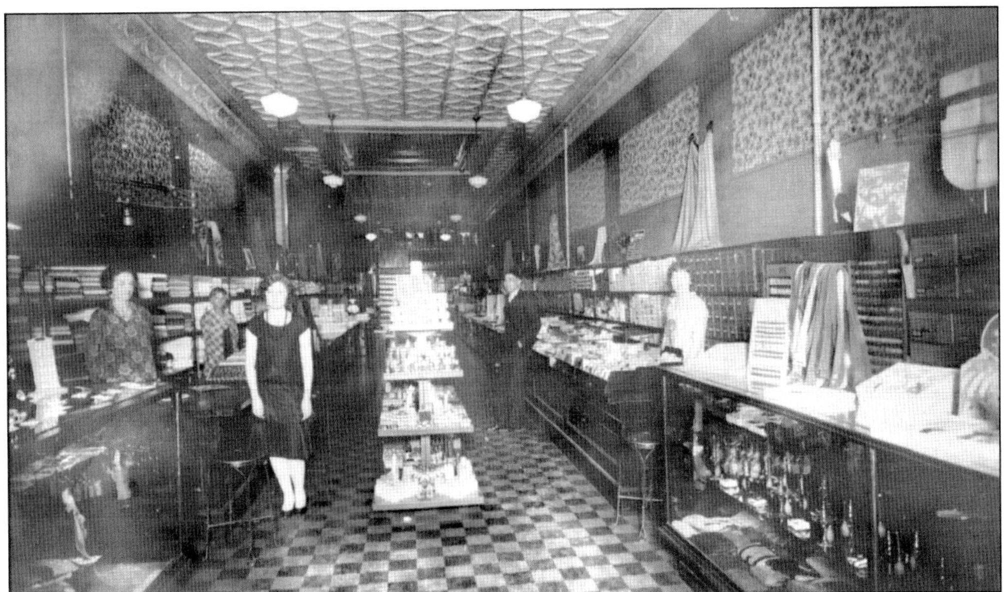

The Harry I. Ward Store was located at 106 South Iowa and remained in operation until the mid-1930s. In the photograph are, from left to right, clerks Loretta Wheelan, Edith Farris, "Dump" Dixon, Harry Ward, and June Arnold Ward.

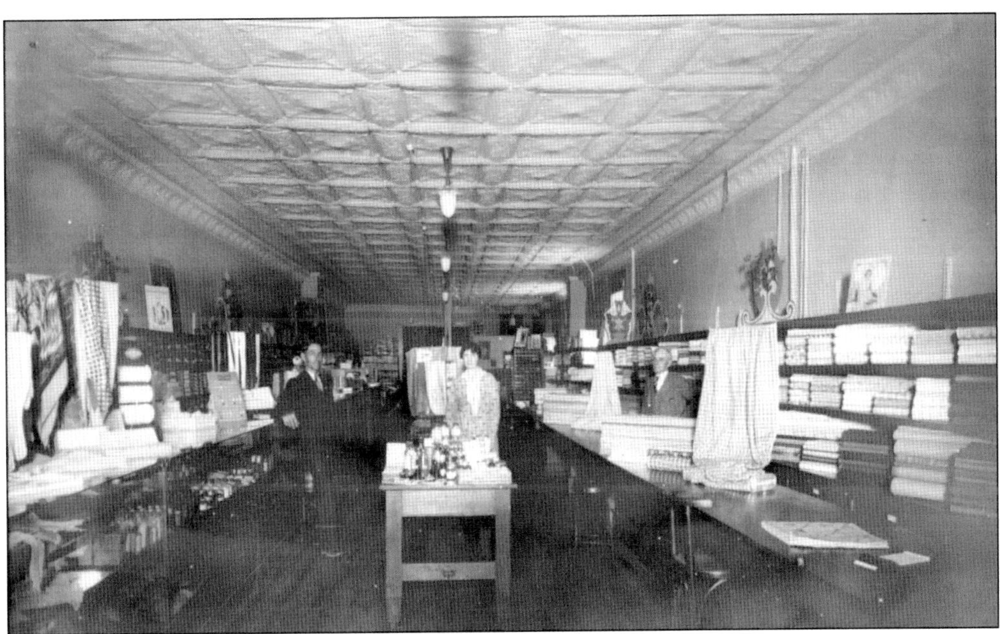

William Blair operated the Blair Store, located at the southeast corner of the square (122 South Iowa Avenue), from 1881 until 1910, when it was purchased by George Ward. Pictured here are Hallie Ward and her father, George Ward. George and Harry Ward were brothers, both in the dry-good business.

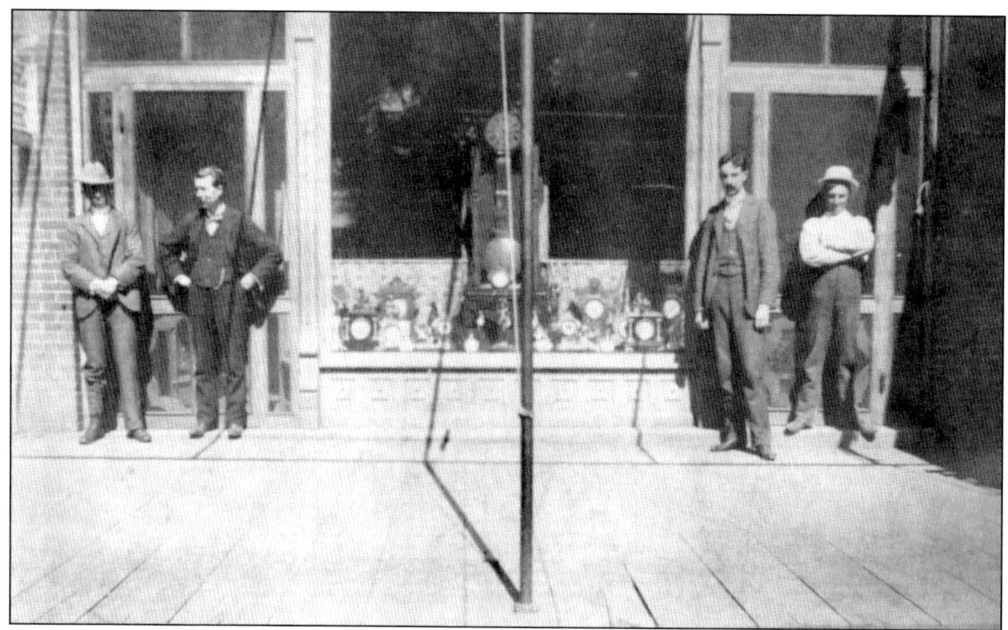

L.D. Robinson (second from left) and C.S. Lemmon (third from left) are pictured with two unidentified men outside L.D. Robinson Jewelers in 1898. A jewelry store has occupied 116 South Iowa since the 1890s, with businesses including Robinson (established in 1892), Lemmon & Lewis (1900), Lemmon (1925), Lemmon & Logan (1957), Logan's (1963), and the current Don's Jewelry. (Courtesy of Jim Logan.)

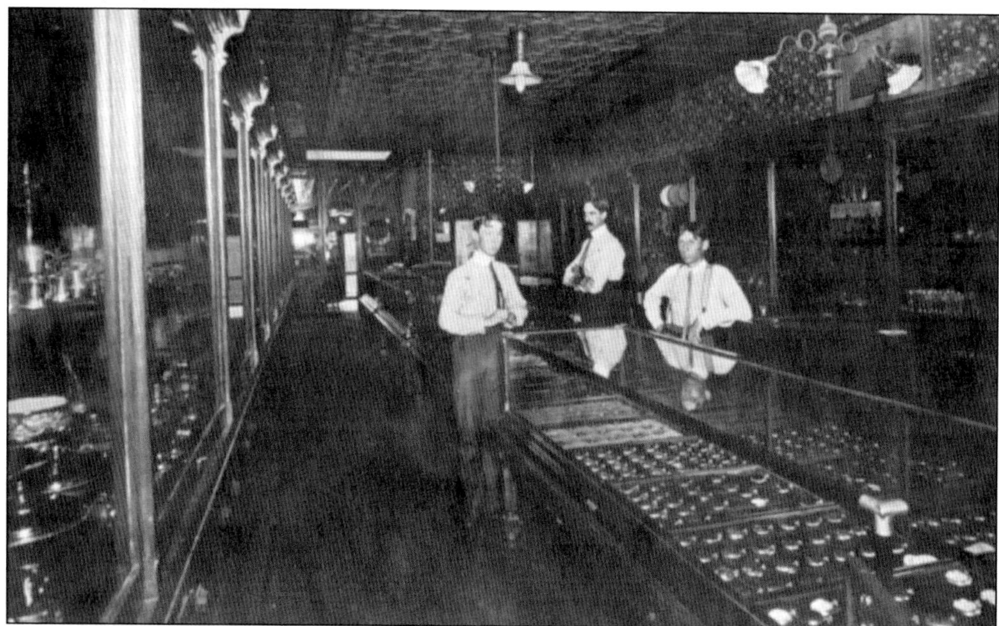

This photograph shows the interior of Lemmon & Lewis Jewelers, located at 116 South Iowa Avenue, as it appeared in 1902. C.S. Lemmon stands in the center. L.D. Robinson opened the store specializing in jewelry and musical instruments in 1895. C.S. Lemmon joined the business in 1898 and purchased it in 1900. Mr. Lewis, an optometrist, joined the business from 1900 to 1925. (Courtesy of Jim Logan.)

John H. Stewart's pharmacy and bookstore opened in 1884 or 1885 at 111 South Marion Avenue and operated until 1907. The site was part of the Union Block/Kendell House that was built in 1856. In 1908, the building was extensively remodeled from three stories to the two-story structure that remains today.

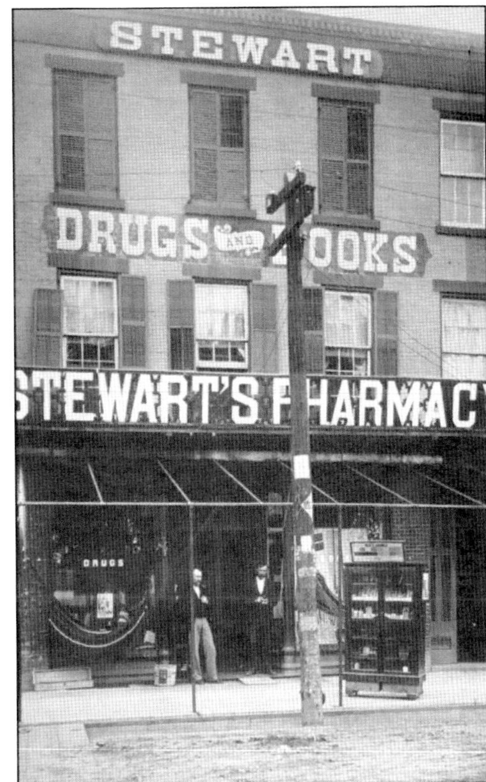

J.E. Lemmon arrived in Washington shortly after graduating from pharmacy school in 1899. He purchased a business on the southeast corner of the square, at 200 South Iowa, in 1902. There, he ran Lemmon's Pharmacy until 1953, when he sold the business to Norman Scoonover. This photograph of the interior shows the new electric lights at the top of the soda fountain. (Courtesy of Tom Dawson.)

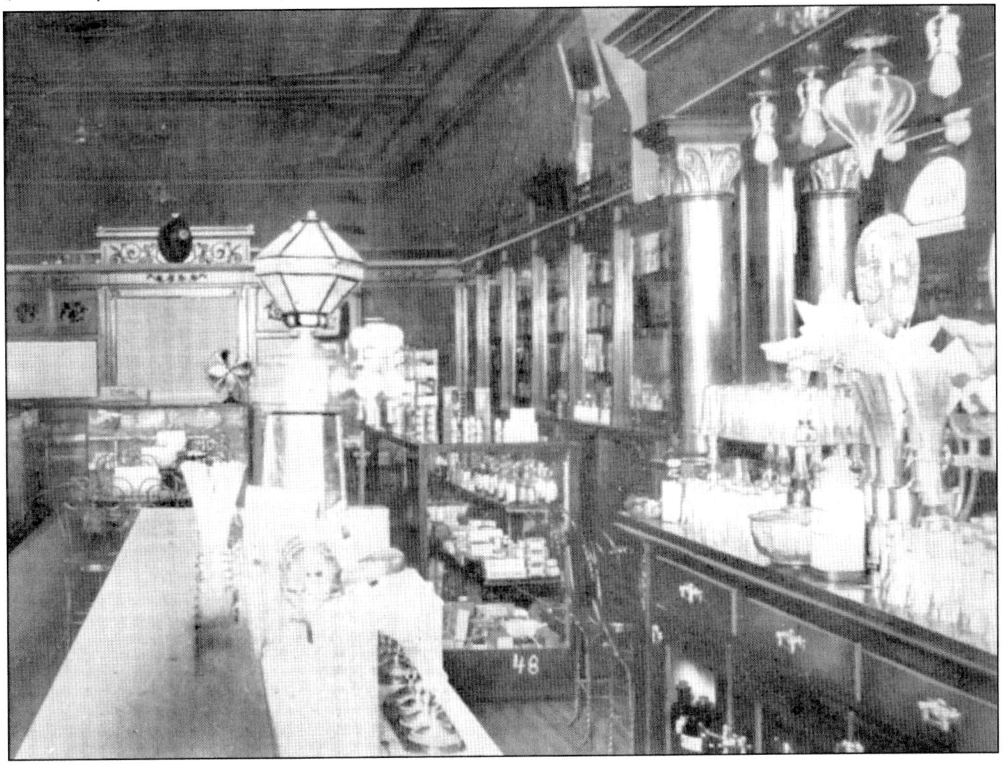

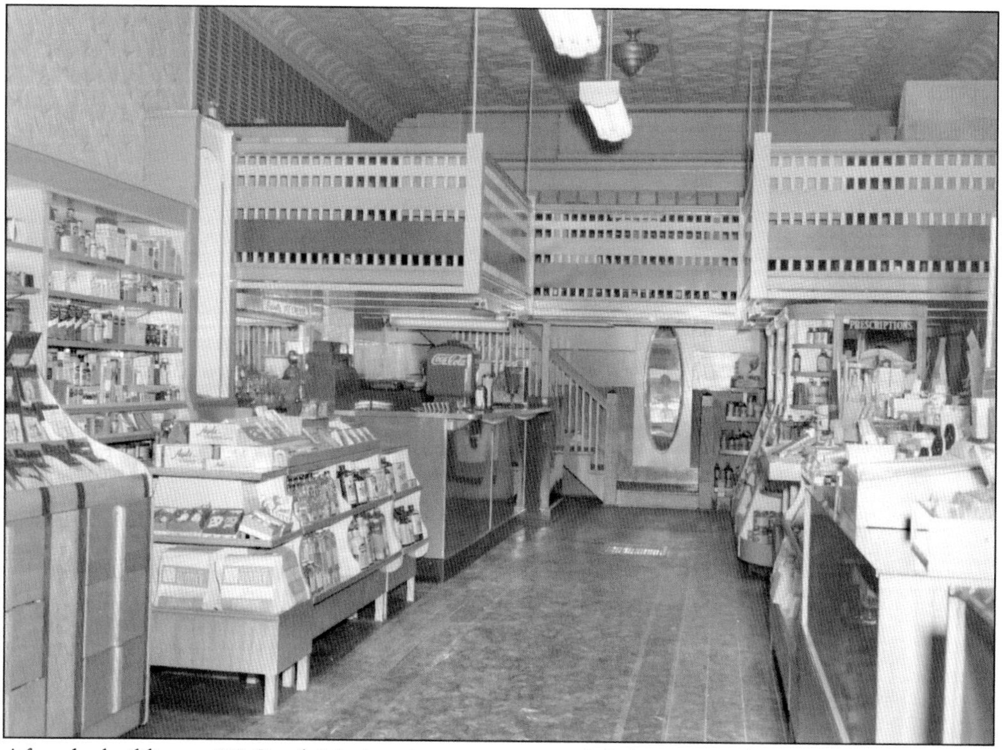

After the building at 111 South Marion Avenue was remodeled in 1908, it housed Ross Drug Store. From 1913 until the 1960s, it was the Philips & Hebner Drug Store. It later became the Phillips Drug Store and then Phillips Pharmacy. The balcony at the rear of the store was a favorite after-school gathering place for local students. Several residents remember "shooting" straw wrappers at unsuspecting patrons below when the manager was not looking. It became the Hub Restaurant from 1967 until 1984 and then operated from 1985 until 1992 under the name BJ's.

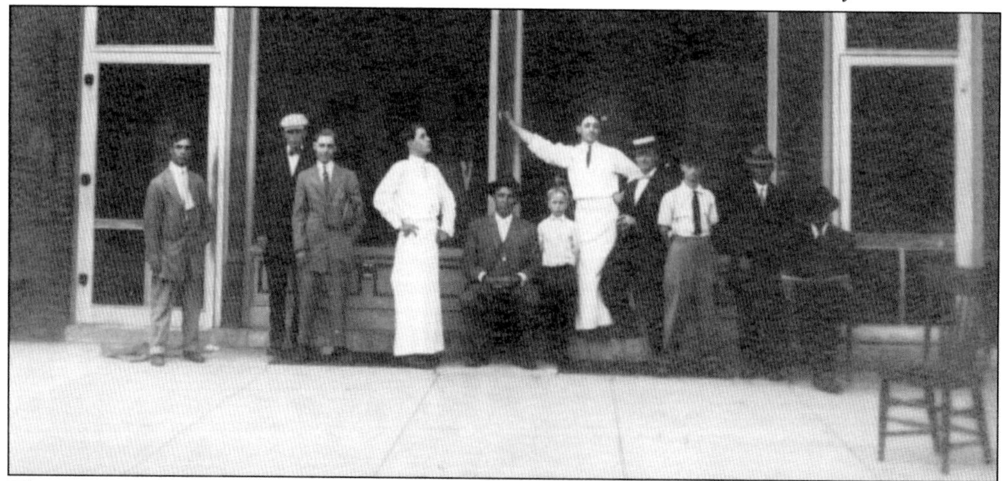

The Harvey & Warfel Restaurant, pictured here in 1897, operated at 108 West Main Street through the early 1900s. David W. Harvey was the commander of Company D, 50th Iowa Volunteers during the Spanish-American War. He later formed a partnership with Rudolph Warfel, and together they operated a restaurant for many years. The site was later the longtime location of Winga's Restaurant.

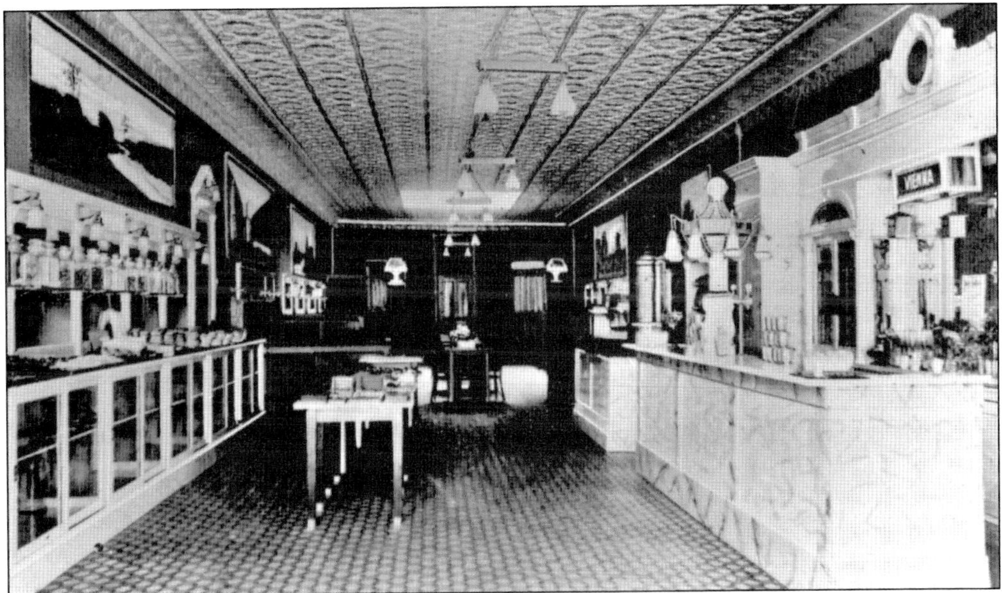

Originally named the Vienna Bakery when it opened in 1905, the Vienna Cafe was located at 114 East Washington Street, across from the opera house. It was moved to 102 South Iowa Avenue in 1913, was sold to Leo Nardy in 1921, and was subsequently renamed the Chocolate Shop.

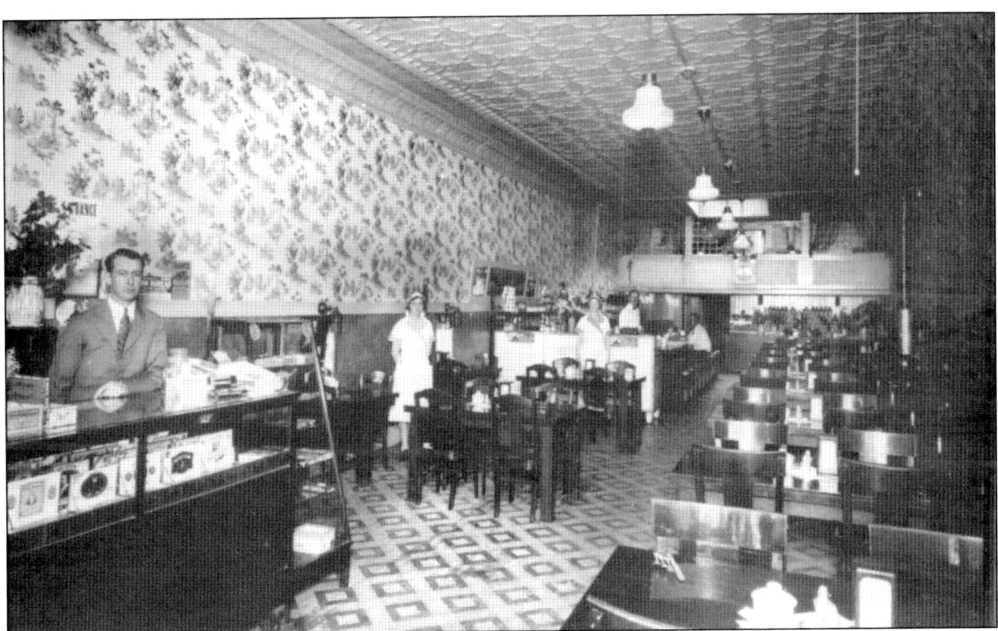

This is a 1933 interior shot of the North Side Café. Later renamed Winga's North Side Café, then Winga's Café, and finally Winga's Restaurant, this location has housed food establishments since the 1870s.

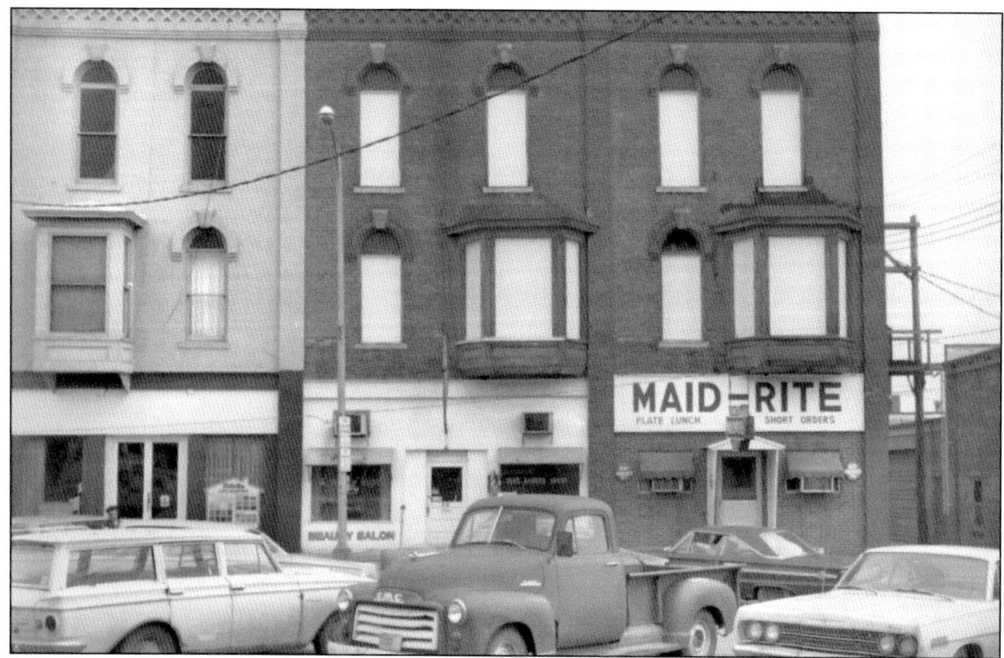

The first Maid-Rite restaurant opened in Muscatine, Iowa, in 1926. A butcher named Fred Angell developed the original recipe for the loose-meat sandwich, and by the end of the 1920s he had franchised four other restaurants. The Washington Maid-Rite opened at 212 South Marion Avenue in 1935 and operated until 1996.

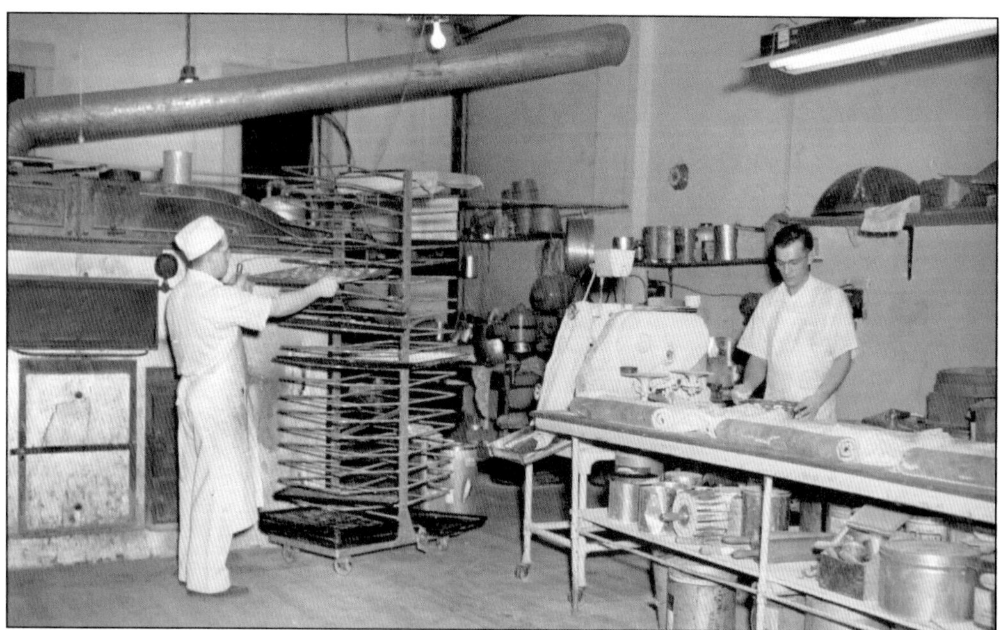

Paul Fern was born in Germany in 1910. After immigrating to the United States, he attended a pastry school and later a cake-decorating institute. He came to Washington in 1944 and established the Fern Pastry Shop at 119 North Marion Avenue, which operated from 1946 until 1972. The shop won several pastry and baking competitions.

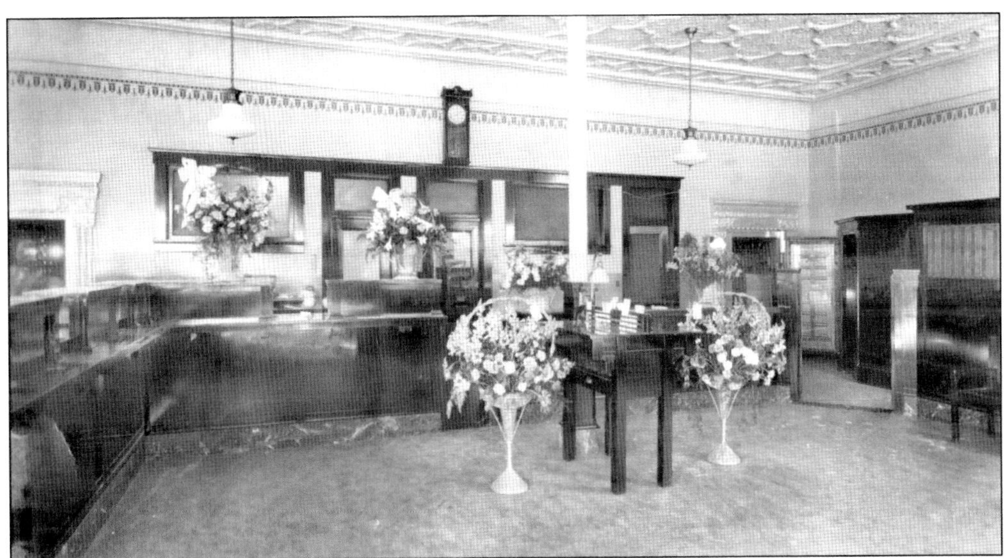

In September 1859, the Washington branch of the State Bank of Iowa was founded with Joseph Keck serving as president. It was reorganized as the First National Bank of Washington County in 1865, and the name changed again to the Citizens National Bank in 1903. It merged with the Washington County Savings Bank to become the Commercial Savings Bank, which closed in October 1931. It reopened as the Washington State Bank on April 18, 1932. Here, the lobby of the Washington State Bank is pictured on its opening day.

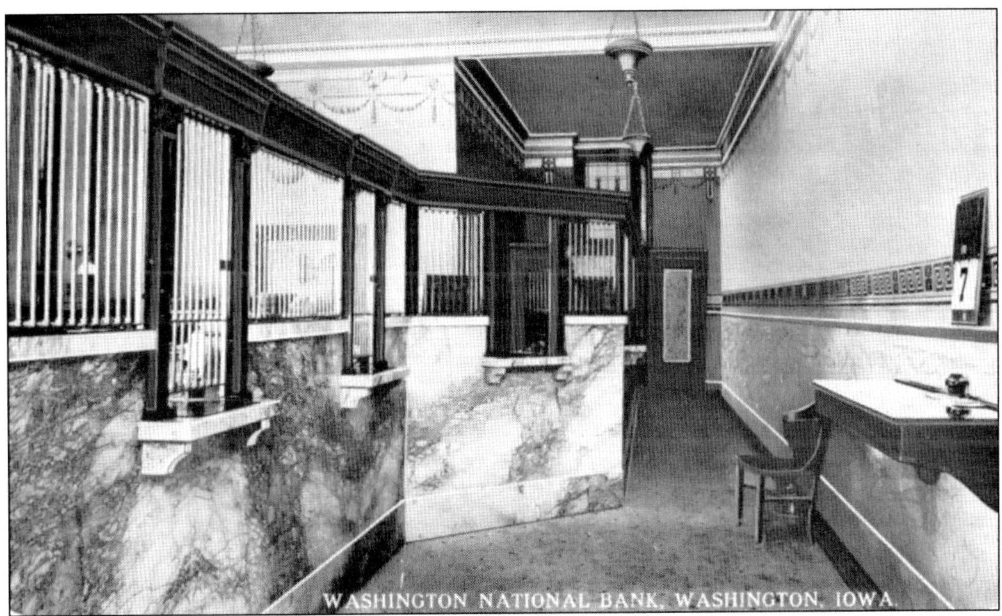

Washington businessman Winfield Smouse became the first president of the Washington National Bank when it was founded in 1871. This postcard image shows the lobby of the bank after its move into the building at the northeast corner of the square.

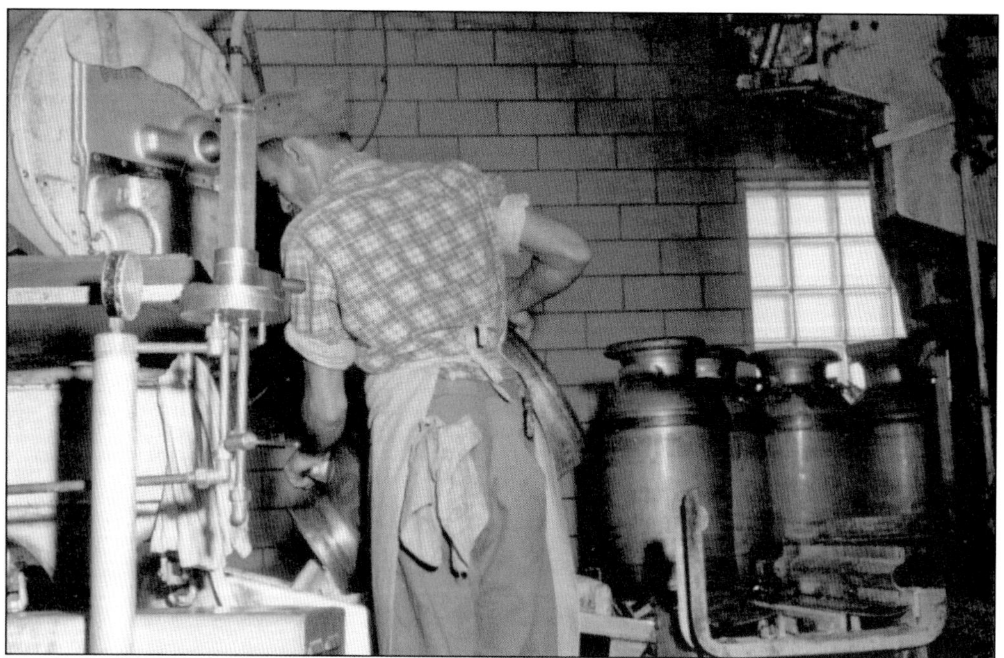

The Griffith-Hebner Dairy operated from the mid-1940s until 1962. The dairy, located at 1000 West Madison Street, expanded to a shop on the square for a few years. Partners John Griffith and John Hebner began producing ice cream in 1947 and expanded to cheese in 1948.

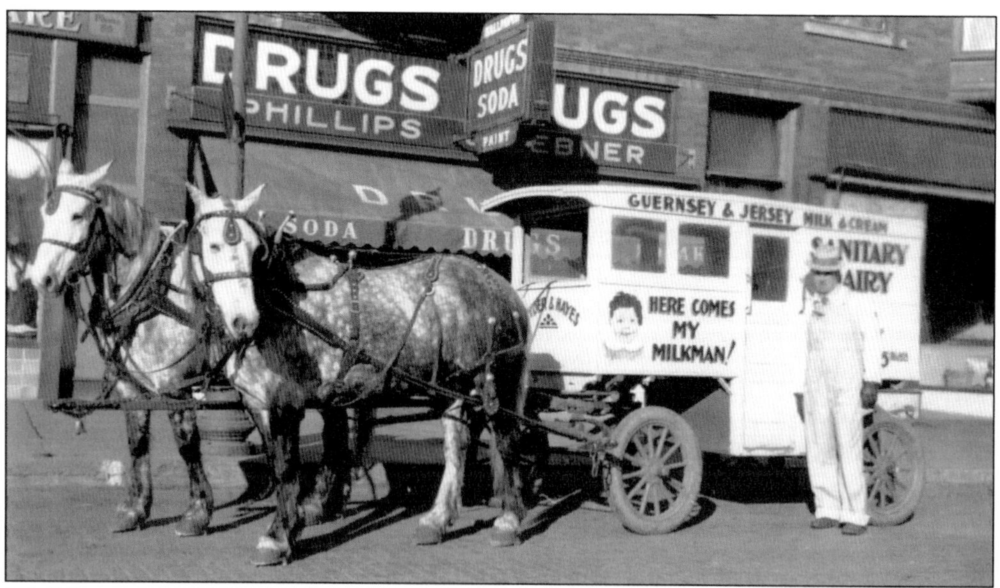

Lyle Havener owned the Sanitary Dairy, located at 1109 South Ninth Avenue, from 1959 until 1969. The business had a shop for a short time at 112 East Washington Street. Their horse-drawn milk wagon is shown here on the west side of the square.

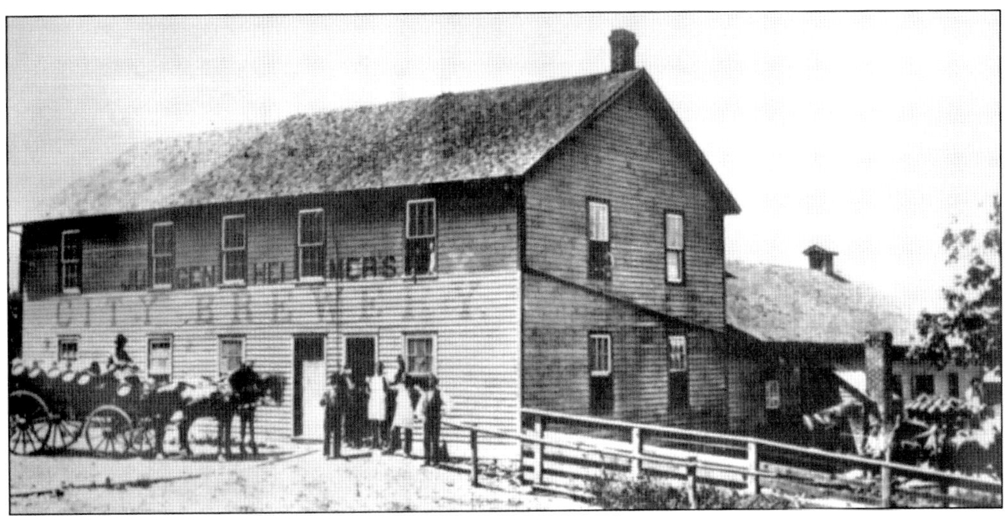

William Juginheimer emigrated from Germany in 1847 and lived in Milwaukee and St. Louis before arriving in Washington in 1871. He established his brewery on the west edge of town, just across from the current fairgrounds.

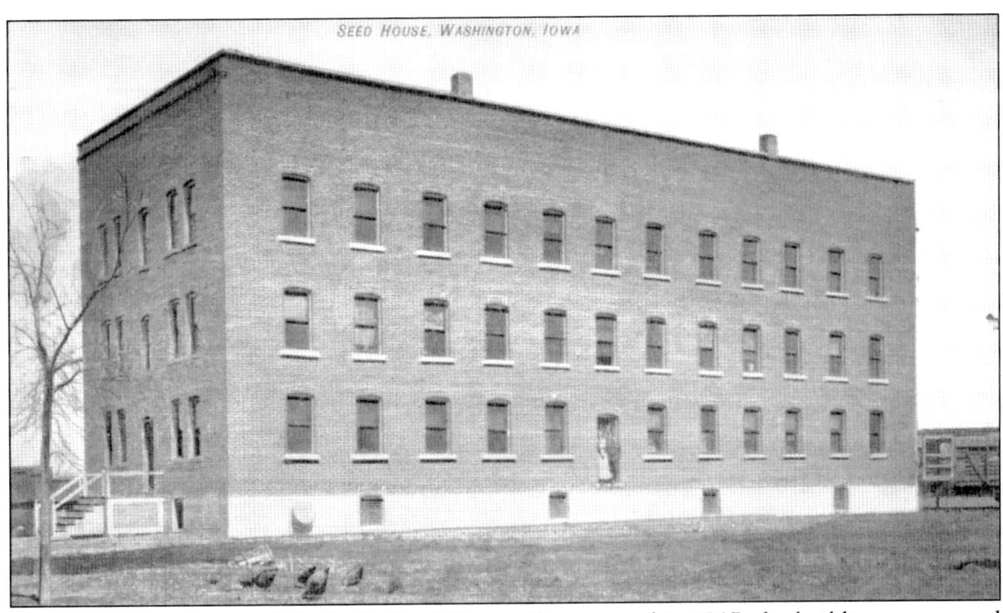

This is a postcard view of the Mills Seed House. Constructed in 1907, the building was moved to a new location on North Iowa Avenue in 2010. The relocation of the structure was featured on TLC's *Heavy Haulers* television program.

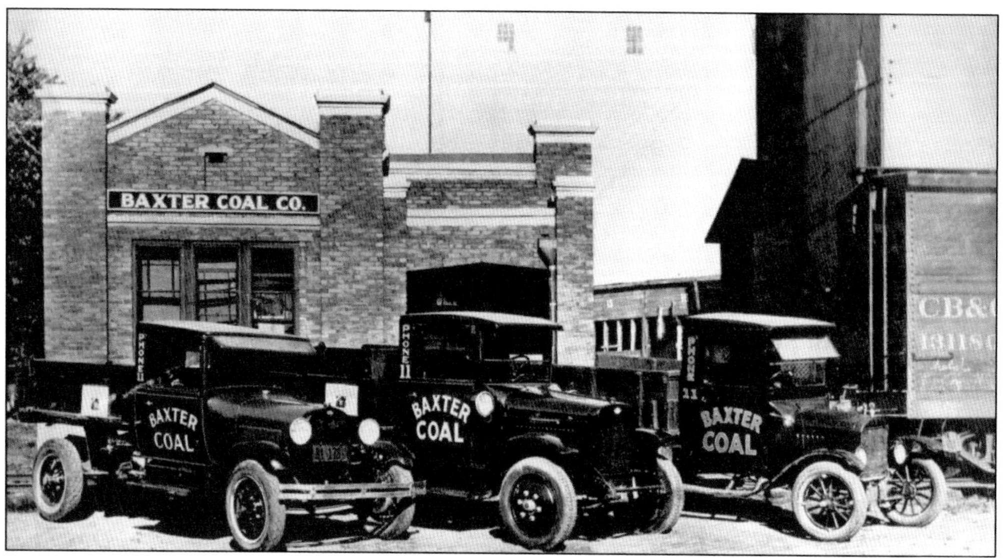

Henry A. Baxter arrived in Washington in 1903 and purchased the Sampson & Livingston Co. at 601 East Third Street. He renamed the business the H.A. Baxter Company and dealt in grain, coal, wood, and building materials. His son Howard continued in the business until 1935. The building, pictured here, is currently used as a weigh station.

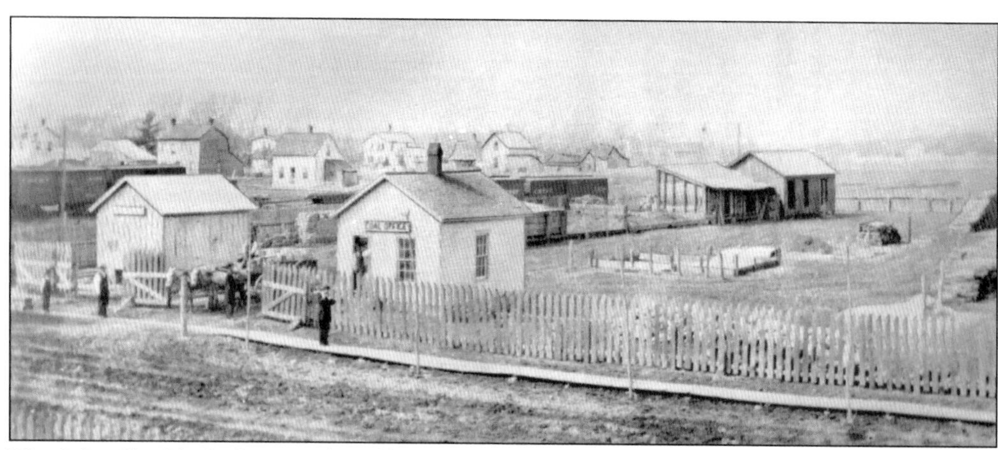

The John Shields & Sons coal and building-materials company operated on the west side of North Marion Avenue, just north of the railroad tracks. It was in business from the early 1870s through the 1930s.

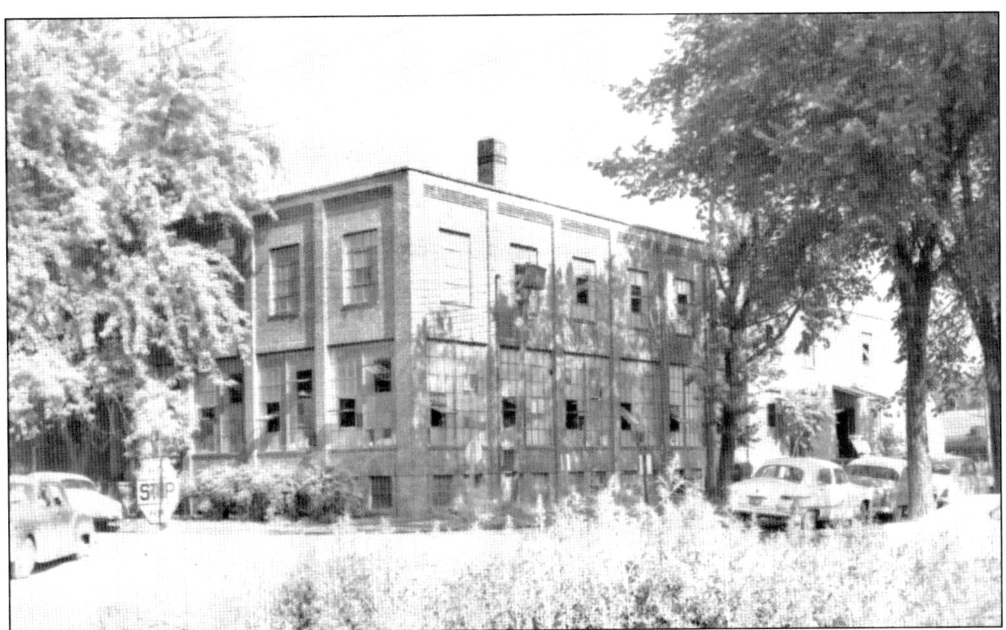

Hugh McCleery began his calendar factory in his basement in 1903, and the company constructed this building at 632 East Third Street in 1924. At its peak season, it had a workforce of 350 people. (Courtesy of Jeff Batterson.)

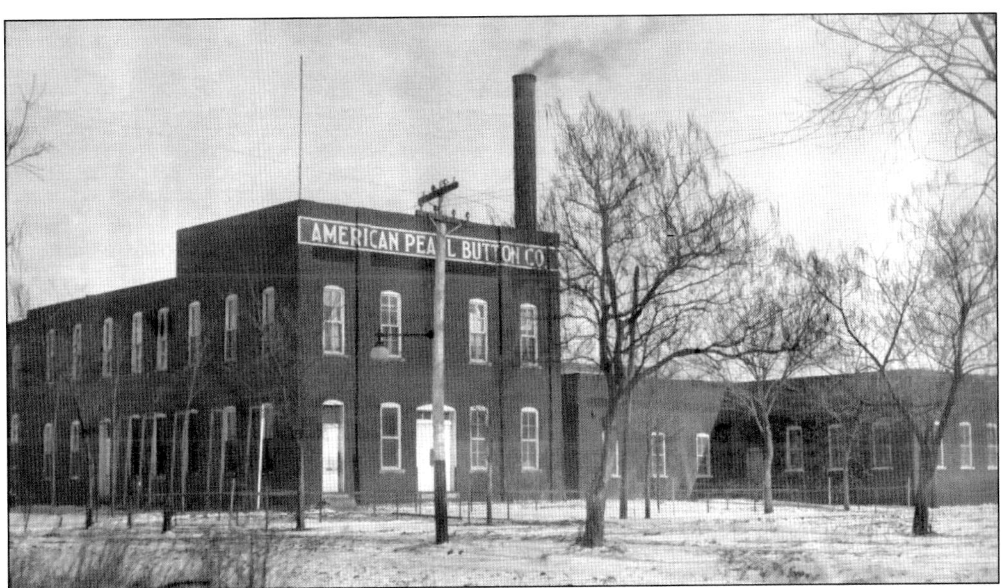

Frank Stewart and Fred Giesler organized the American Pearl Button Factory in 1908. By 1936, it employed about 230 people. In addition, many families did "carding," sewing the button on cards, at home. The buttons were cut from shells that were imported into town, but the post–World War II popularity of plastic buttons brought an end to the industry.

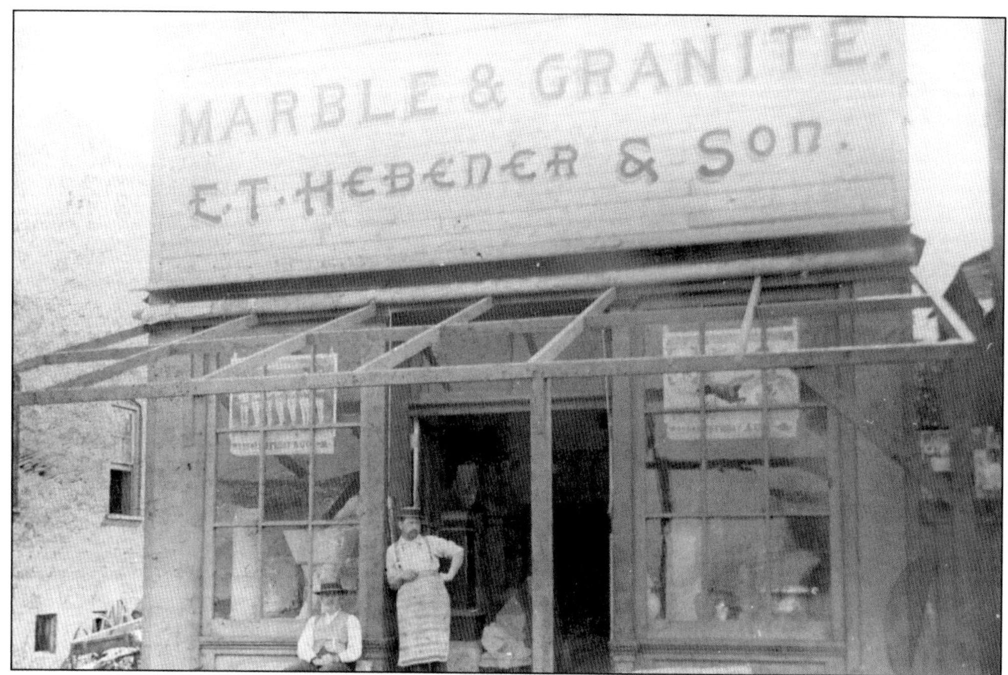

E.T. Hebener & Son Marble & Granite advertised in newspapers as early as 1862 and continued in business until 1938 at 110 North Iowa Avenue. Charles Hebener entered the enterprise with his father and continued after his E.T.'s death, ultimately spending over 60 years in the business. Charles, who as an 11-year-old had played the fife during recruitment meetings, was an honorary member of the national Civil War veterans' organization the Grand Army of the Republic (GAR).

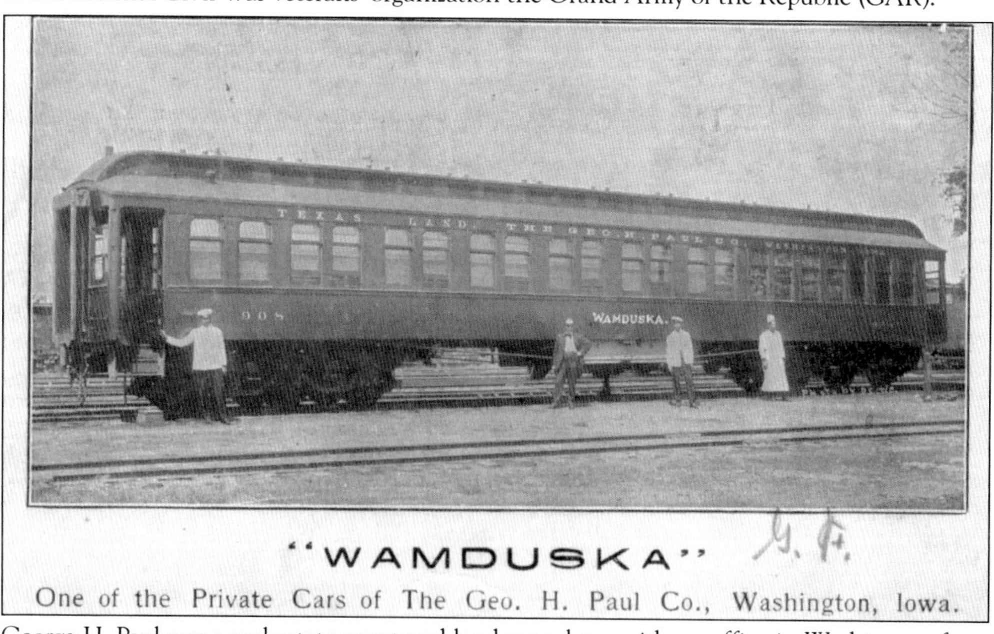

George H. Paul was a real estate agent and land speculator with an office in Washington from 1908 until 1914. His company bought thousands of acres of land in Texas and Florida and then resold them to settlers. This is one of his excursion railroad cars, which carried potential buyers to visit the properties.

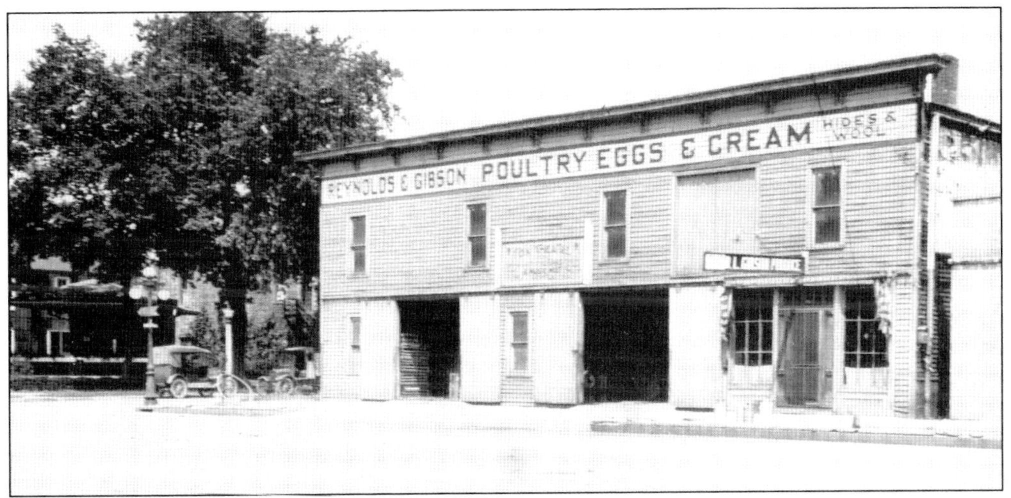

The Reynolds & Gibson (later Gibson's) poultry and produce company operated at the southeast corner North Marion Avenue and West Second Street in the 1920s and 1930s. The site had previously been the 1860s location of Sanford's livery and exchange barn.

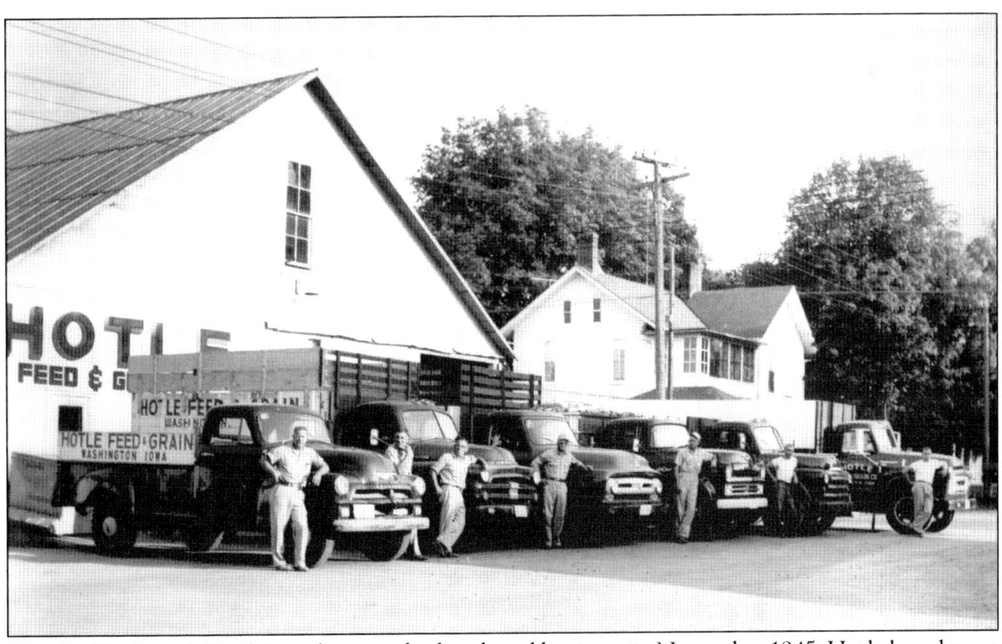

Charles Hotle and Cecil Long began a feed and seed business in November 1945. Hotle bought out Long in January 1949 and continued the business until his retirement in 1979. This photograph is from around 1958.

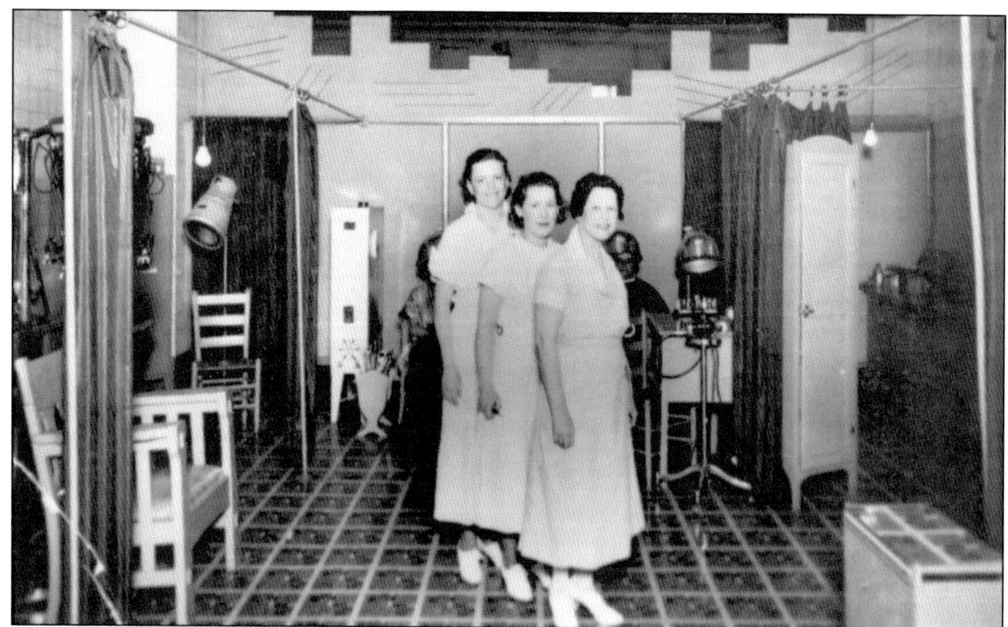

Sadee Shrader McAvoy opened the first beauty shop in Washington County in 1924. Pictured in this c. 1933 image are, from left to right, beauticians Pauline Peters, Melba McAvoy, and Sadee McAvoy. To the left, partially hidden by a curtain, is an early electric hair-curling machine.

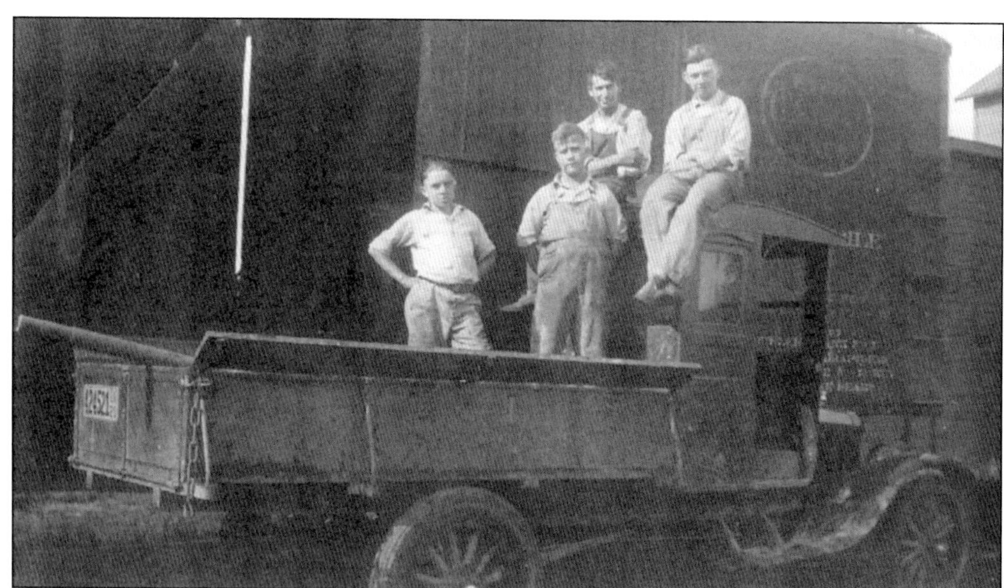

The Mose Levy Company, at 421 North Iowa Avenue, began in the scrap-metal business in 1939 and later, in 1958, became a distributor of new steel. Morris "Mose" Levy is pictured third from the left. (Courtesy of Mary Levy.)

Three

Home Life

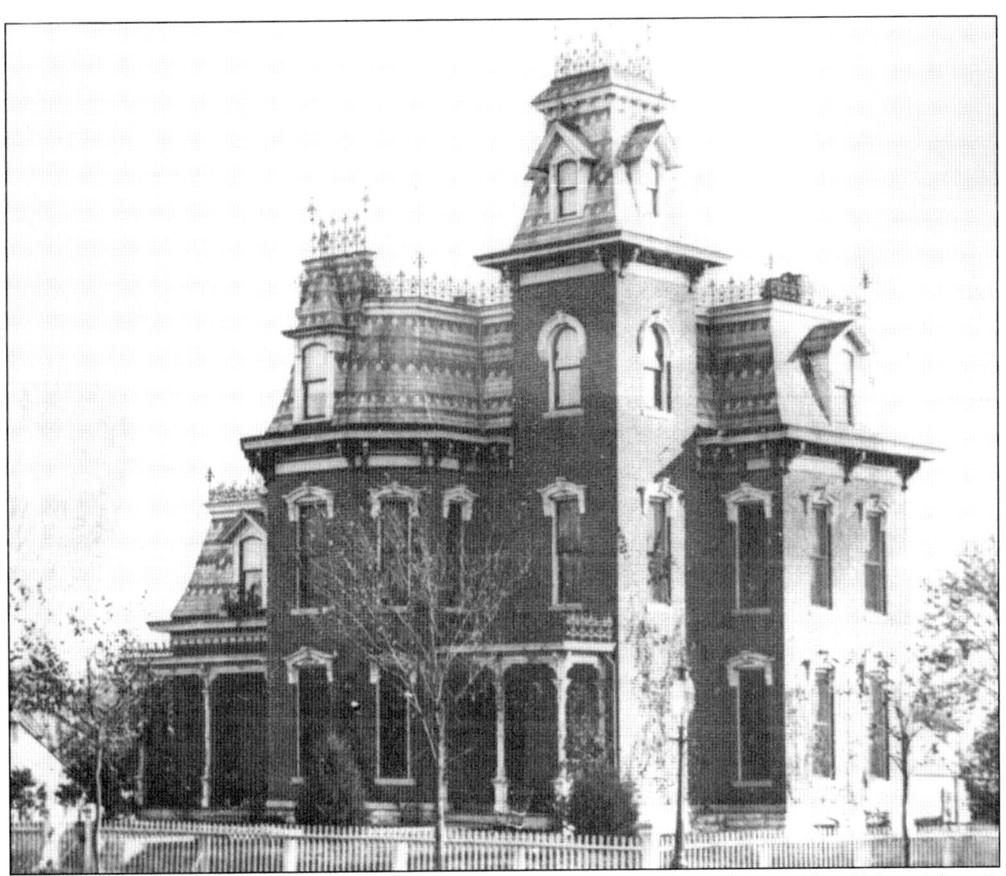

The Blair House was built around 1880 by Winfield Smouse and was later sold to Edwin Blair. It became the headquarters of the Commercial Club in 1903 and served as Washington City Hall from 1925 until 1974. After being rescued at the last minute from demolition, it currently houses offices and a public meeting room.

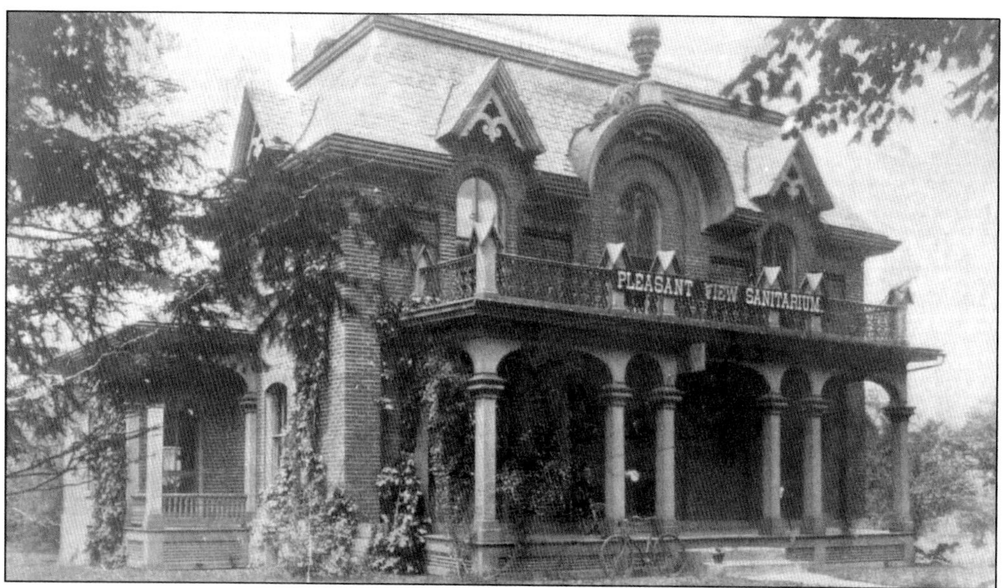

John and Jane Jackson built this house at 504 West Washington Street in 1845. Their daughter Elizabeth married Joseph Keck in the home's kitchen. The structure was added on to in 1856 and, after 1906, operated for a few years as a five- or six-bed hospital named Pleasant View Sanitarium. It is now listed in the National Register of Historic Places.

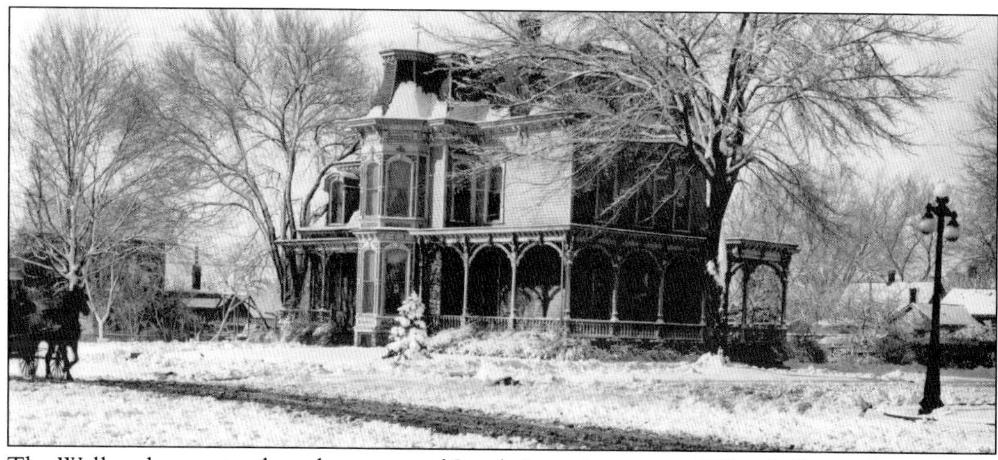

The Wallace house stood on the corner of South Iowa Avenue and West Jefferson Street at the present-day location of the medical building. In later years, it was known as the Dora Jones house. It was torn down in the mid-1960s.

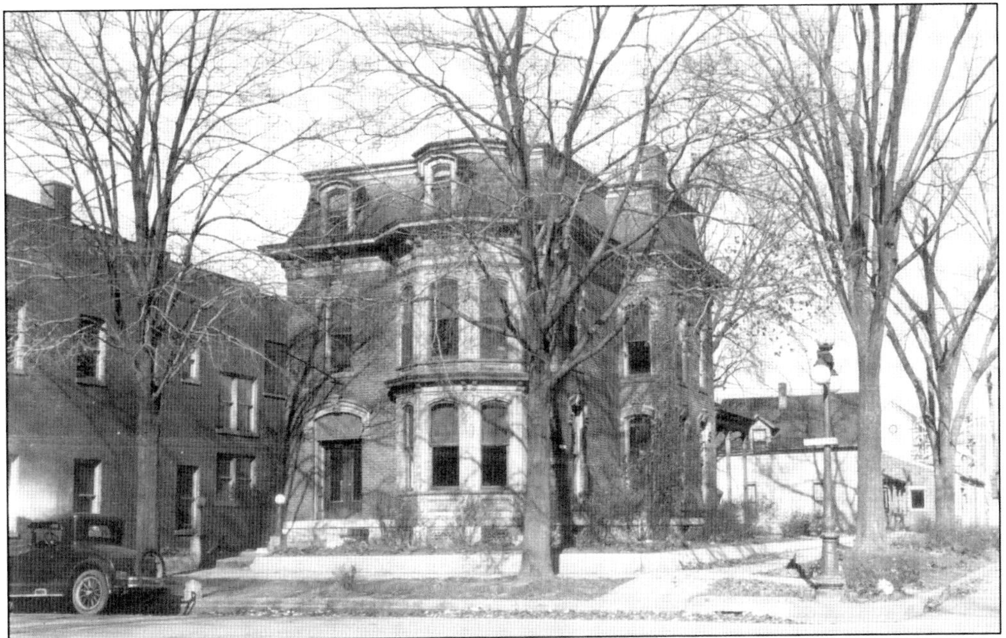

In 1901, Jane A. Chilcote, widow of Dr. Alexander Chilcote, bequeathed her home at 120 East Main Street to the City of Washington for use as a public library. The building was demolished in 1952 to make way for a new facility.

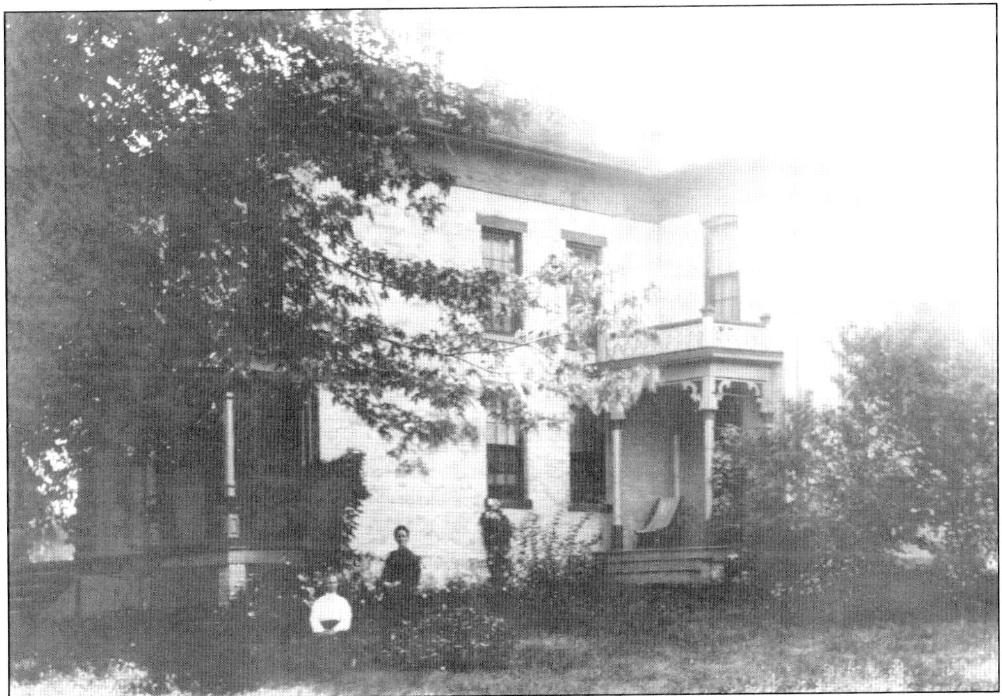

The R.T. Wilson House stood at the corner South Fourth Avenue and East Jefferson Street. Wilson owned a dry-goods store on the north side of the square for many years. The house was demolished prior to 1918, and the location became part of the site of high school (now middle school) building.

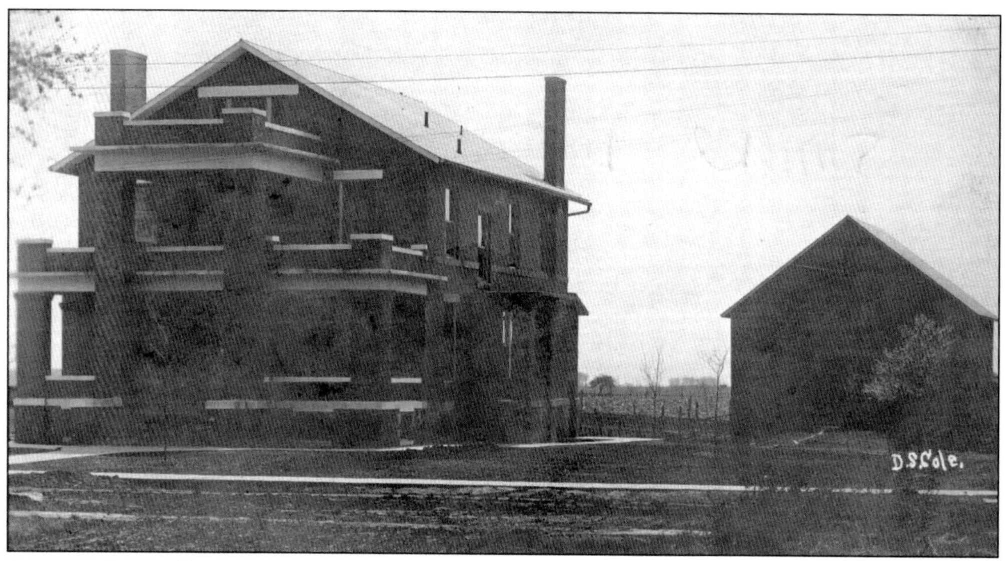

Sen. Smith Brookhart built his home at 1203 East Washington Street in 1919 at a cost of $35,000. He was terrified of fire, so the entire house, including the roof, was built of concrete, tile, and brick. It is now part of the United Presbyterian Home.

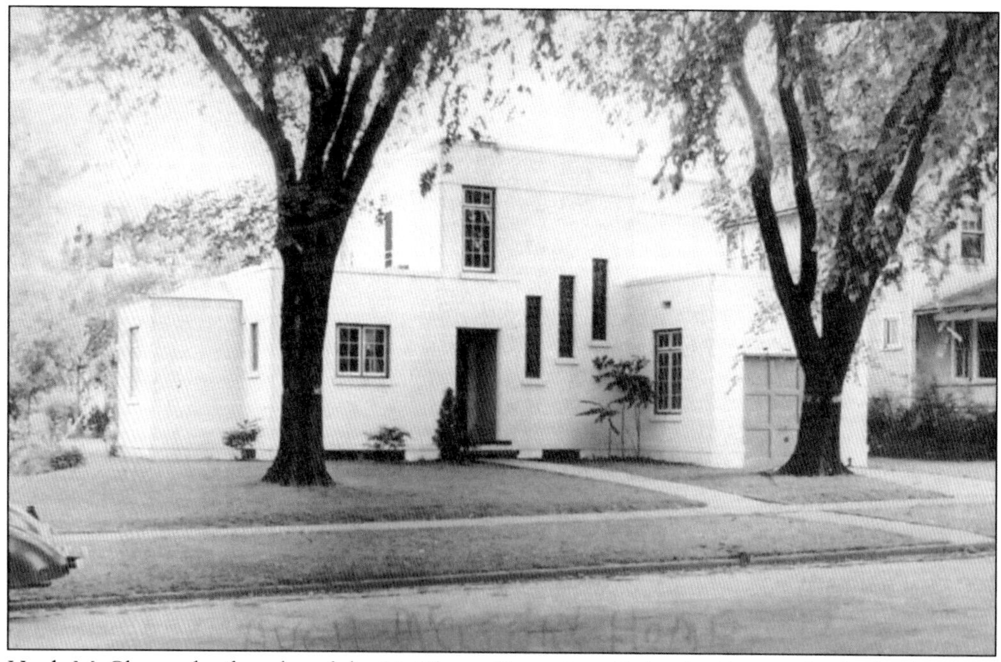

Hugh McCleery, the founder of the McCleery-Cummings Calendar Factory, built this home at 215 East Main Street, and his widow, Ola, lived there for many years after his death. It was one of the few Art Deco–style homes to be built in the city. It was torn down in the early 1970s, and the location is part of the site of the current United Presbyterian Church.

This image, from a collection of photographs found at the Frank Stewart house at 603 West Washington Street, shows the dining room of a typical Victorian home. It does not, however, appear to be of the house in which it was found. (Courtesy of Mary Patterson.)

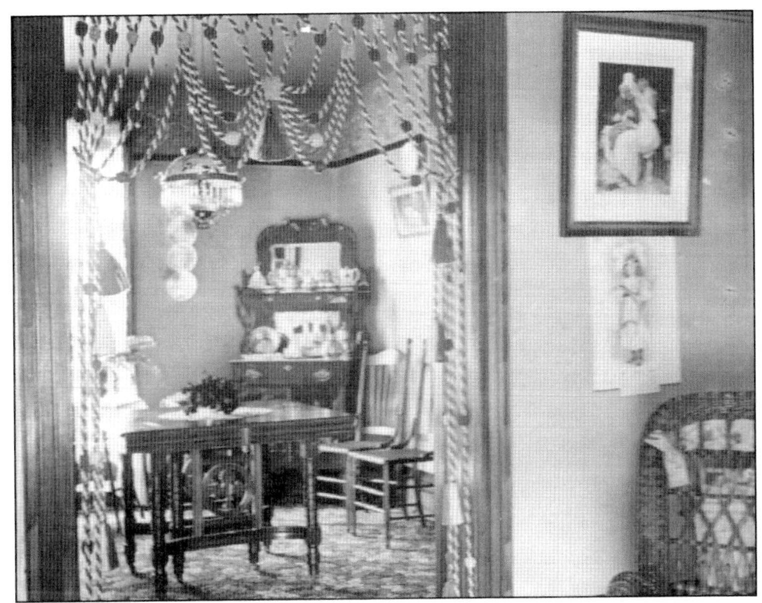

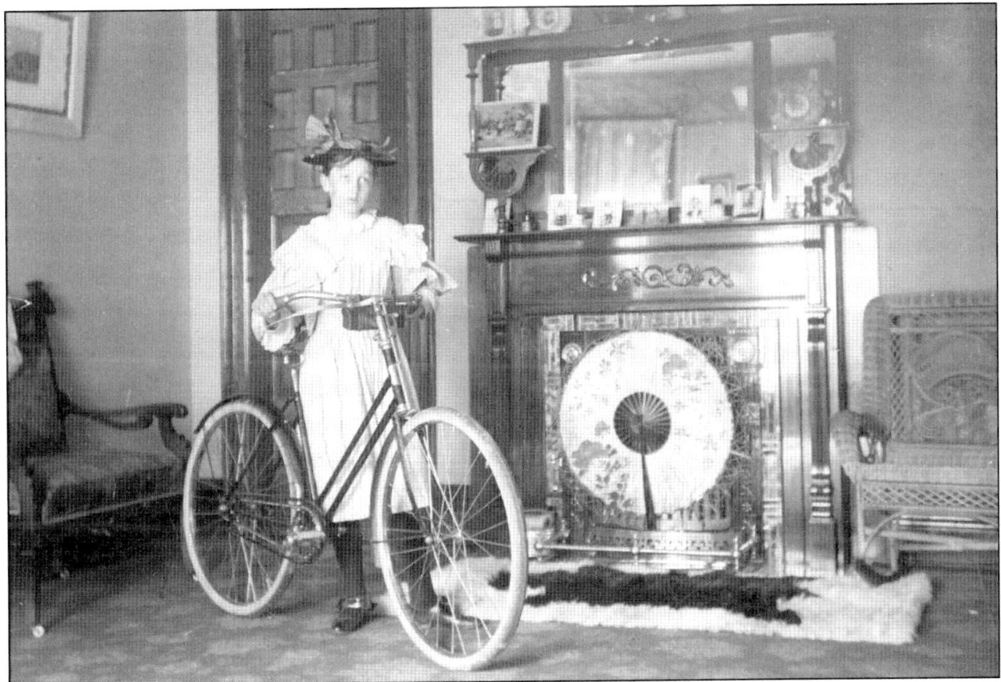

Marian Virginia Stewart (1882–1967) was the daughter of Franklin and Juliet Washburn Stewart. She is shown with her new bicycle in the parlor of their home on West Washington Street. Marian married Delbert Roscoe Bailey, 20 years her junior, at the Little Brown Church in Nashua, Iowa, in November 1930. (Courtesy of Mary Patterson.)

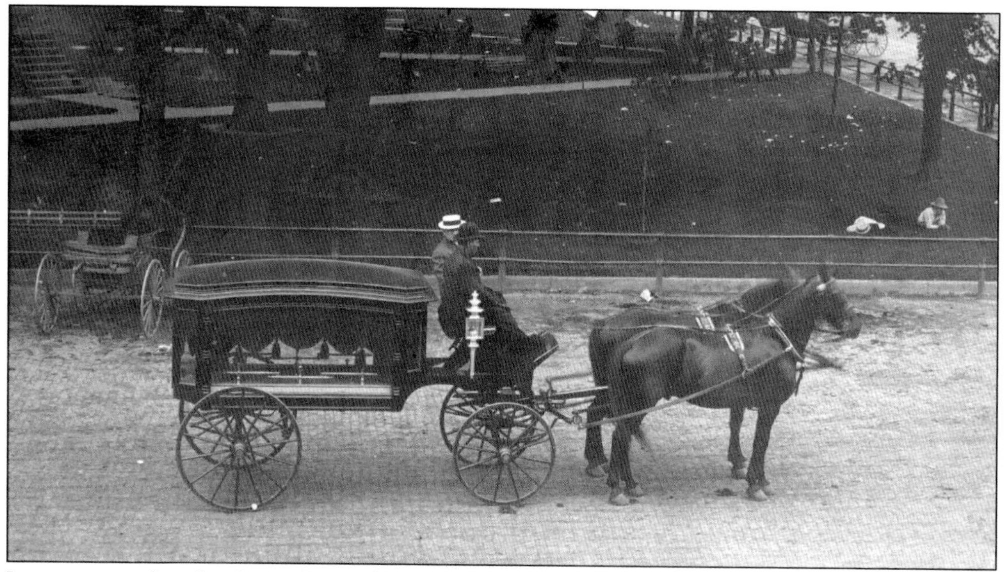

Longtime undertaker Louis Jones (wearing the white hat) is pictured with the Jones Funeral Home hearse in front of Central Park. Jones became a funeral director in 1914 and moved to Washington in 1917. He purchased the Charles Woodford funeral business at 116-118 East Main Street in 1924. Note the metal rail surrounding Central Park; it replaced an earlier wood fence erected to keep animals from grazing in the park.

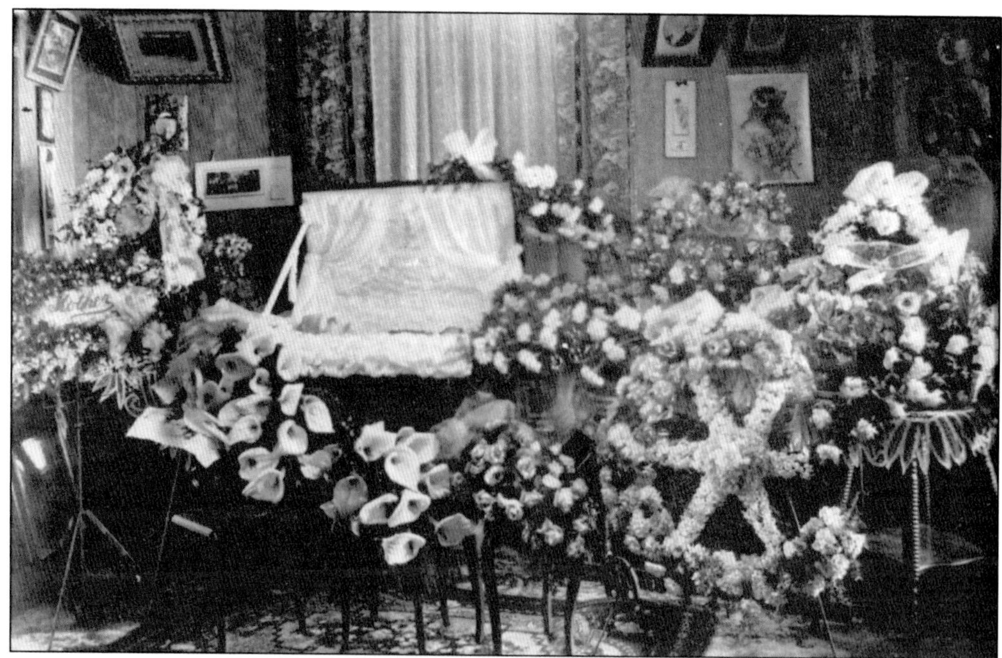

In the 19th century, it was a common practice to have funerals in the home of the deceased; the location of this particular one is unknown. When Wilber Miller constructed his funeral home in 1911, it was the first building west of the Mississippi River to be specifically erected for such a purpose. The Miller Funeral Home building now houses the Jones Funeral Home.

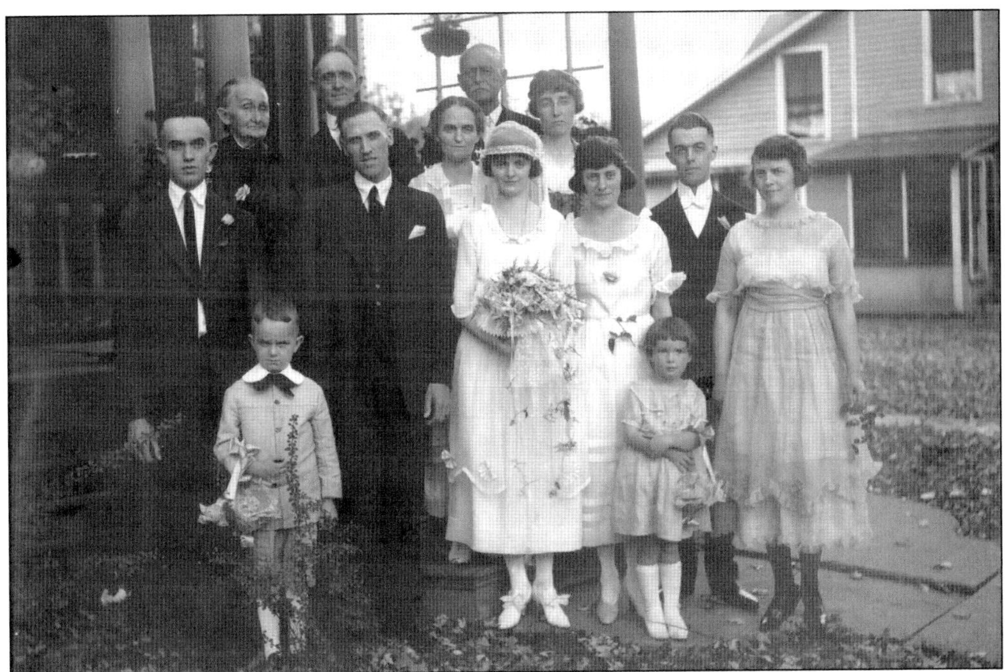

The wedding of Hazel Stewart to Oral W. Albertson occurred on October 18, 1920. Pictured from left to right are (front) ring bearer William Stewart and an unidentified flower girl; (back) George Stewart, unidentified, Fred Stewart, Oral Albertson (groom), Mrs. Fred Stewart, unidentified, Hazel Stewart (bride), unidentified, Ruby Stewart, and two unidentified people.

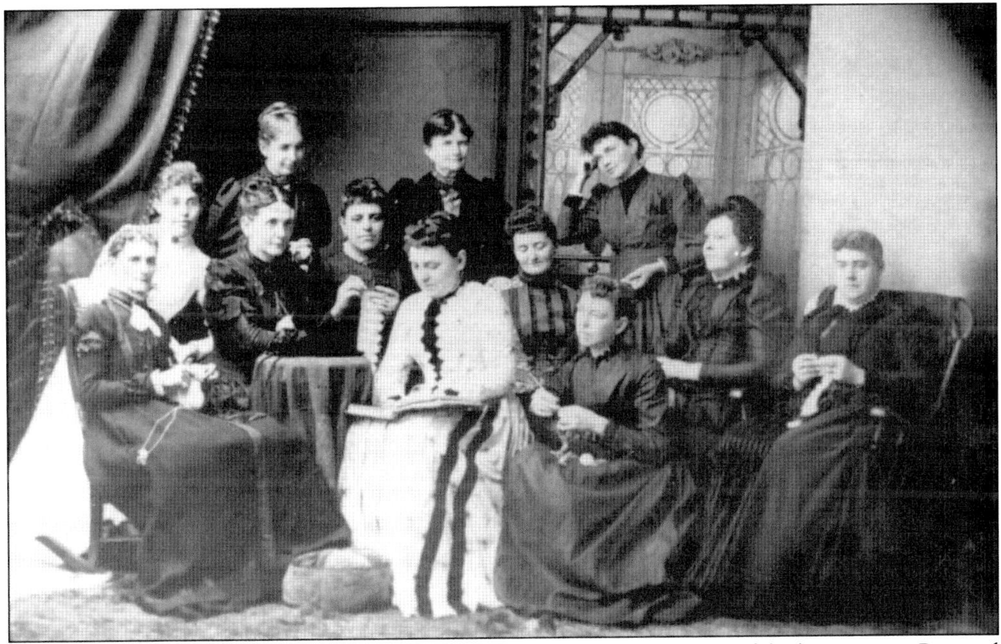

Reading circles, predecessors of today's book clubs, were popular at the turn of the last century. Pictured are, from left to right, Mesdames (first row) H.A. Burrell, F.H. Graves, and Mack Ackley; (second row) E.J. Meacham, A.H. Wallace, C.H. Wilson, C.N. Stinson, William Scofield, and E.R. Jenkins; (third row) Norman Everson, A.W. Chilcote, and A.R. Dewey. (Courtesy of Mary Patterson.)

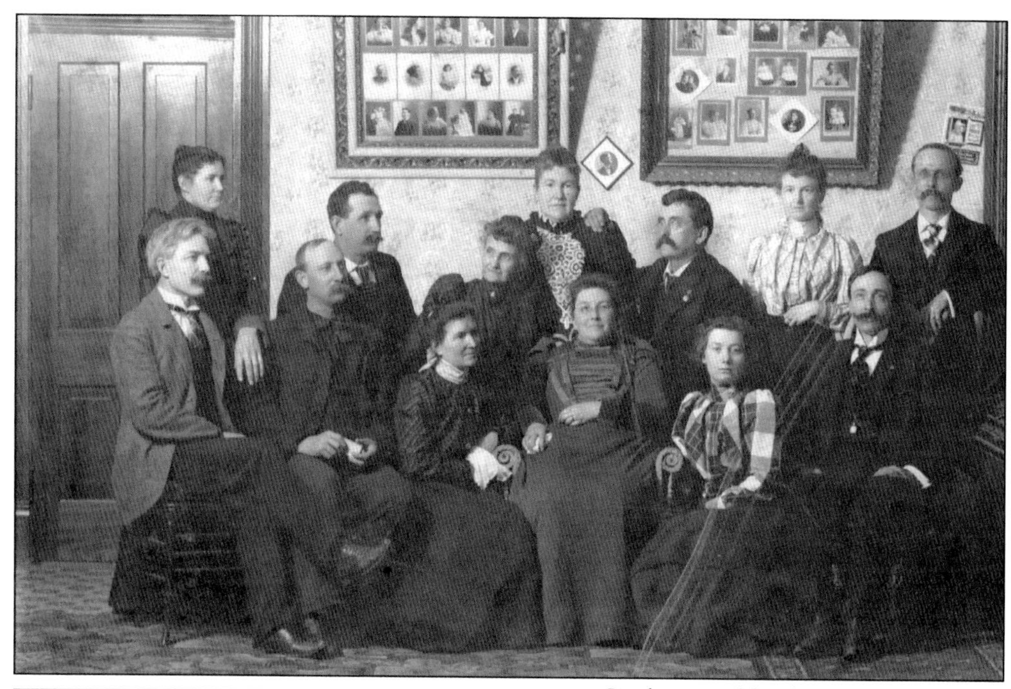

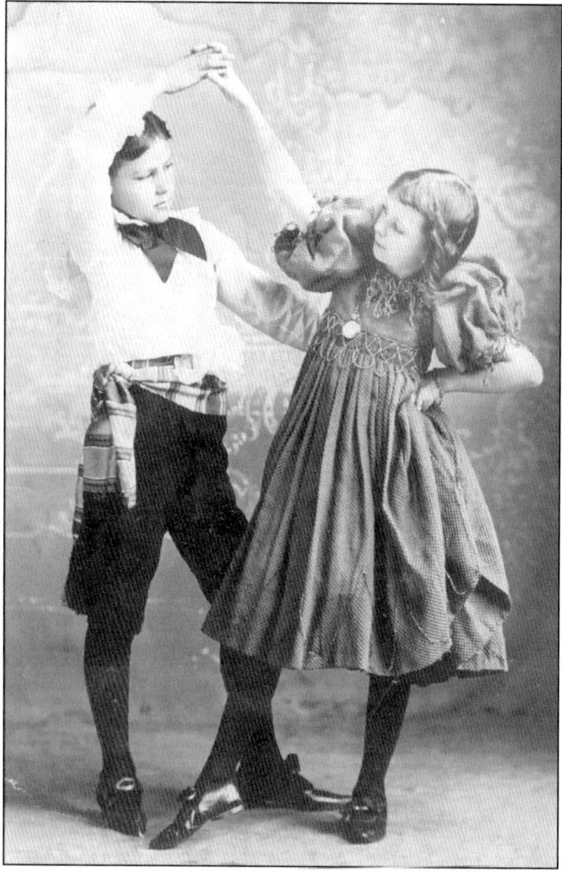

Card parties like this one were another popular form of home entertainment. Pictured here are, from left to right, (first row) Mr. Reynolds, Charles Hebner, Mrs. Morris, Mrs. Slirader, Katherine Wilson, and James Glasgow; (second row) Mrs. Reynolds, Mr. Slirader, Mrs. Charles Hebner, Mrs. Manners, Mr. Manners, Mrs. Glasgow, and Mr. Morris.

Edward Raguet and Vera Rogers are shown in their costumes for a dance recital in the 1890s. The Raguet family moved from Washington by 1910, and Vera Rogers later married John Bailey.

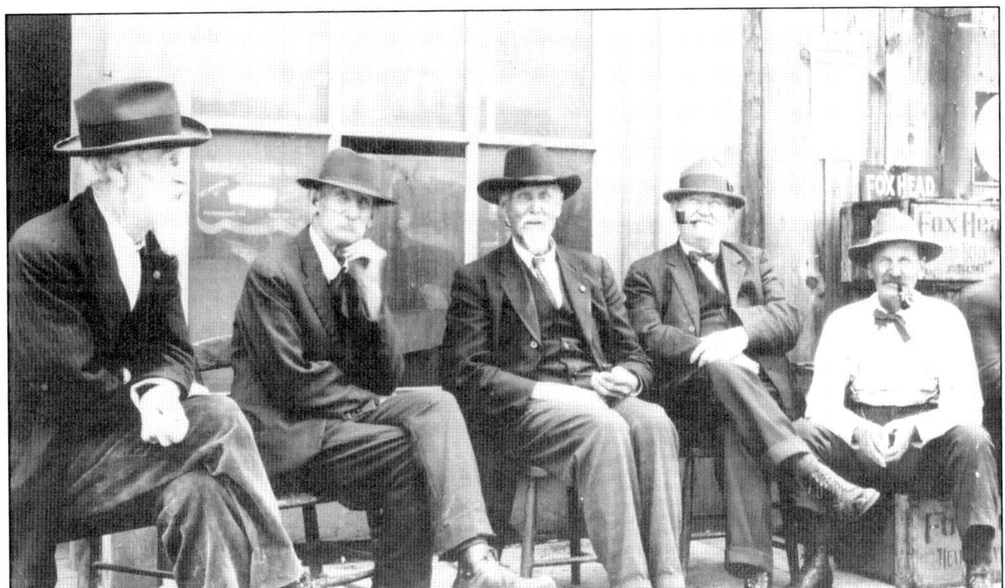

These men, who called themselves the "Shady Rest Club," are visiting in front of the Charles Hebener Monument Works at 110 North Iowa Avenue. They are, from left to right, Joe Purvis, Charles Hebener, Henry Parkinson, Lisle McGugin, and Mart Yockey.

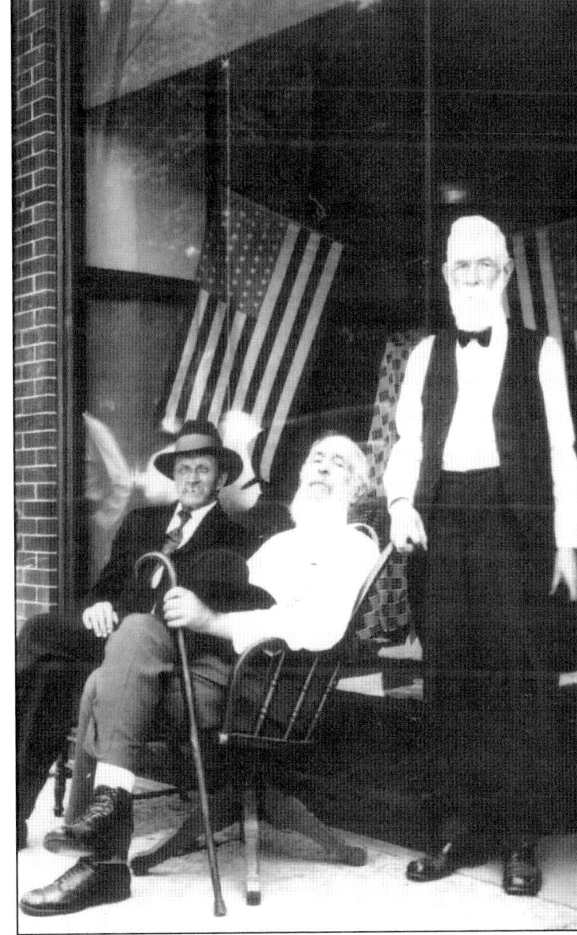

Tom Thompson (left), William Blair (center), and C.H. Wilson are pictured in front of Blair's Dry Goods Store on the south end of the square's east side. The store operated from the 1860s until 1925. William Blair lived in what is now known as the Blair House. Thompson was a self-taught veterinarian, and Wilson was a prominent attorney.

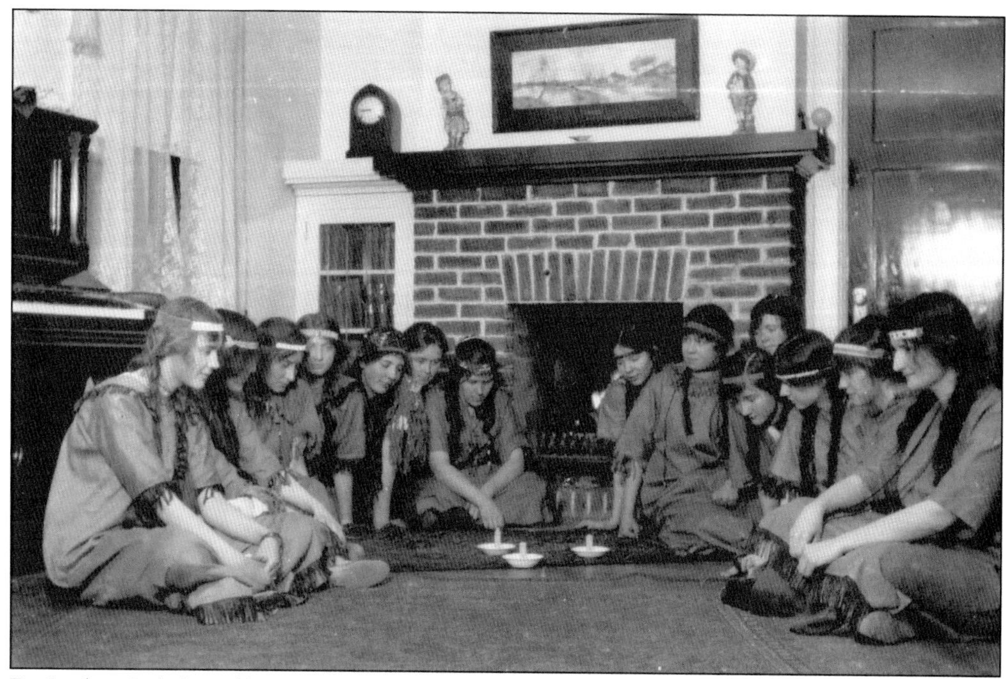

Dr. Luther Gulick and his wife, Charlotte, founded the national Campfire Girls organization in 1910. Its first chapter was the Wahwahtaysee group, founded in 1929. The Nawakahmoka group began in 1932. The girls in this image are unidentified, but they appear to be meeting in the home of one of the members.

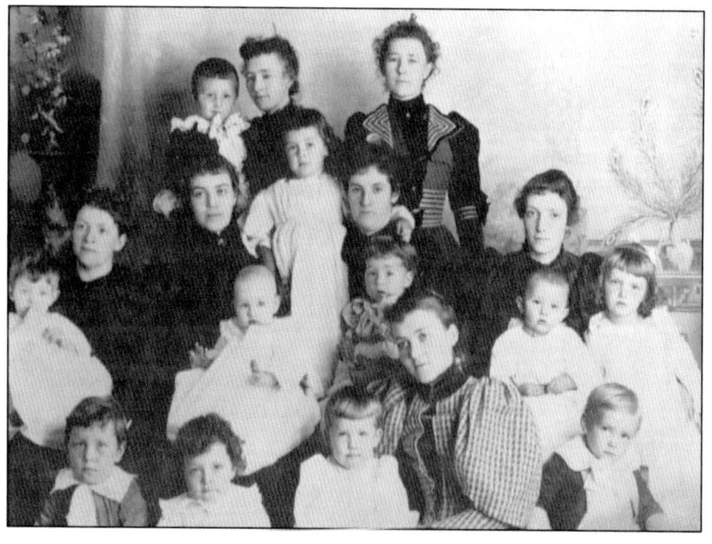

The individuals in this photograph are descendents of brothers Hiram and William Scofield. In the back row are sisters Clara and Cora, daughters of Hiram. Cora Scofield wrote a two-volume history of England's Edward IV that is still considered the definitive history of the monarch. For several years, she taught history at Wellesley College near Boston, Massachusetts.

Four

EDUCATION

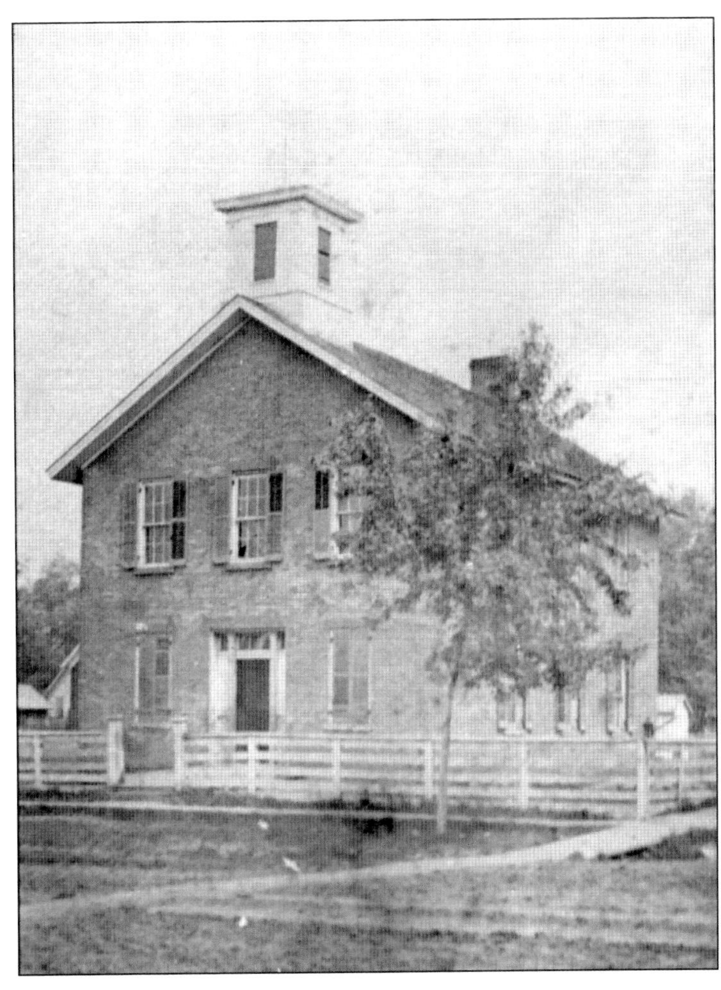

It is likely that the earliest school in the city was taught in a log structure. A one-story brick school was erected in the 1840s, and the building seen here was constructed at the corner of West Main Street and Avenue C in 1857.

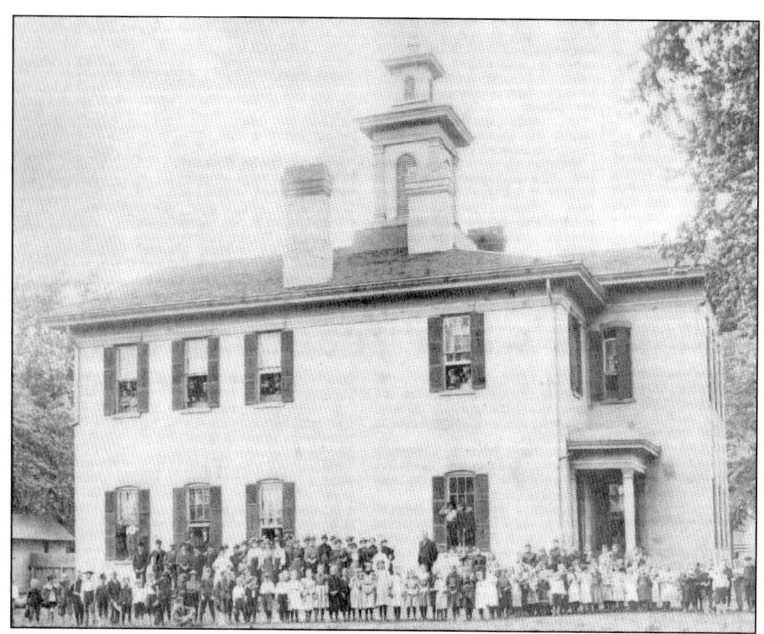

A bond issue for a new school passed by 17 votes in March 1865. The two-story, six-classroom, brick building was completed in 1867. Named South School, it was located at 604 South Iowa Avenue.

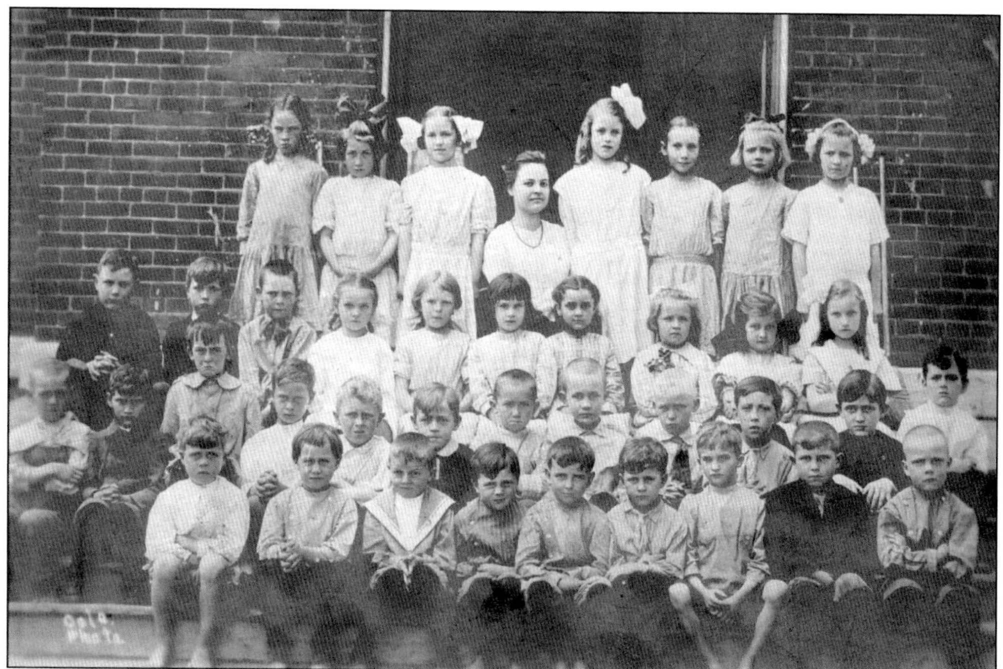

These students are pictured outside the old South School. The building burned in 1899, and the old Lincoln School was erected on the site. This image was taken sometime after 1894, the year that D.S. Cole began taking photographs, and 1899, when the building burned.

Heights School, located on North Second Avenue, was built in 1884 at a cost of $8,000. The flat land north of the railroad tracks had been called "The "Heights," hence the school's name.

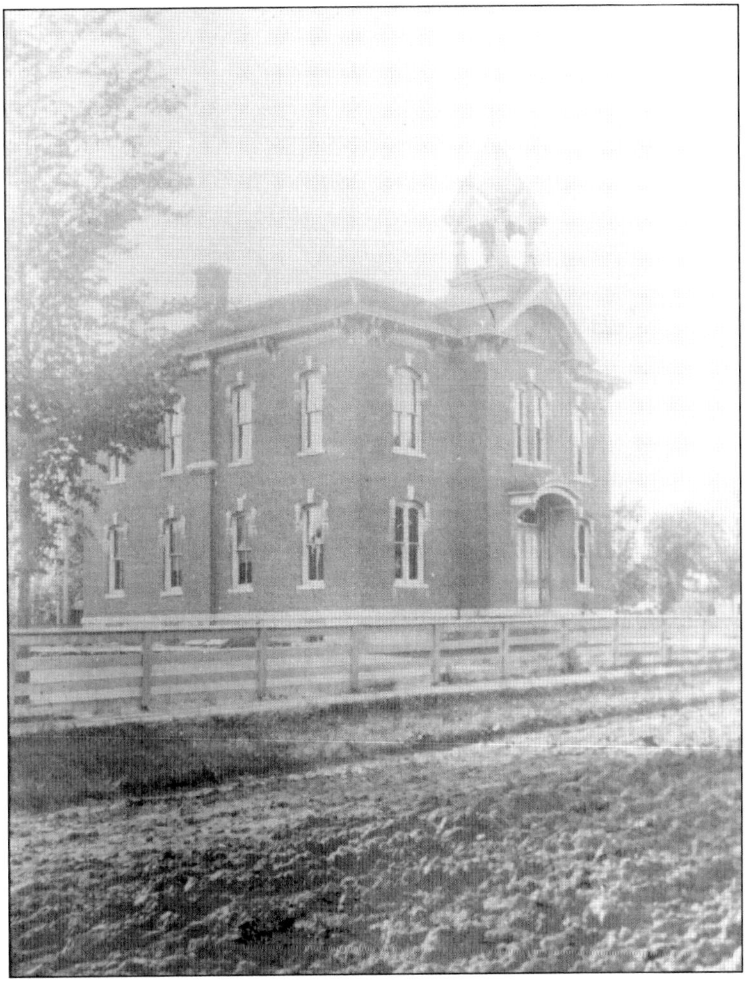

These students pose in 1911 outside Heights School with their teacher, Maud McCreedy (upper right). The school had a capacity of 200 students.

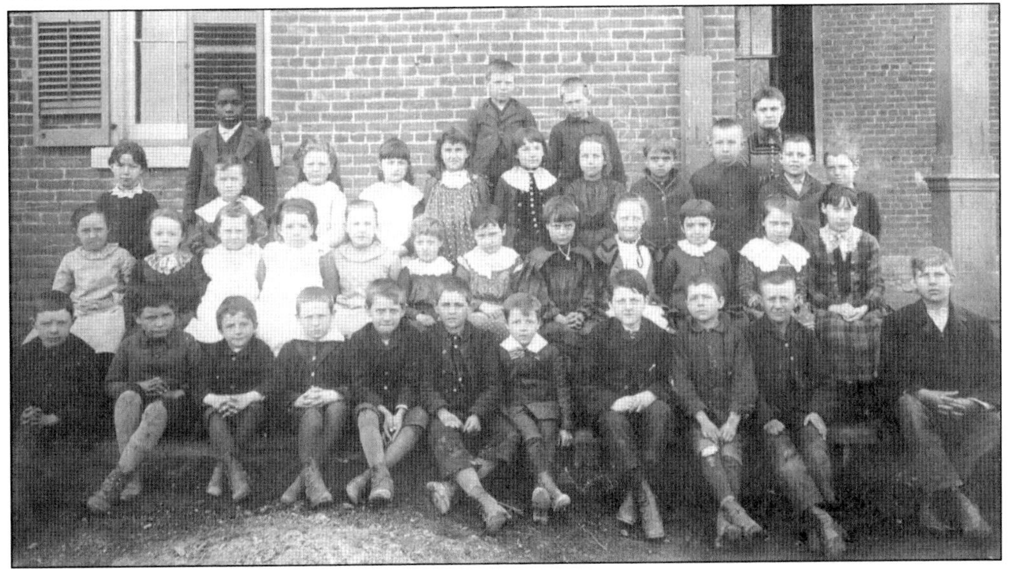

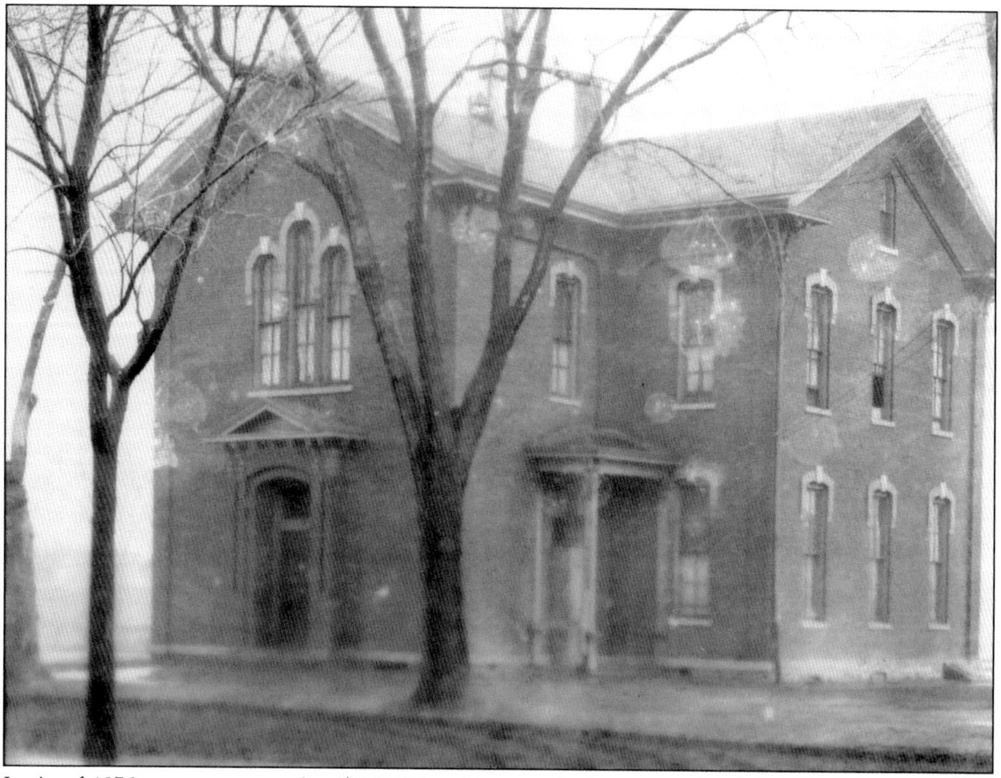

In April 1876, voters approved an $8,000 bond issue to build a new school on West Monroe Street. It was named Centennial School, in honor of the nation's centennial.

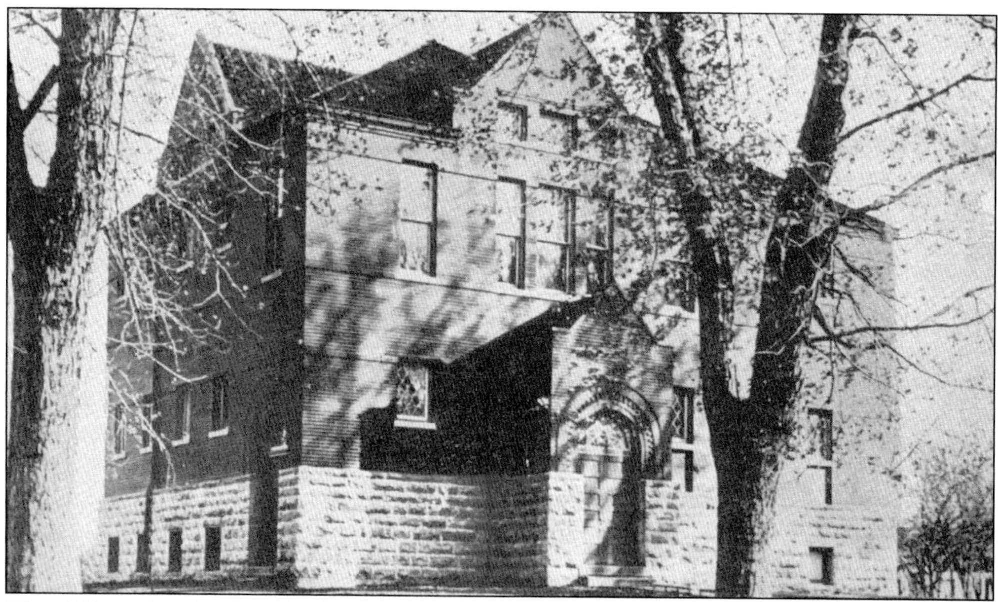

The old Lincoln school was built in 1889 on the former South School site. After being extensively remodeled, it served as the Church of the Living Word for several years and later became Hamakua Place, a teen center.

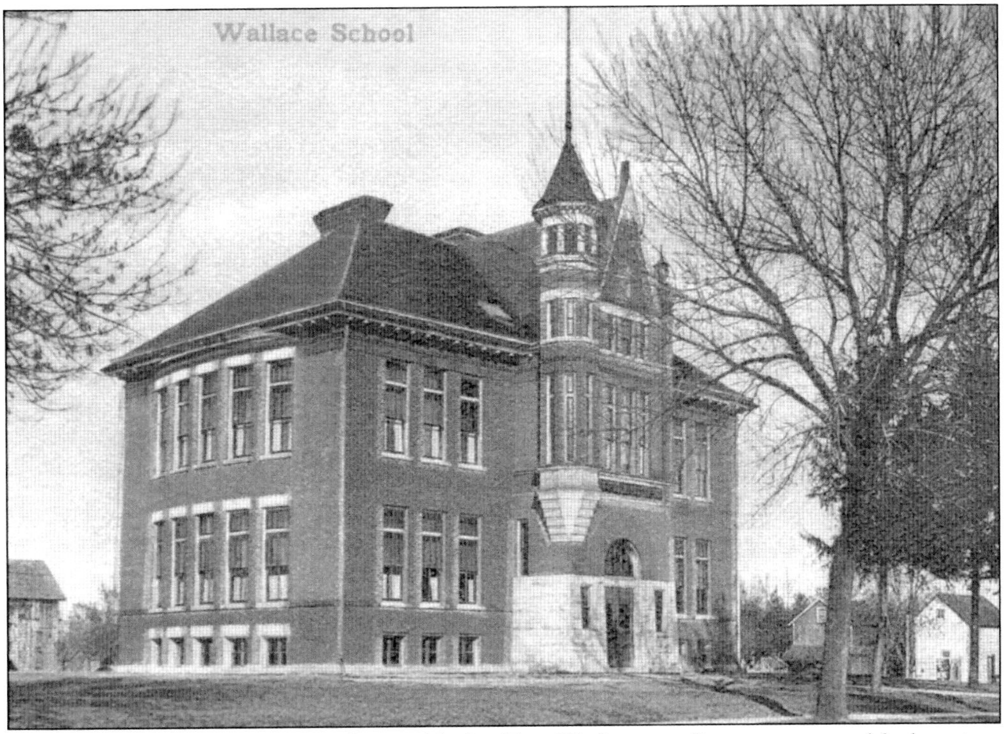

Wallace School

Wallace School, built in 1896 on the 900 block of East Washington Street, was named for longtime school board member A.H. Wallace. Wallace owned a lumberyard in town for many years.

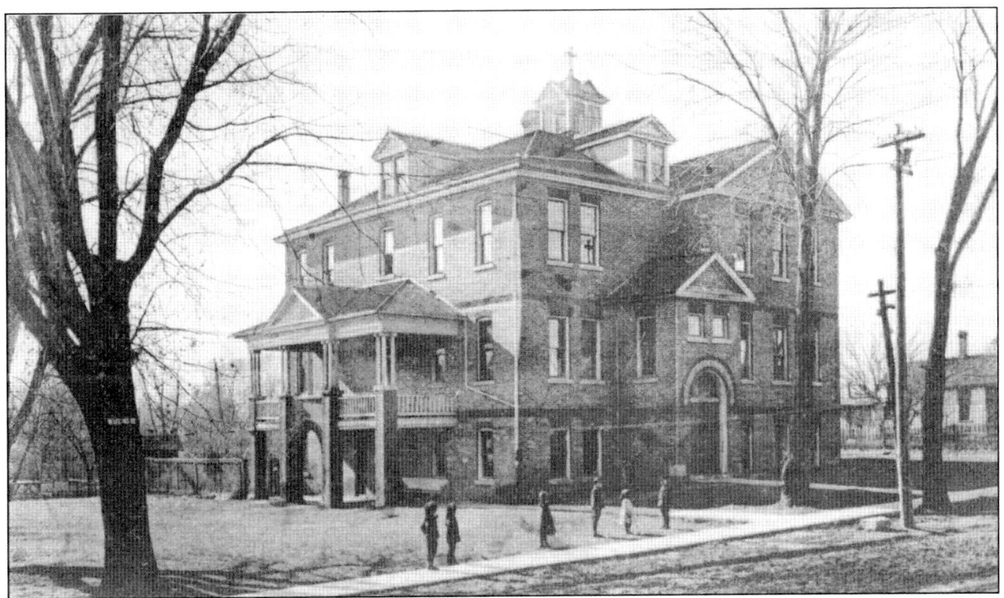

The first St. James School was built in 1876. This is the second St. James, constructed in 1901. A one-story brick building for elementary students replaced this structure in 1956.

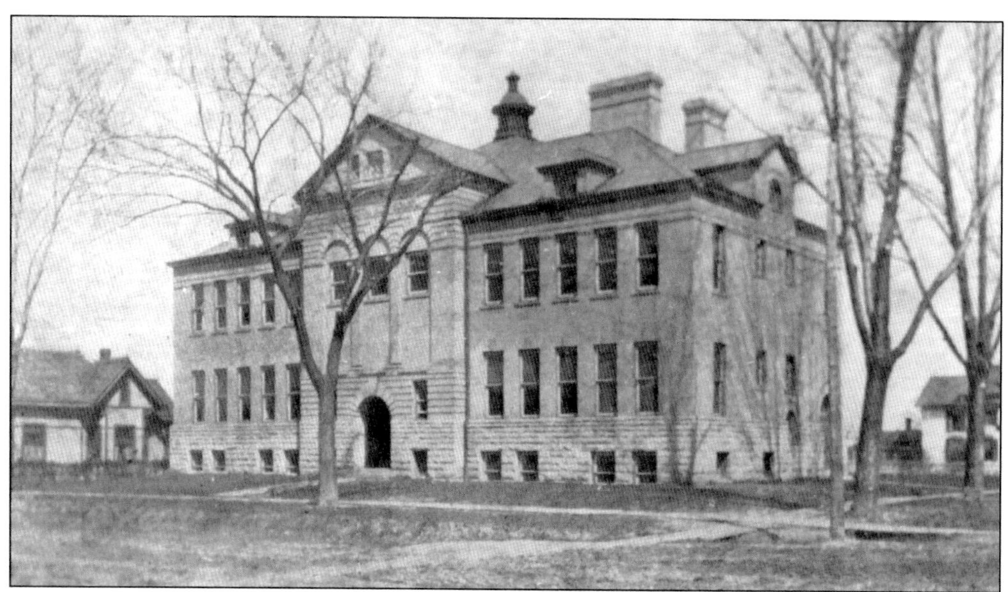

The old high school was constructed in 1899. Located at 404 West Main Street, the building was later used as the junior high. It was torn down in the 1960s, and the site is now the home of the Washington School District central offices.

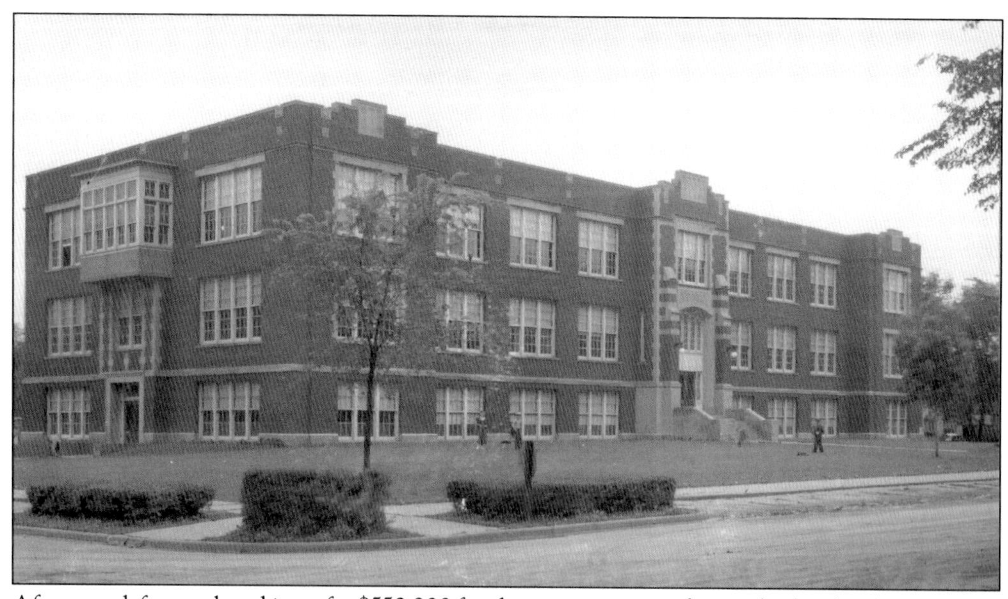

After two defeats, a bond issue for $550,000 for the construction of a new high school was passed. The community held the cornerstone-laying ceremony on November 15, 1918, and the new school opened on September 15, 1919. In 1953, a new addition was constructed, and in 2012 the building became Washington Middle School.

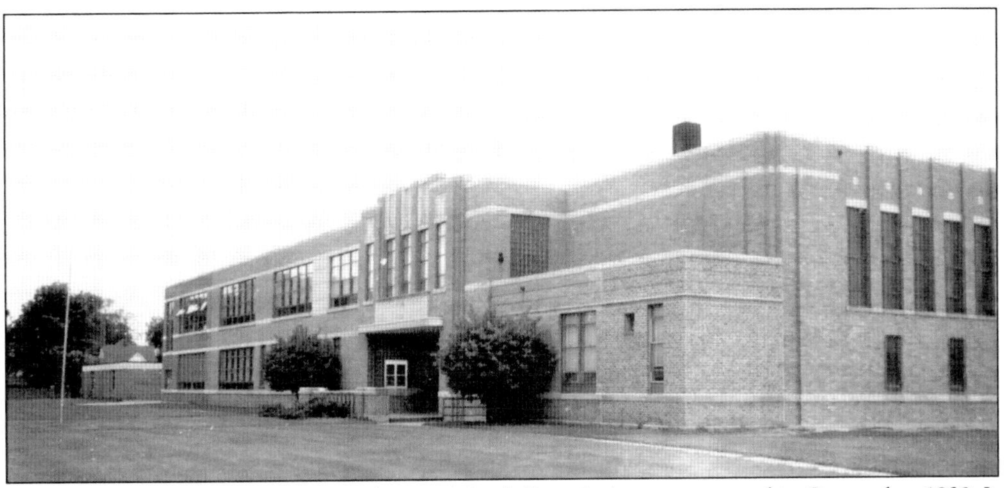

Stewart Elementary School, located at 821 North Fourth Avenue, opened in September 1939. It was a project of the Public Works Administration, one of Pres. Franklin D. Roosevelt's programs to put unemployed citizens back to work.

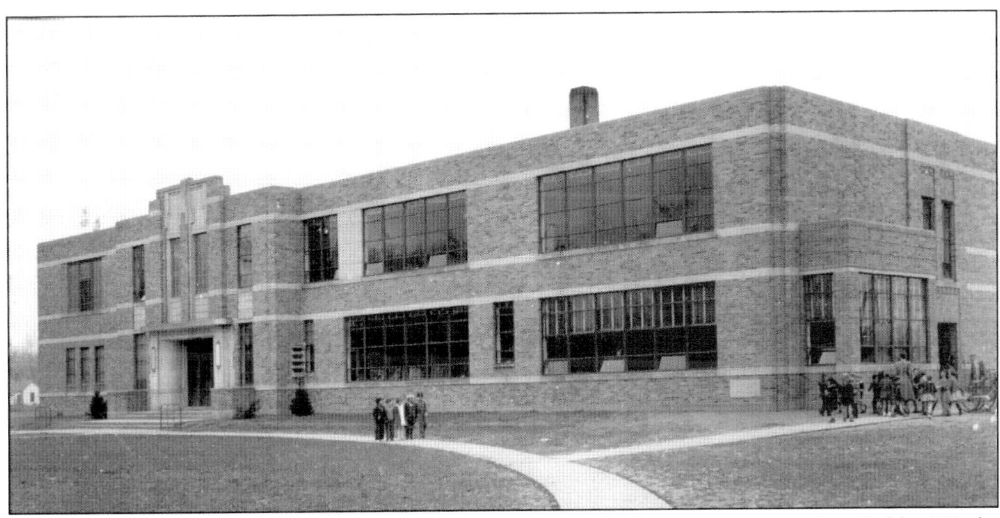

Lincoln Elementary School, located at 606 South Fourth Avenue, was another Public Works Administration project. In 1938, the citizens of Washington approved a $127,369 bond issue for the construction of two elementary schools. Lincoln opened in December 1939. The school board held a formal dedication for both schools on January 9, 1940.

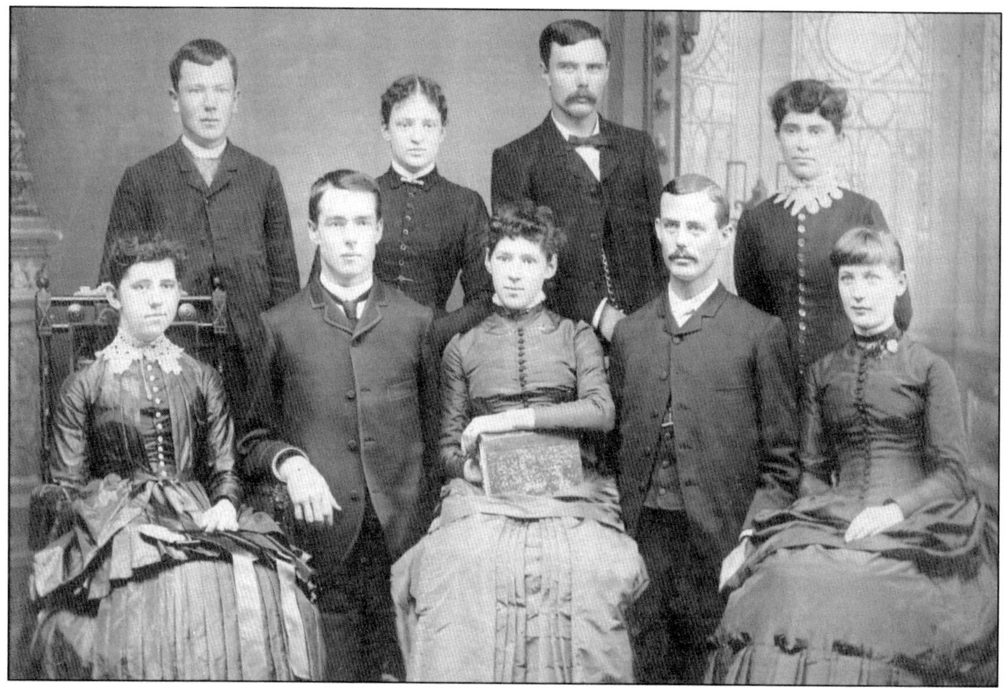

This is the 1885 graduating class of the Washington Academy. The man with the moustache in the back row is D.W. Lewis, the superintendant of schools.

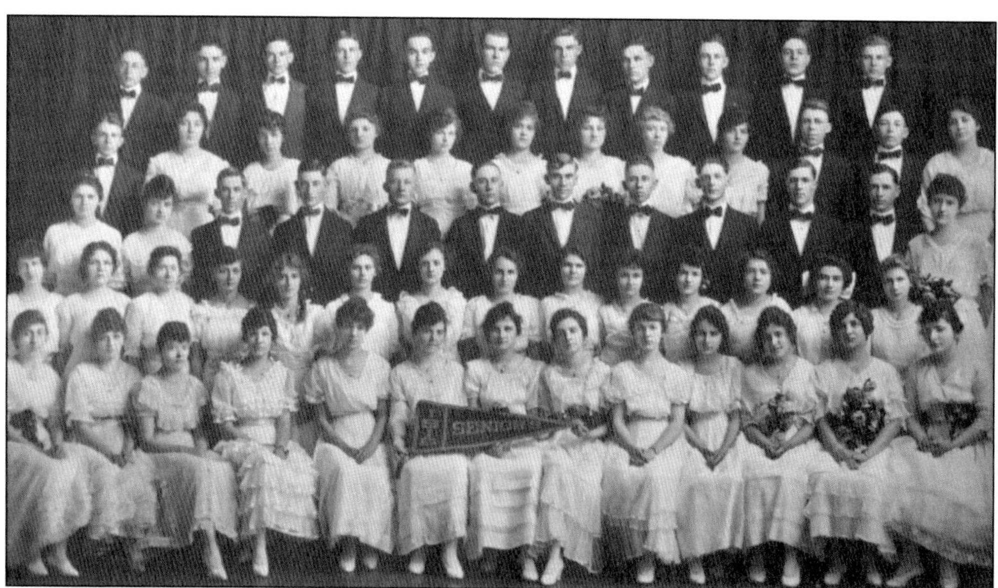

The Washington High School class of 1916, with 62 students, was the largest to graduate up to that time. Here, class members pose at their commencement on June 2. The class president was Charles Graber, the vice president was Bertha Hay, and the secretary/treasurer was Reed Sailaday.

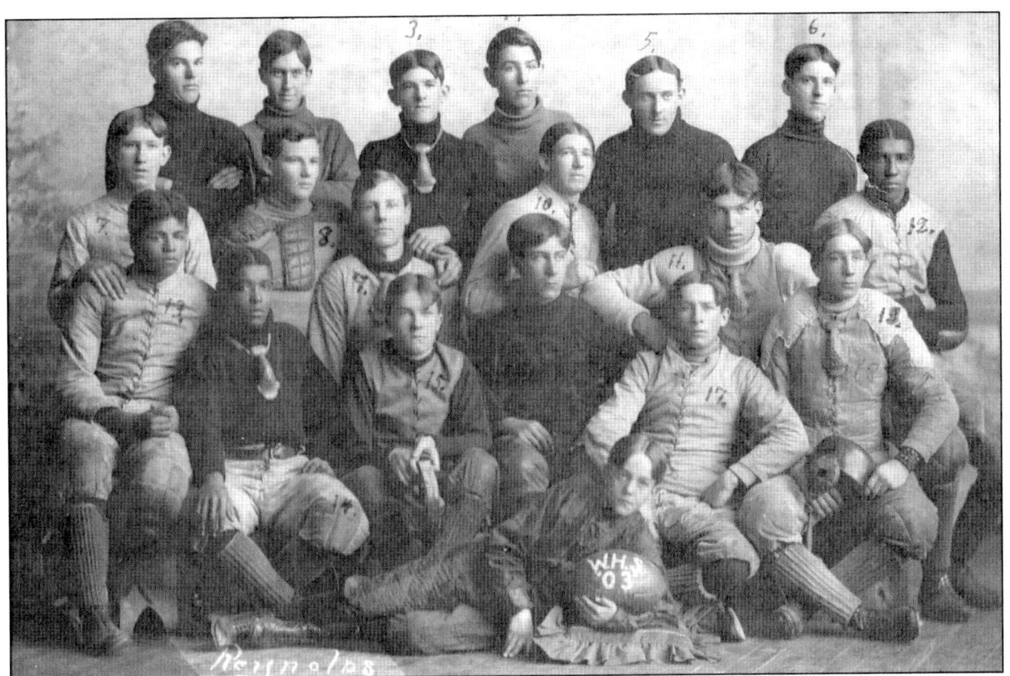

The 1903 Washington High School football team had an undefeated record. Members included, from left to right, (first row) James Crump, Robert Motts, Harold McElhinney, ? Snider, Tom Bailey, and Harold McWilliams; (second row) Laudi Koss, Frank Buckley, Arthur Ingham, Lloyd McCall, Lawrence Wilson, and captain Ralph Motts; (third row) ? Lynn, ? Guthrie, Verge Irwin, Glen Abdill, manager John Bailey, and Rodney Crail.

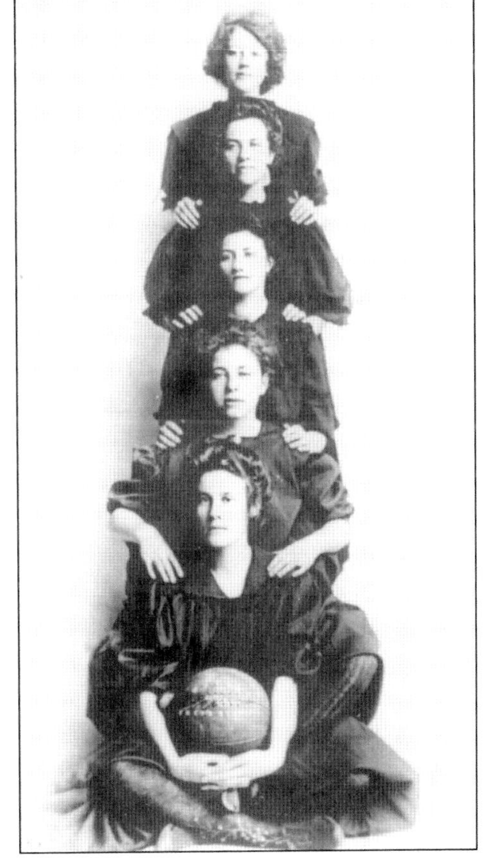

One of Washington High School's earliest girls' basketball team poses for a photograph in 1908.

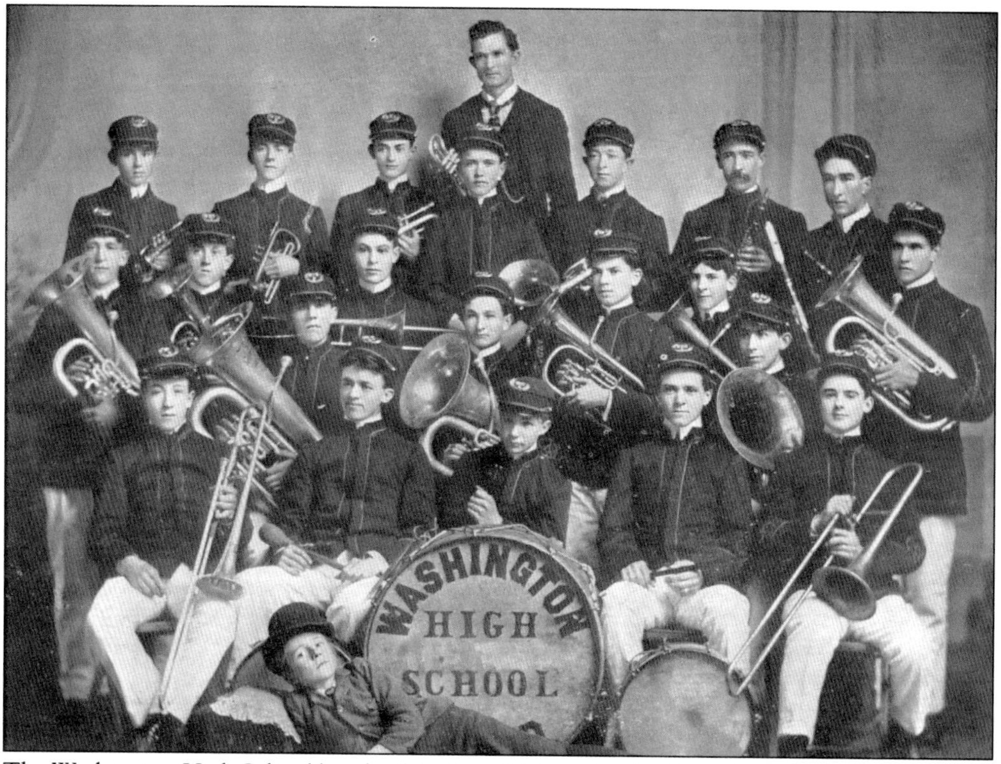

The Washington High School bands of the late 1890s and early 1900s did not include any female musicians. Charles Langenberg, the band director, can be seen at the top of this image, and Clyde Bickford, the mascot, is at the bottom. Also pictured are, from left to right, (first row) Cleveland Dayton, Lloyd Bickford, Phillip Crail, unidentified, and William Harwood; (second row) Homer Nichols, Louis Moyer, Lloyd Neal, Ralph Junkin, Frank McClean, Earl Corbin, Verle Isenhart, Rodney Crail, and Charles Hayes; (third row) George McClean, Paul Allen, Charles Chance, Fred Ferguson, Bob Stewart, "Doc" Dagel, and Glenn Zaring.

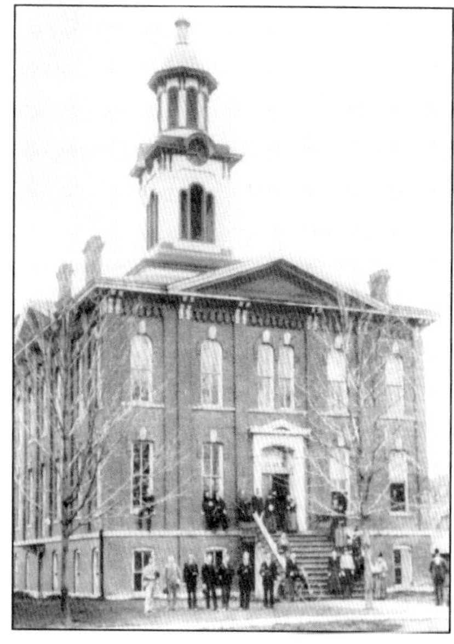

The first Washington Academy was established in 1854. Pictured here is the Washington Academy's second building, which was built in 1874 and later became known as McKee School. In 1910, it was used by the Washington School District for a grammar school and the manual-training program. The structure was torn down in 1920, and the YMCA/YWCA now stands on the site.

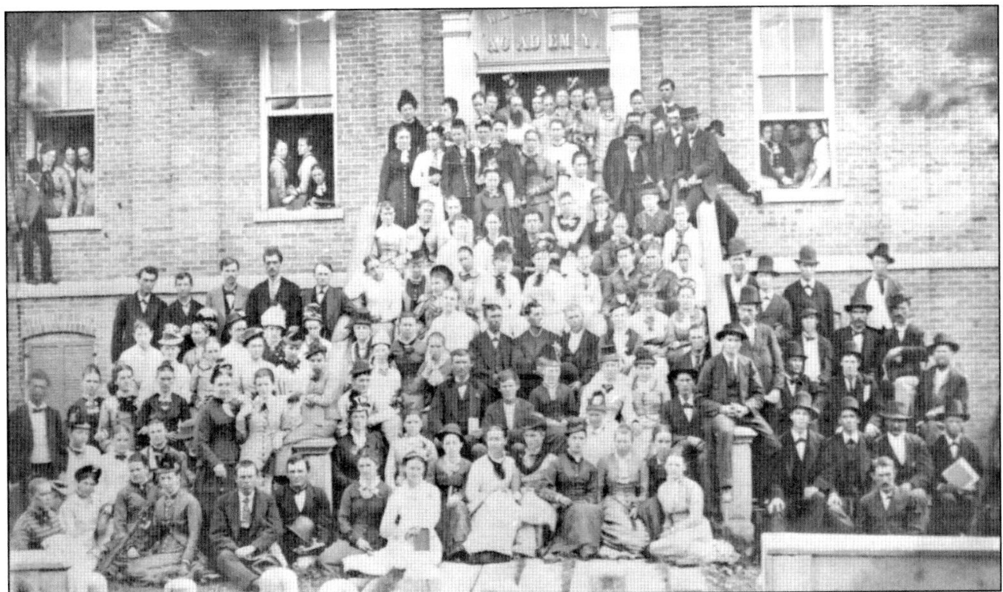

The Washington Academy graduating class of 1885 seen here included members Sadie Boyd, Litia Townsley, Ida Roberts, Anna Fleming, Flora Glenn, George Robb, A.W. McCausland, R.G. Gibson, and J.T. Mauhers.

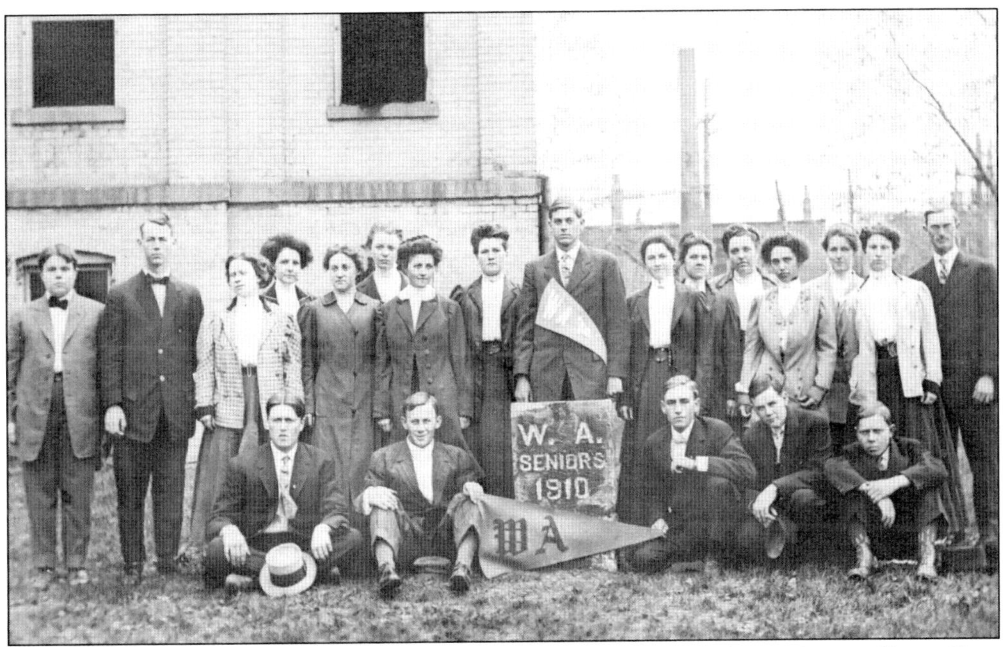

The 1910 graduates of Washington Academy, pictured here, included Enor Hayes, Cloyce Kerr, Jesse Busby, Irene Simpson, Clara Wallace, Clarence Dodds, Wallace Carson, Margaret Carson, Harry Taylor, Stella Meek, Anna Wilson, Vesa Rickery, Martha Porter, Hill McCleary, Elsie Wallace, Edith Cherryholmes, Ora Starr, Barclay Miller, Esther Strom, Alice Dennison, and Melo Shalla.

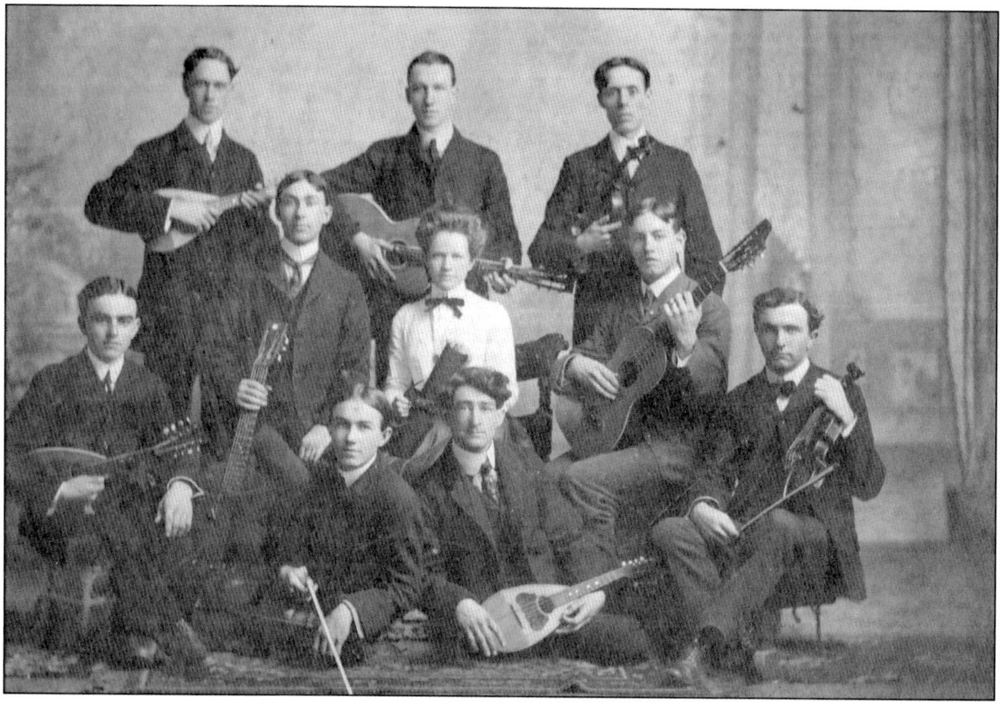

The Washington Academy Magnet Mandolin Club members included, from left to right, (bottom row) Fulton Masson, Marion Anderson, and two unidentified; (middle row) Harvey McCall, Ara Matthews, and Bert Smith; (top row) Lawson Fisher, John Fisher, and unidentified. The group chose the name Magnet to represent "drawing power."

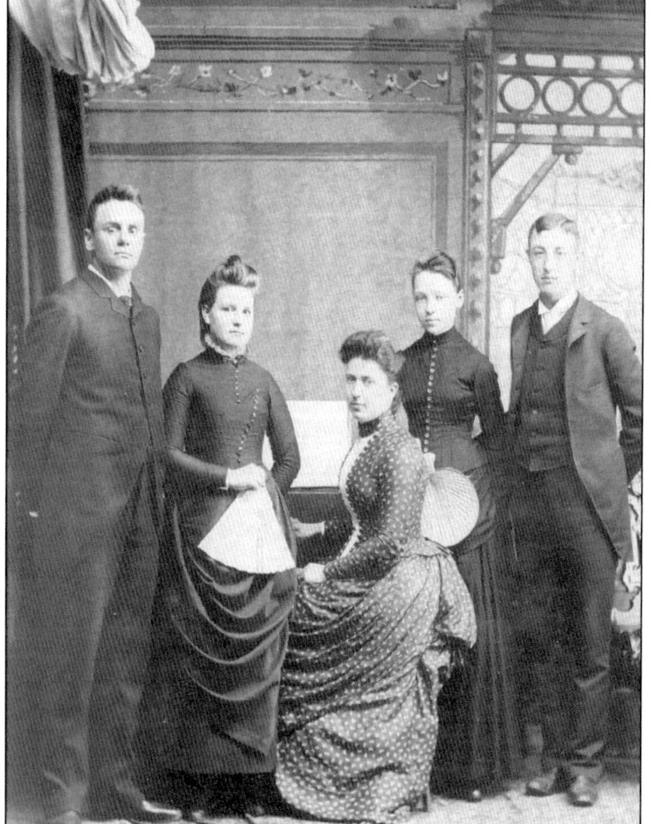

The Washington Academy had many music groups. This 1888 photograph shows one of the quartets with its accompanist. Pictured are, from left to right, bass John Beamer, alto Nellie Doolittle, organist Ella May Brown (Thomas), soprano Nellie Anderson (Wallace), and tenor John Ferguson.

Five

Religion

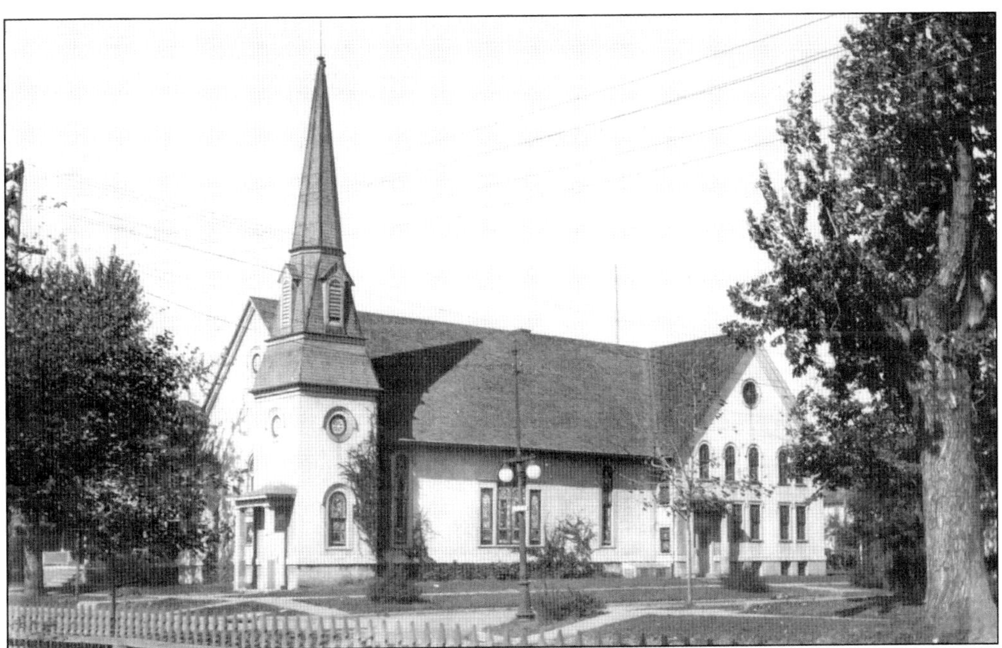

The First Baptist congregation was organized on October 2, 1841. The original church, dedicated in 1851, became part of a new structure built in 1871. Located on the corner of North Second Avenue and East Second Street, the church has been remodeled numerous times. In 1925, a tower replaced the original spire.

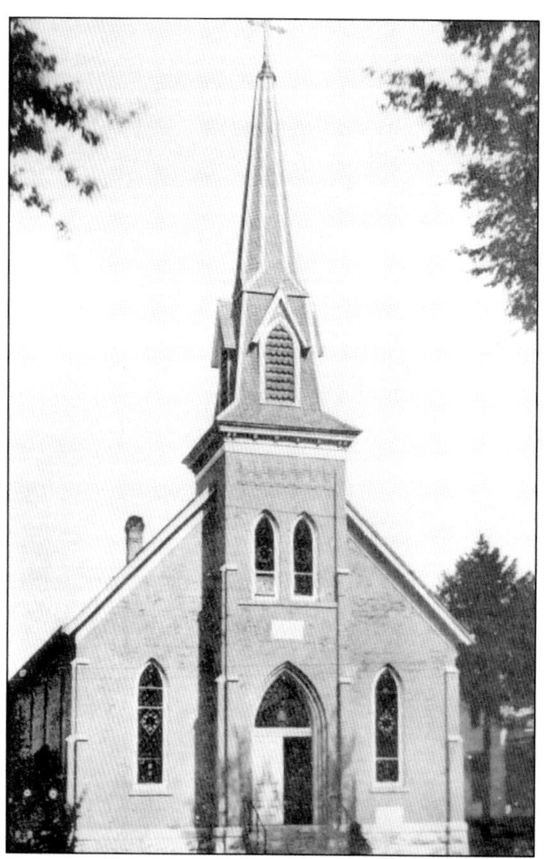

The first St. James Church was a log structure built in 1865. The second, pictured here, was constructed in 1892; it was demolished in 1960 after the construction of the current church, located near the site of the first two buildings.

This is the interior of the old St. James Catholic Church. Two of the statues and two stained-glass windows from the old structure were incorporated into the new church.

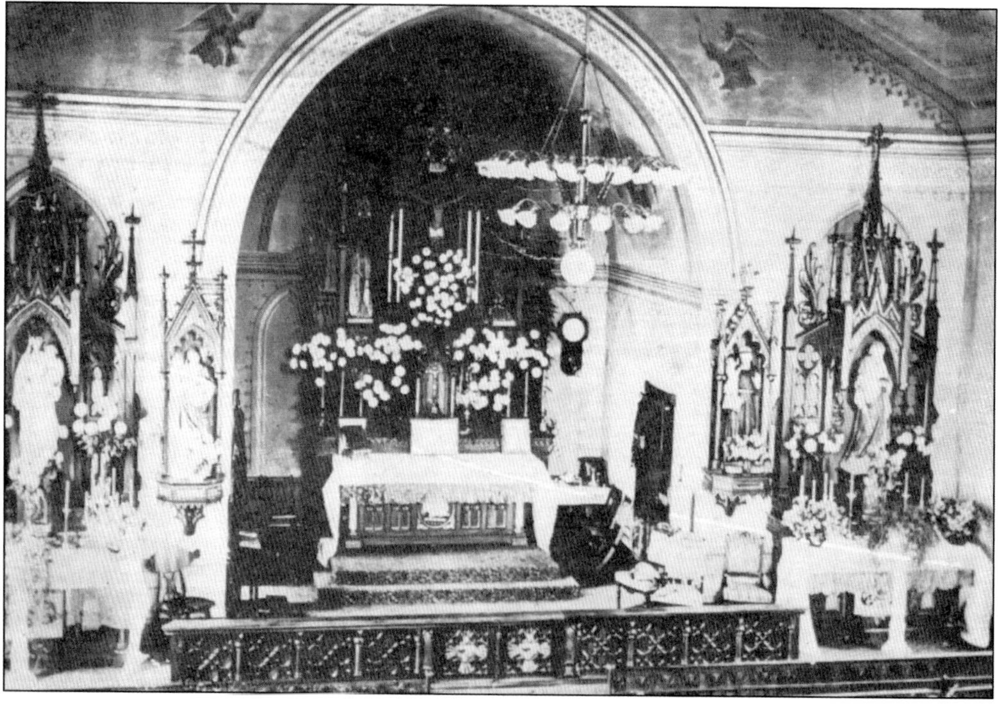

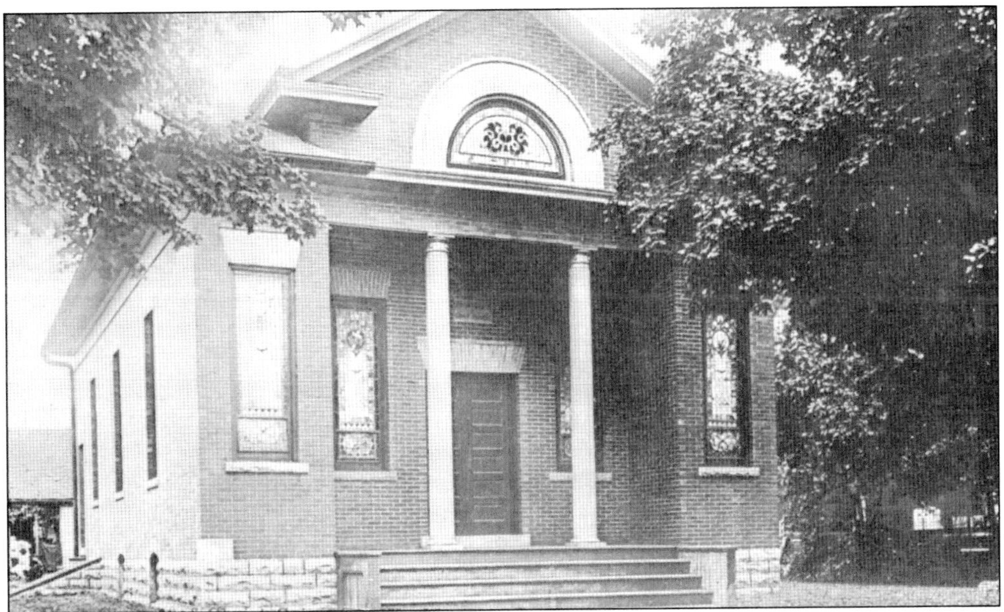

The Christian Scientists formally organized in Washington in September 1897. In 1899, Mrs. E.E. Everson donated a lot south of the square as the site of a church building. Construction began in 1904 at 221 South Iowa Avenue, the current location of Marshall's Furniture.

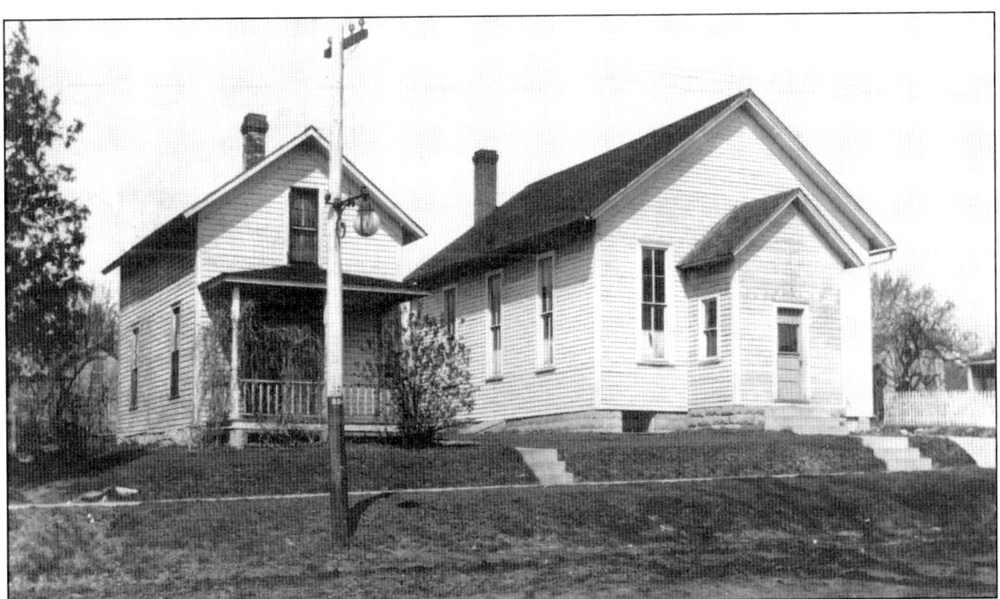

Built in 1870, the African Methodist Church and parsonage stood on the 500 block on the west side of South Avenue C. The church was originally known as the Shorter Chapel. Both buildings were torn down in 1972.

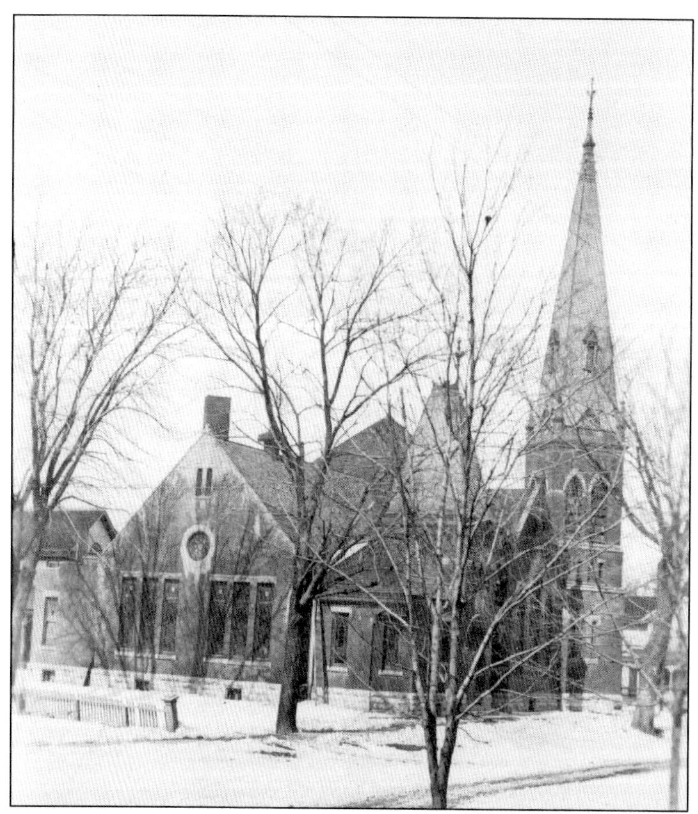

Construction on the third Methodist church in Washington began in 1891, and the dedication occurred on April 10, 1892. The spire was later removed, and the building, located at 301 West Second Street, is now the First Christian Church. The present Methodist church was built in 1912 after the congregation outgrew this structure.

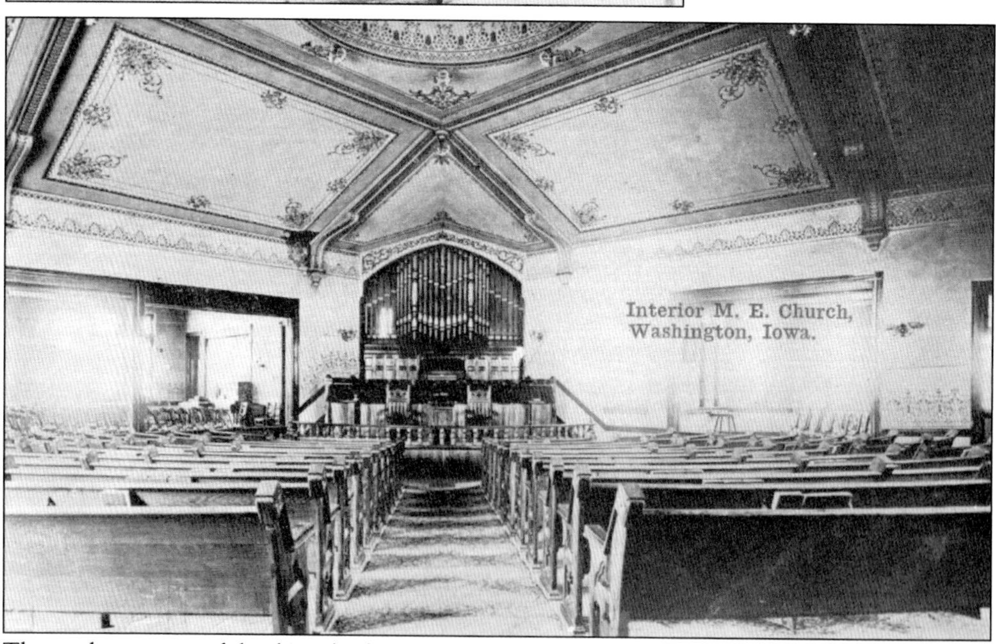

This is the interior of third Methodist church as it appeared when first built. Note the opening into a large room on the left: this design feature was common for churches of the period, allowing for additional seating and also serving as a stage for various pageants and special presentations. The sanctuary has been significantly remodeled through the years.

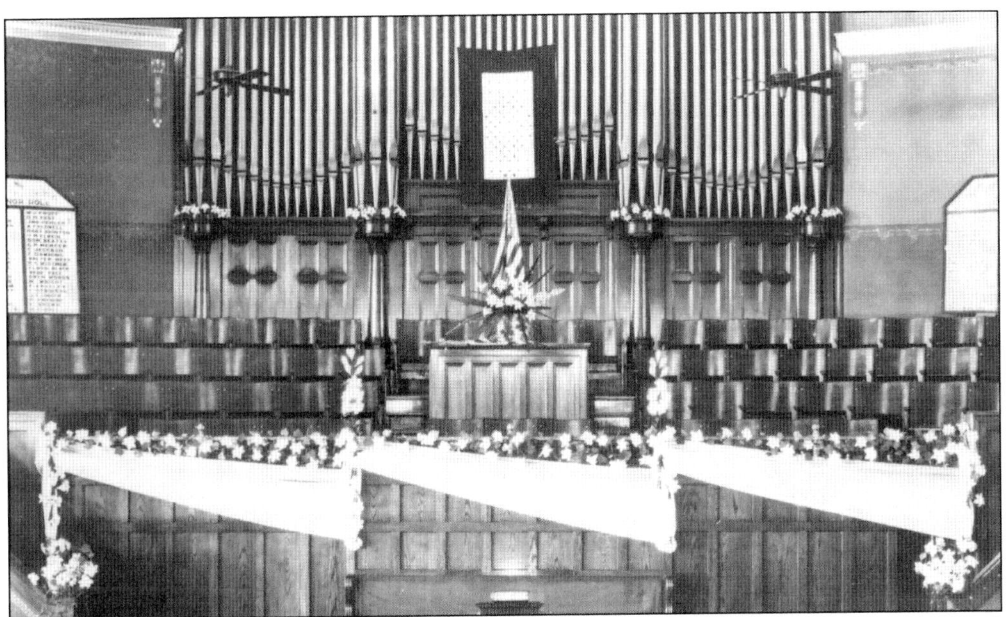

This is the choir loft of the old Methodist church. The flag hanging at the center of the organ's pipes was the honor roll of men serving in World War I.

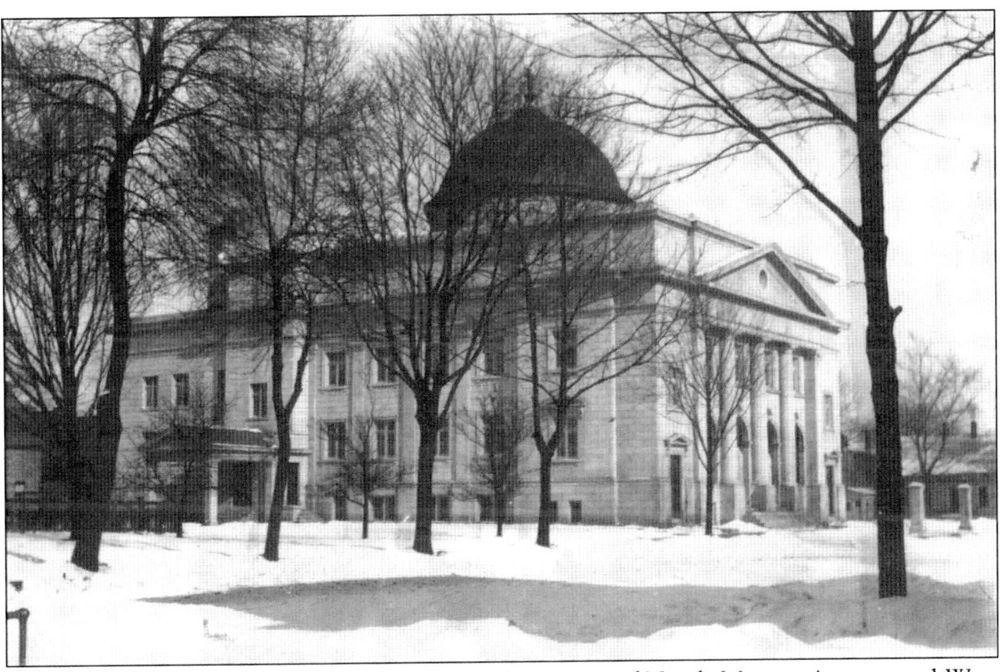

The current Methodist church is located on the corner of North Marion Avenue and West Second Street. Built in 1912 at a cost of $85,000, it originally had a carriage drive on the west side. The ground breaking for the educational building, just west of the church, took place on July 3, 1977.

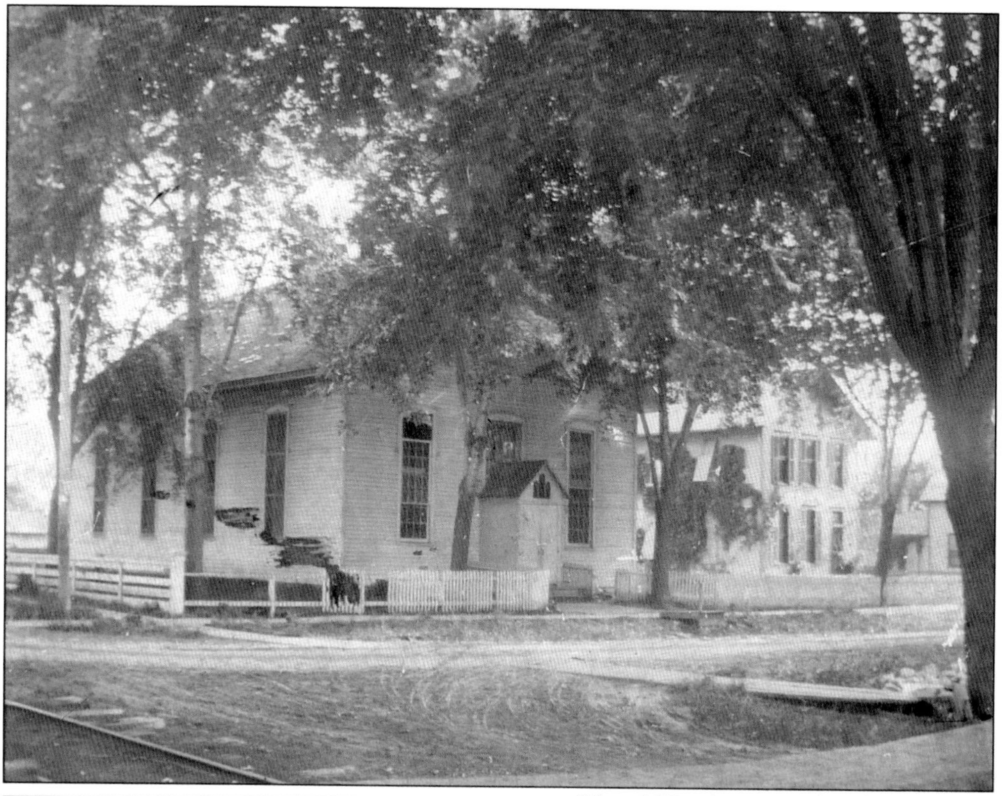

The old Presbyterian church and parsonage were on East Washington Street. Built in 1865 at a cost of $3,000, it continued in service until a new church was dedicated on May 29, 1892.

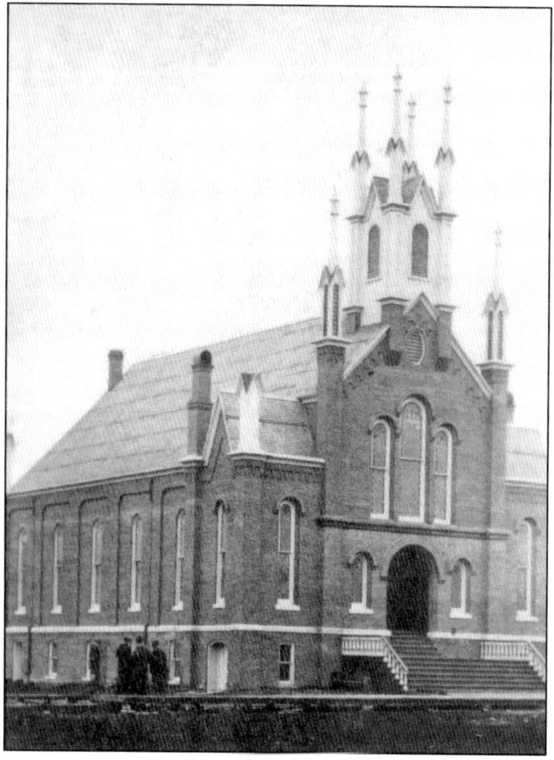

The First United Presbyterian Church at 215 South Marion Avenue was dedicated on May 29, 1892. On May 17, 1970, the Marion Avenue United Presbyterian Church united with the First Presbyterian Church to form the present United Presbyterian Church. Ground was broken on October 10, 1971, for the new church on the site of the old First Presbyterian Church at the corner of East Main Street and Second Avenue. The building pictured is now the Marion Avenue Baptist Church.

This is the interior of the First United Presbyterian Church, now the Marion Avenue Baptist Church, at 215 South Marion Avenue. Many of the original architectural features remain.

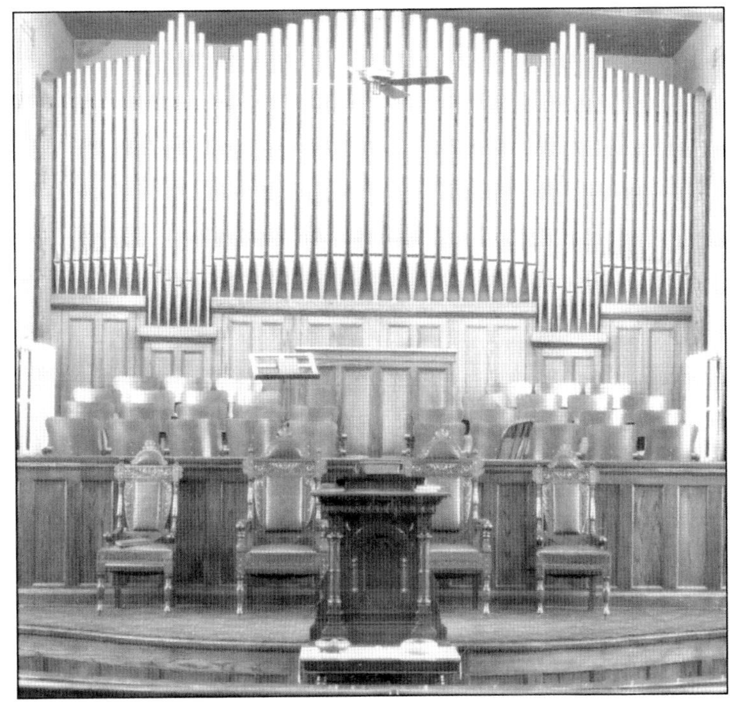

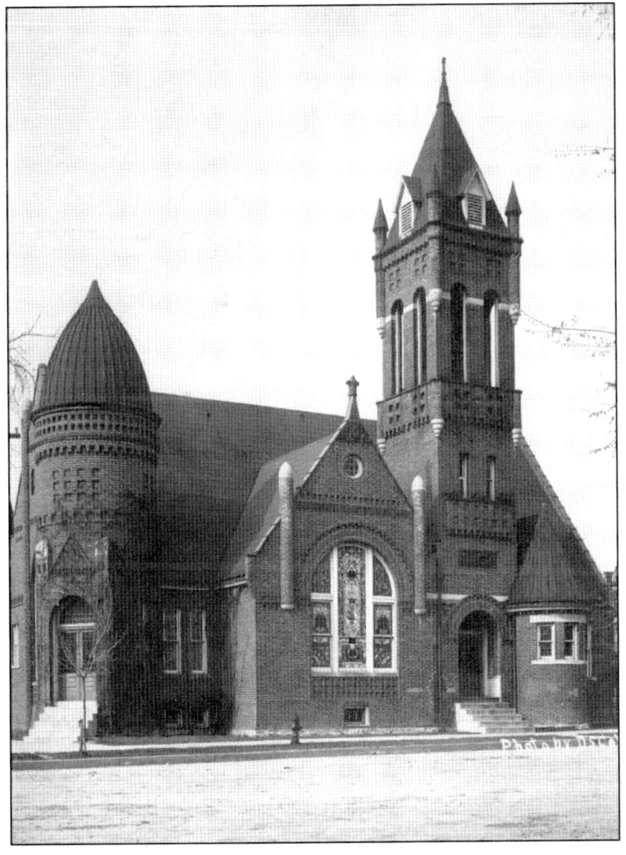

The Second United Presbyterian Church, located at the corner of West Washington Street and South Avenue B, was built in 1891. It was torn down in 1927, the year that the Second United and First United Presbyterian congregations joined and moved to the Marion Avenue church.

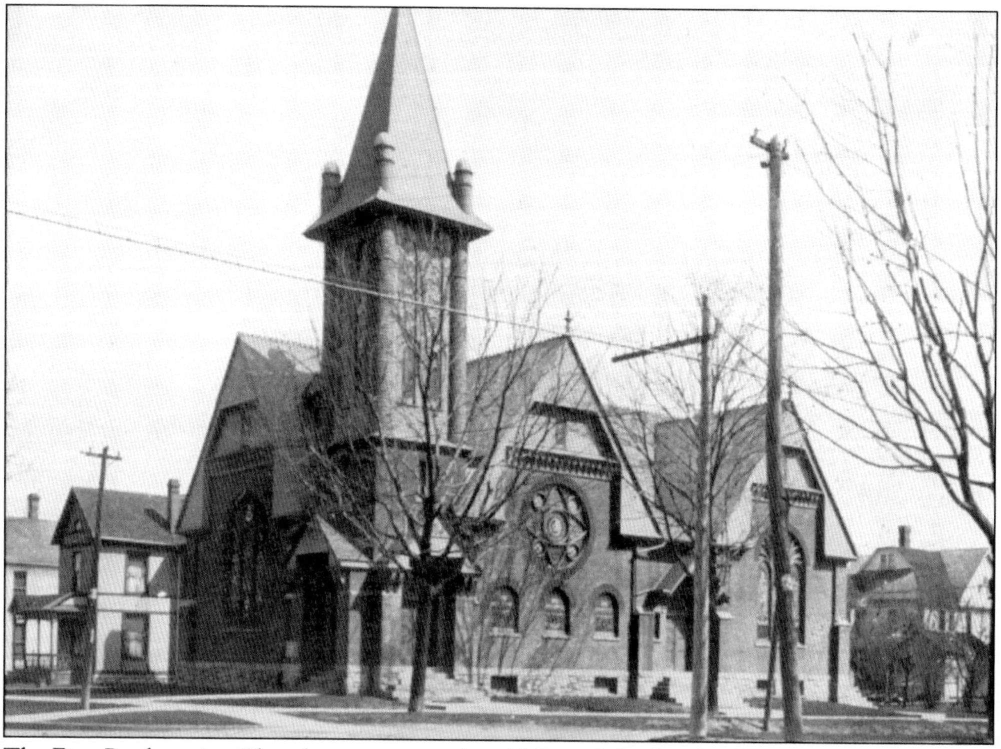

The First Presbyterian Church was organized in 1843, and the first building was erected in 1846 at the corner of East Main Street and South Second Avenue. The congregation's third church (pictured here), built in 1893, was torn down in 1971 to make room for the present United Presbyterian Church.

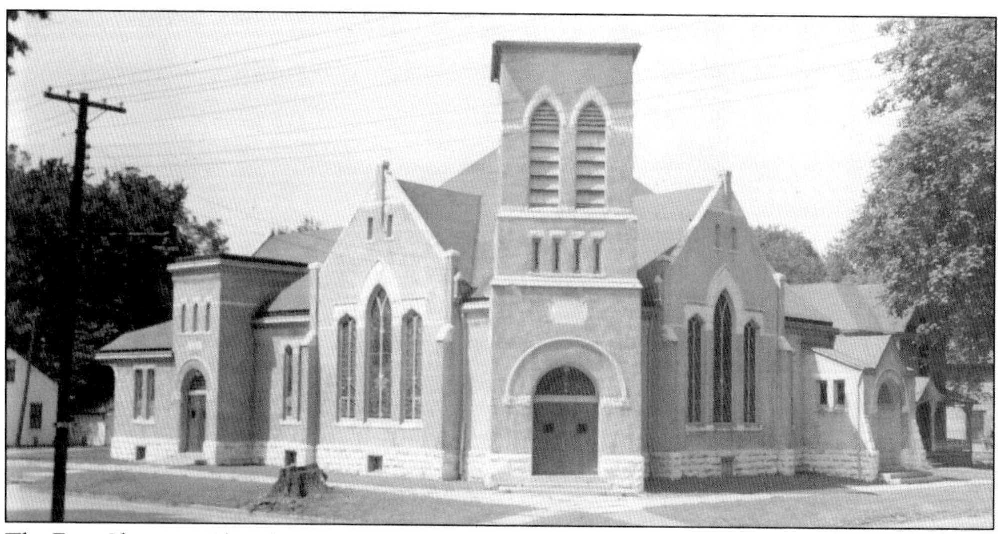

The First Christian Church in Washington was incorporated on October 16, 1892. A new church, since demolished, was built in 1914 and remained in use until 1921, when the congregation bought the old Methodist church at 301 West Second Street. At that time, the spire was removed, and extensive remodeling was done.

Six

Transportation and Communication

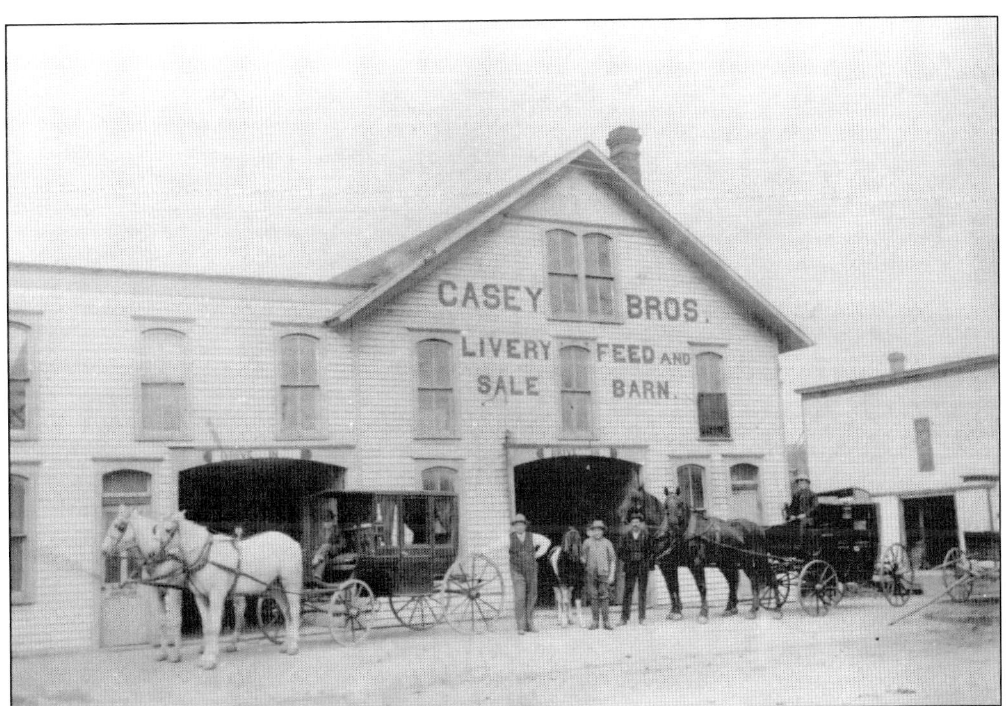

The Casey Brothers Livery Stable was one of many located near the railroad tracks. It was at the corner of North Iowa Avenue and West Second Street in the early 1900s. The door to the left, behind the two white horses, was the door to the Ladies Parlor.

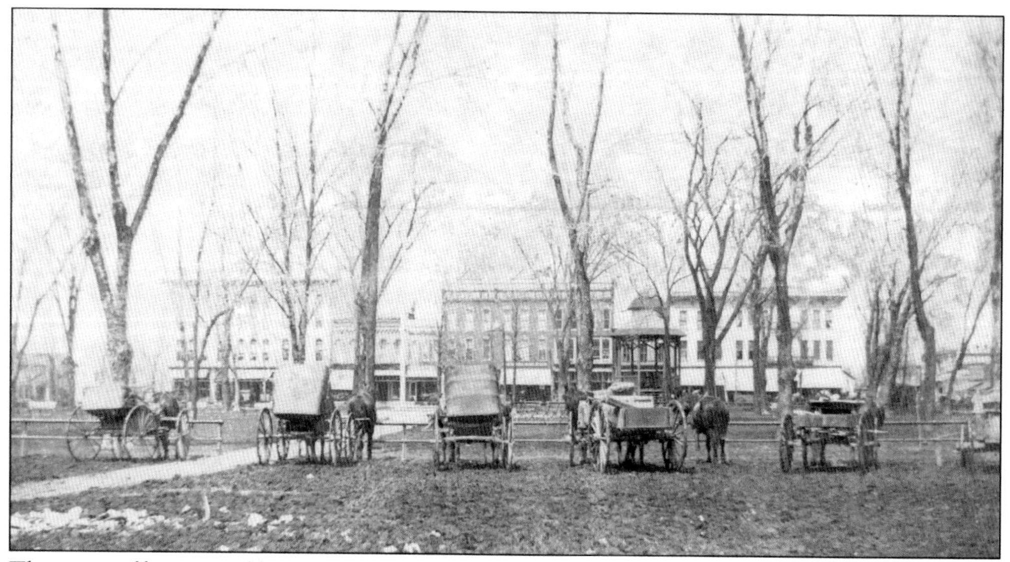

This view of horses and buggies on the edge of Central Park is from 1898. The north side of the square can be seen in the background, and the building on the left is Everson's Block, which once held the opera house and later the Masonic lodge. It burned in 1930 and is now the site of the current Masonic Lodge. The building to the far right is the Bryson House, later the Colenso Hotel. The second bandstand is near the park's center, and the hitching rail that once enclosed the park is visible.

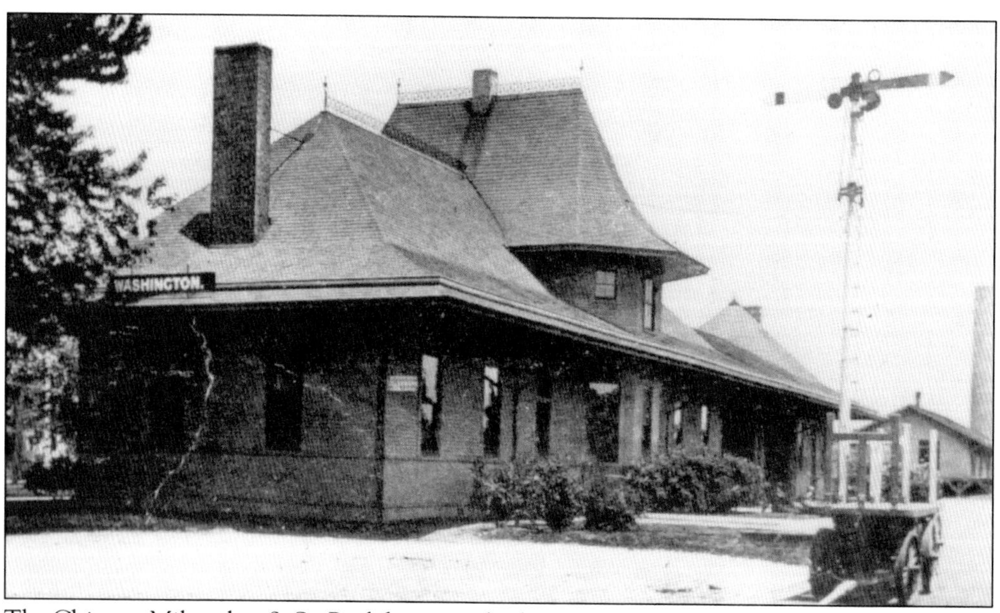

The Chicago, Milwaukee & St. Paul depot was built in 1902. Later renovated, it currently houses businesses on the ground floor and a residence on the upper level.

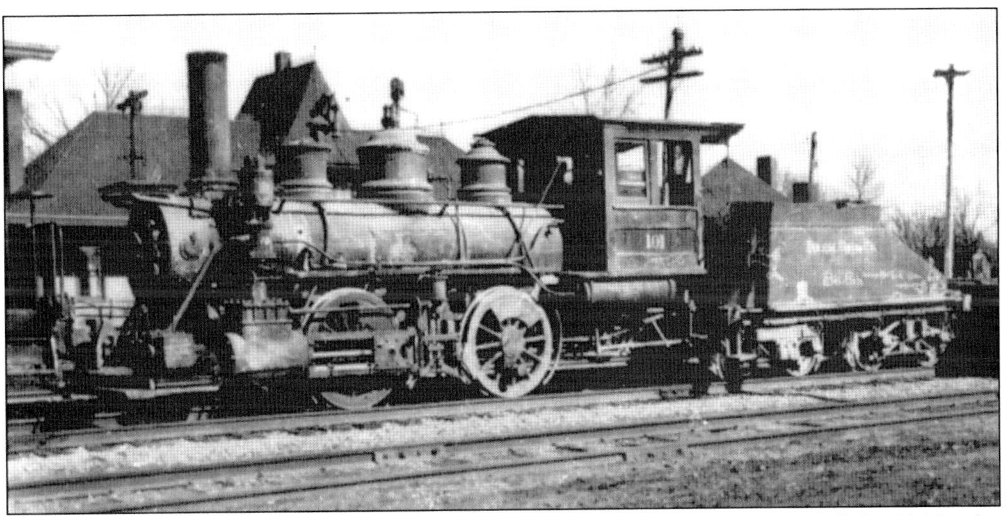

In this photograph, a steam engine waits in front of the Milwaukee depot. Until the 1940s, the station was open 24 hours a day, seven days a week. At that time, four passenger trains stopped in Washington each day. (Courtesy of Jeff Batterson.)

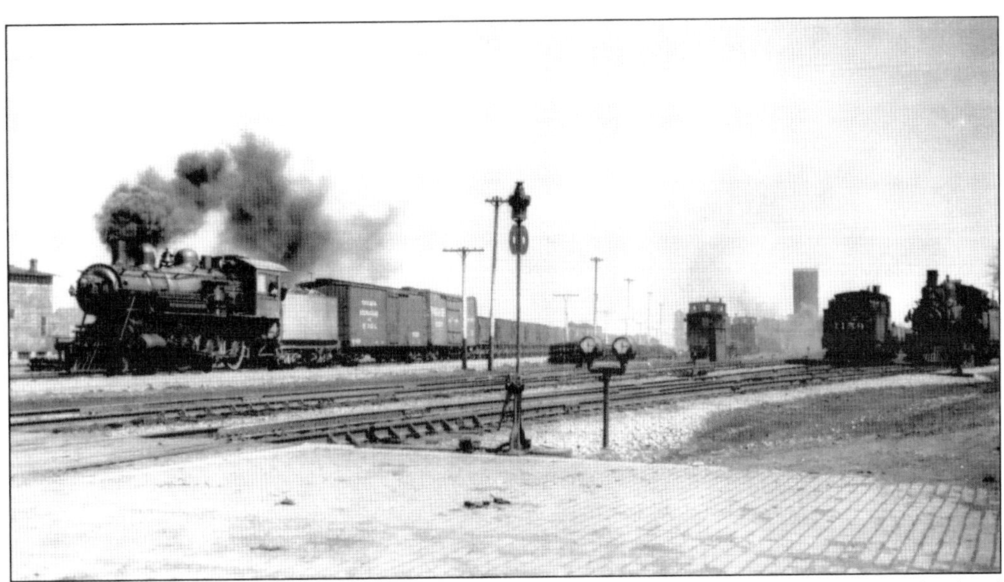

Several trains are pictured in the Chicago, Milwaukee & St. Paul and the Chicago, Rock Island & Pacific yards between East Third and East Fifth Streets and North Second and North Fourth Avenues. (Courtesy of Jeff Batterson.)

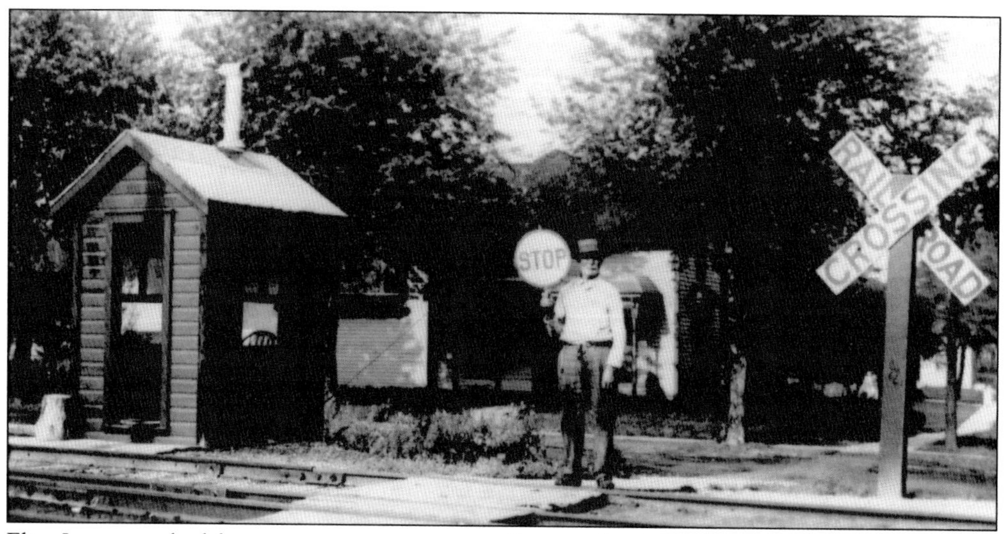

Elias Lowry worked for many years as a crossing flagman for the railroads. He is shown here, on the job, in 1911. The crossing is likely at North Marion Avenue.

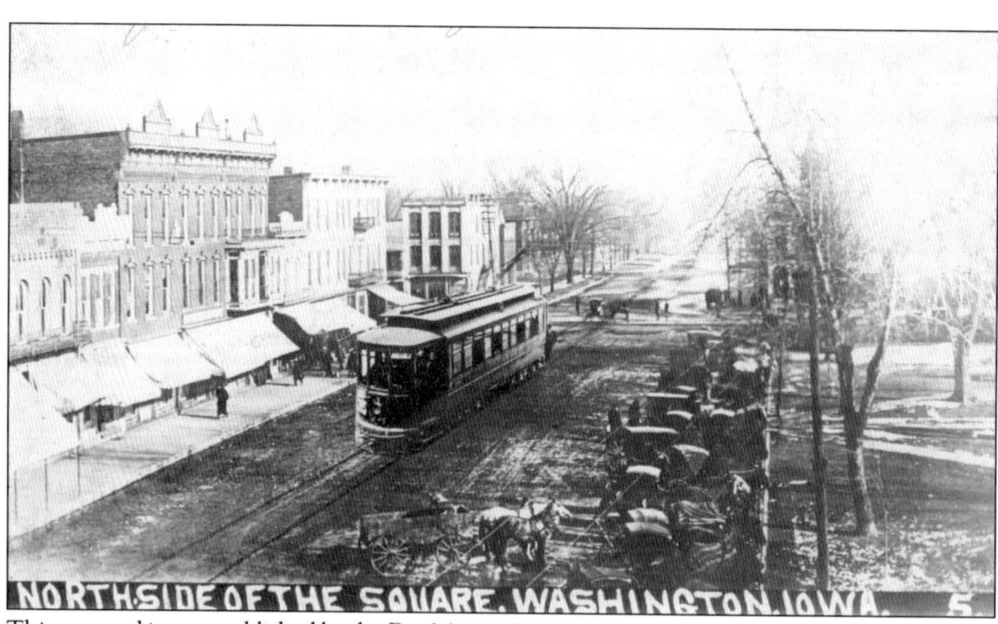

This postcard image, published by the Des Moines Post Card Company, shows the north side of the square at the end of the 19th century. It is a doctored photograph, though, because Washington never had a streetcar line.

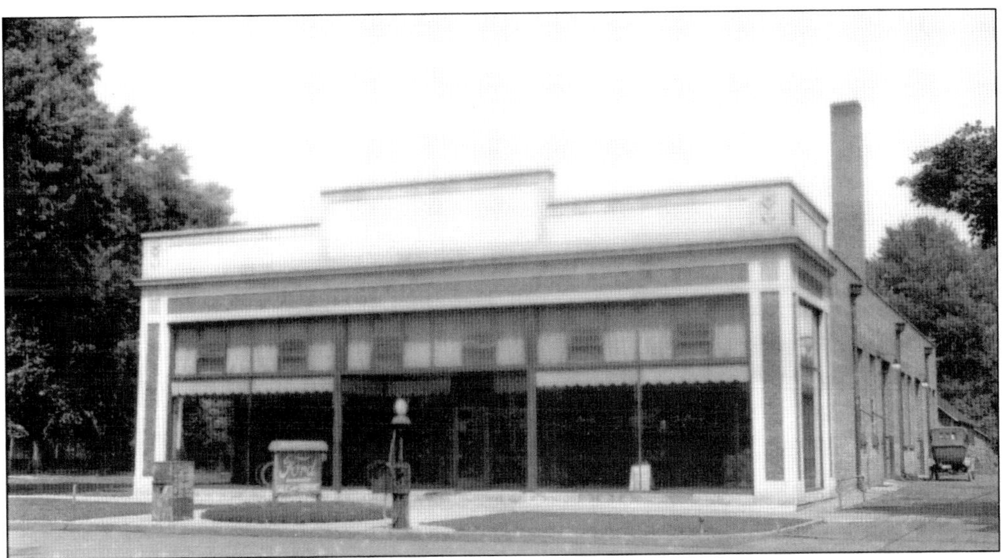

The Ford Garage, located at 212 North Iowa Avenue, was known for many years as the Mace Motor Company. It later housed the Washington Chamber of Commerce and Washington Economic Development offices when it was destroyed by fire in 2008.

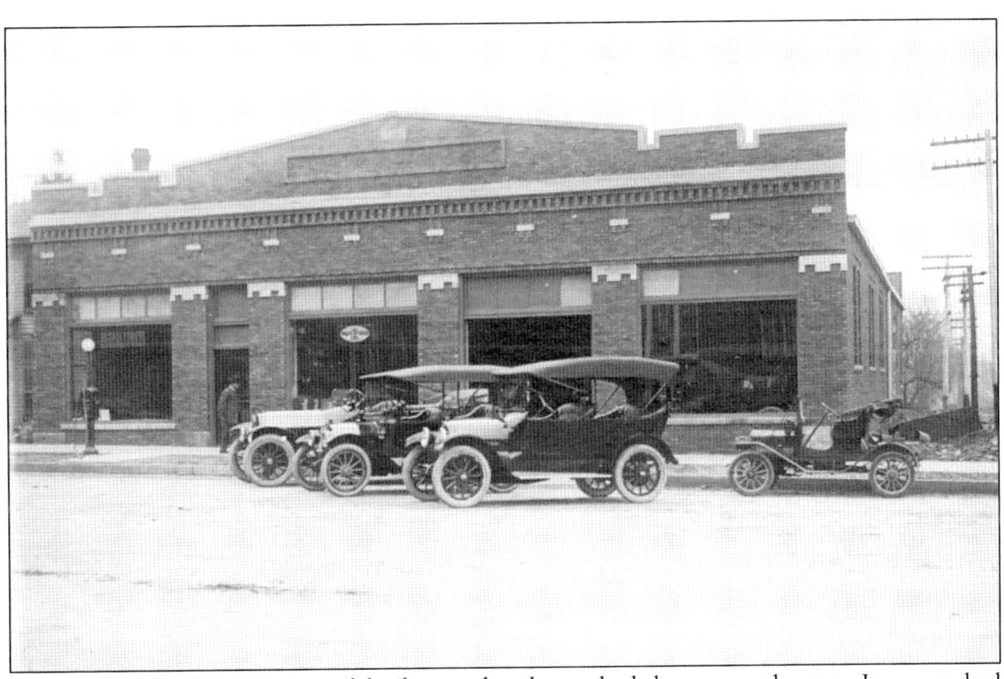

The Great White Way was one of the first roads to be marked clear across the state. It was marked in Washington County in June 1913. The White Way Garage, named for the road, was located at 221 West Washington Street. In later years, it was Perdock's garage. The building collapsed in 2011.

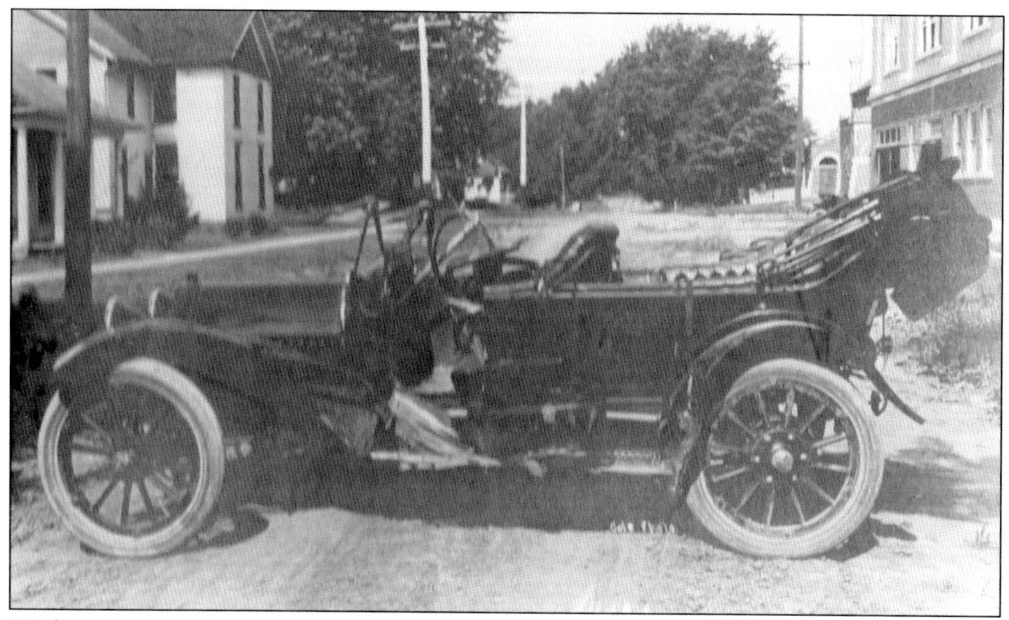

Washington's first automobile fatality occurred on July 3, 1913. A.P. Hayes, a demonstrator and salesman for the Buick Motor Company, died in his 1913 Buick, seen here after the accident, when it hit a bridge railing east of town.

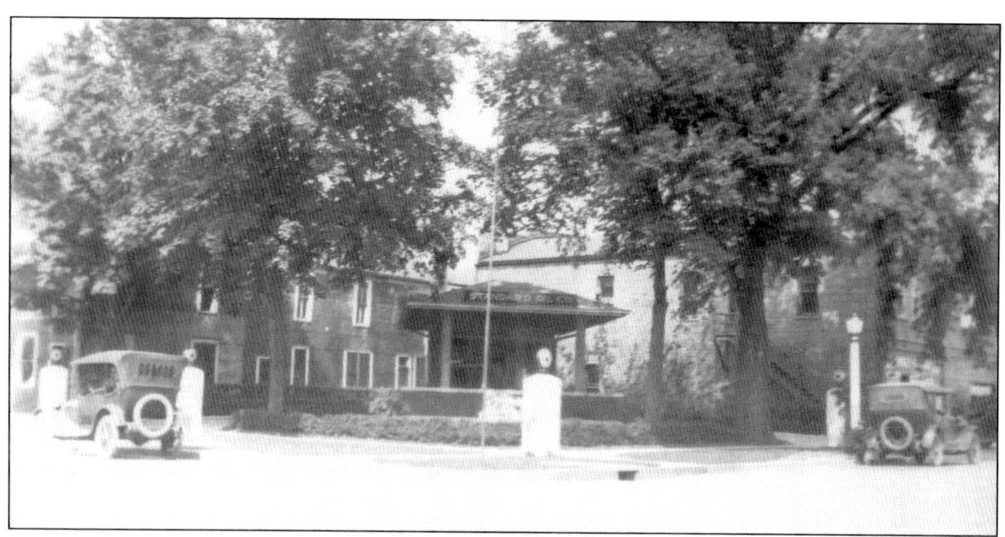

Located at the corner of North Marion Avenue and West Second Street, this Standard Oil station is believed to be the first gas station constructed in Washington. The building to the left is the Phoenix Hall, built by David Donovan to house dances. The building to the right is the Western Hog Oiler Company.

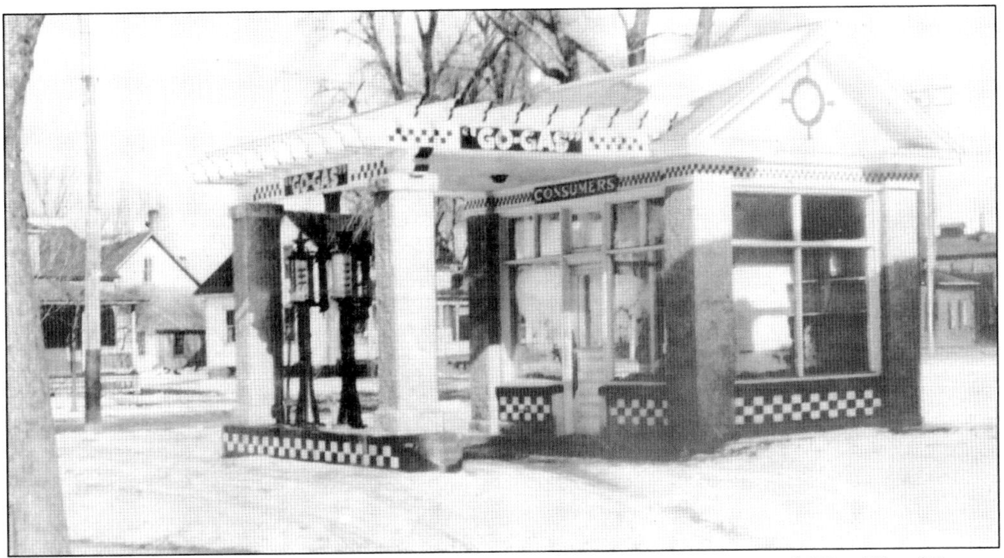

The Go-Gas station was located on the corner of North Marion Avenue and West Third Street. In the 1930s, four gas stations were within a block of each other: two at the corner of North Marion and West Third, one at the corner of North Marion and West Second Street, and one at the corner of West Second and North Iowa Avenue.

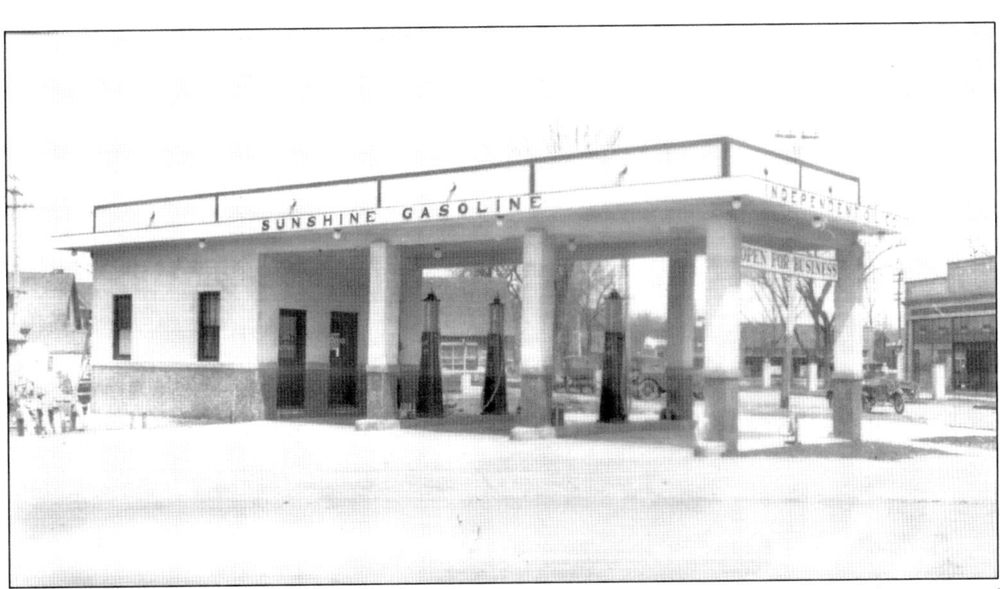

In the early 1930s, the Sunshine Station was located at 201 North Iowa Avenue, at the corner of North Iowa and East Second Street. In the 1940s, it was known as the Tankar Station.

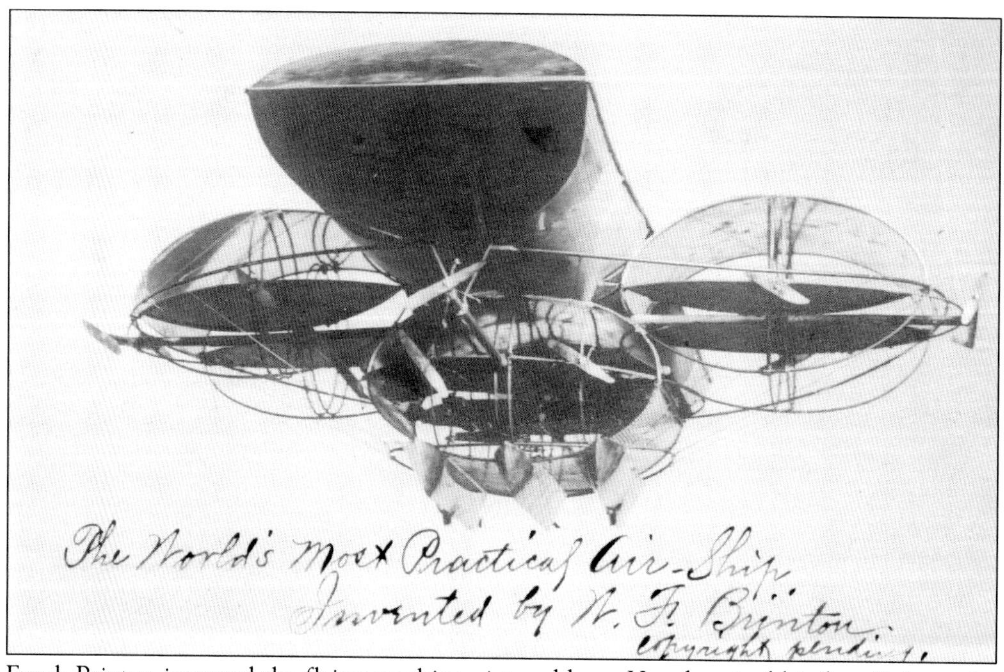

Frank Brinton invented the flying machine pictured here. He advertised his first flight at the fairgrounds on September 20, 1899, charging admission to witness the event. The plan was to have a balloon inflated to lift the aircraft, which would then fly; however, the generator to make hydrogen for the balloon never arrived.

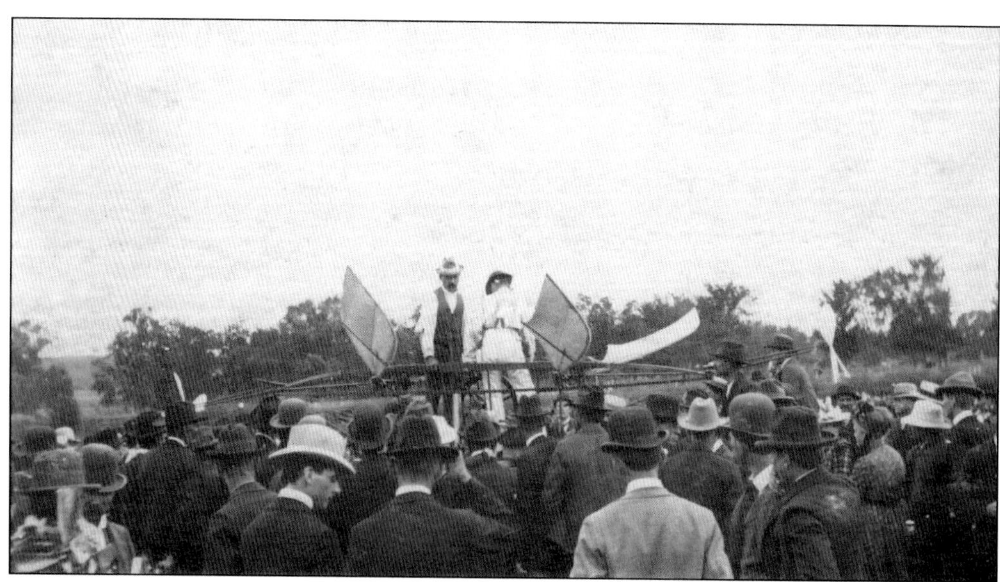

This is Brinton Day in 1899. When the flight did not happen, the angry crowd tore the aircraft to pieces. Later, authorities that reviewed Brinton's plans said that the aircraft might actually have been capable of flying. (Courtesy of Mike Zahs.)

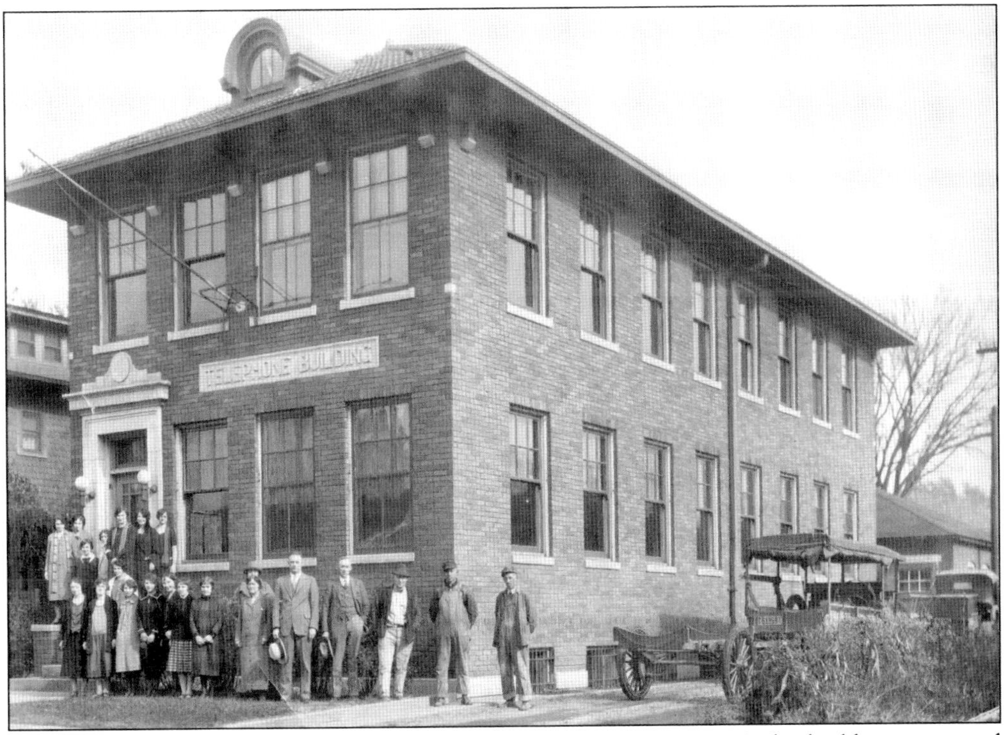

Constructed to house the Iowa Continental Telephone Company in 1910, this building continued to house local telephone operations until 1956, when it was remodeled into apartments. It is located on the 100 block of North Second Avenue.

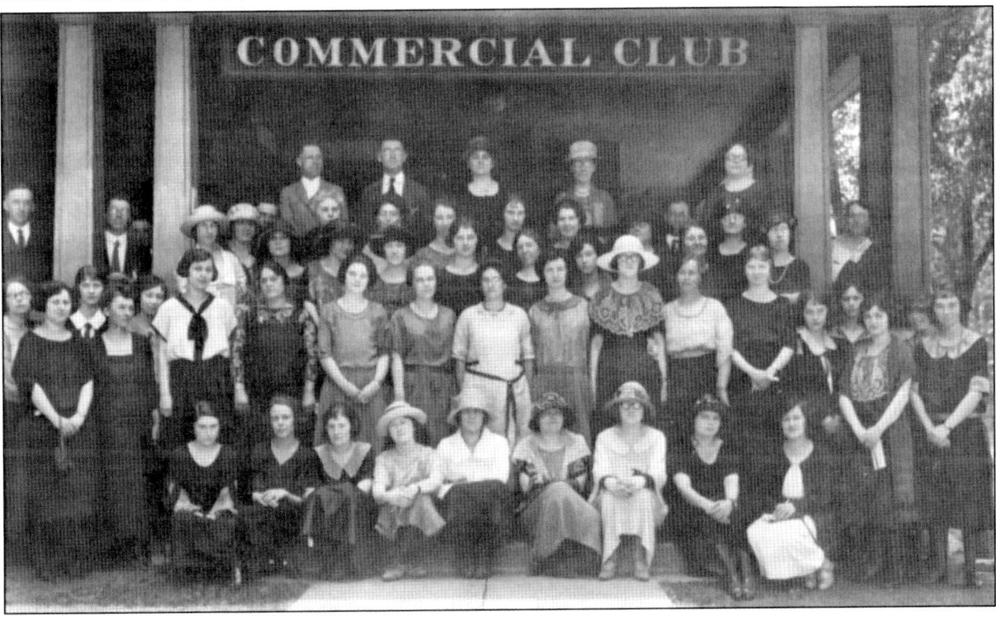

The first telephones arrived in Washington in 1879. Here, the county telephone operators are pictured in front of the Commercial Club, the predecessor of the chamber of commerce, during a 1923 gathering. The building, which later functioned for many years as the city hall, was restored in 1976 and is now known as the Blair House.

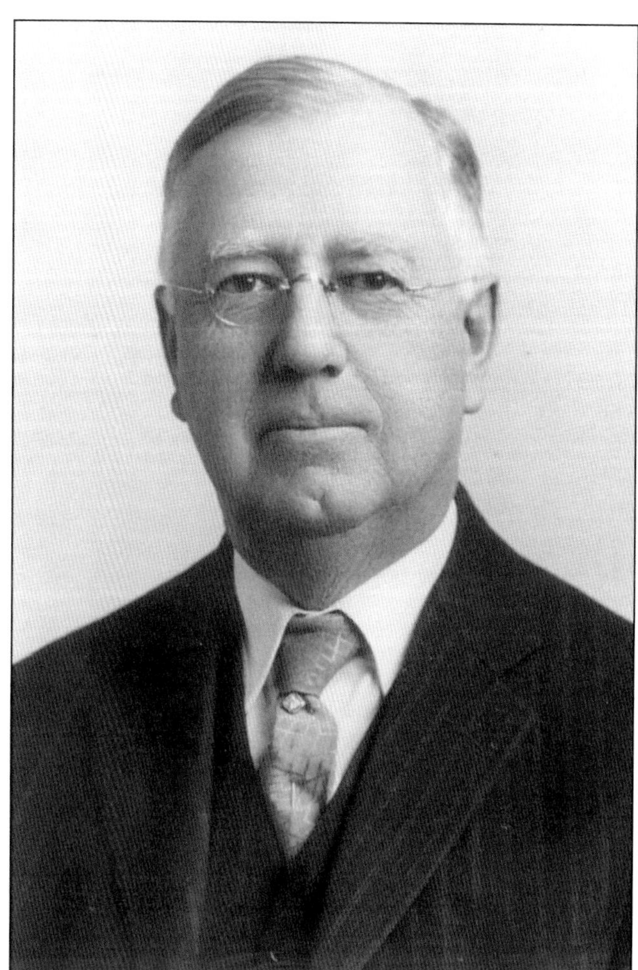

Washington's first daily newspaper, the *Daily Hustler*, appeared on February 15, 1893. The owner changed the name to the *Washington Evening Journal* in 1894. Orville Elder, who arrived in Washington in 1894 to go into the grocery business, purchased the *Journal* in 1906 and served as editor until his death in 1940.

The Washington Evening Journal moved into this building in October 1930.

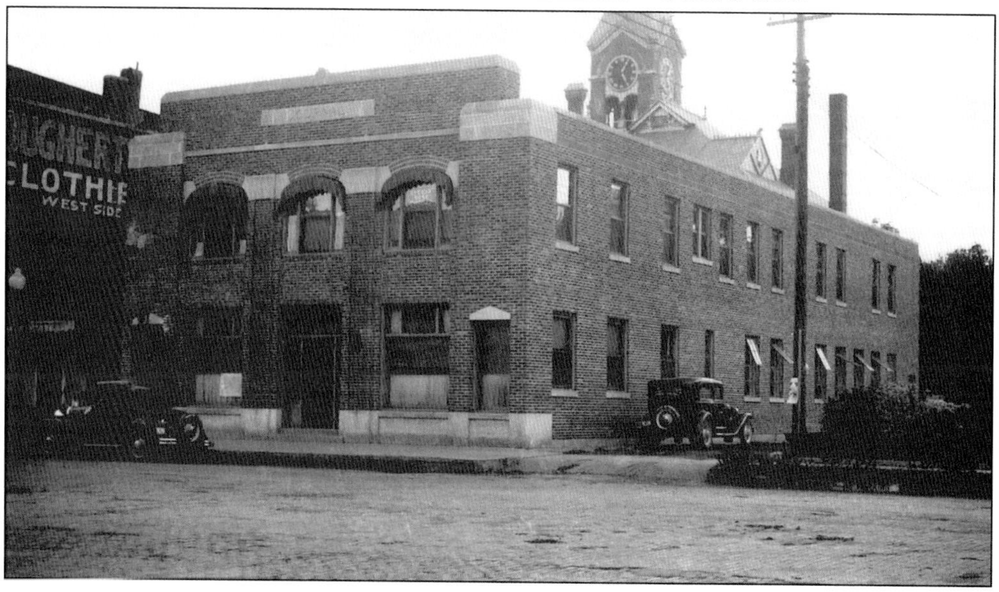

Seven

WAR

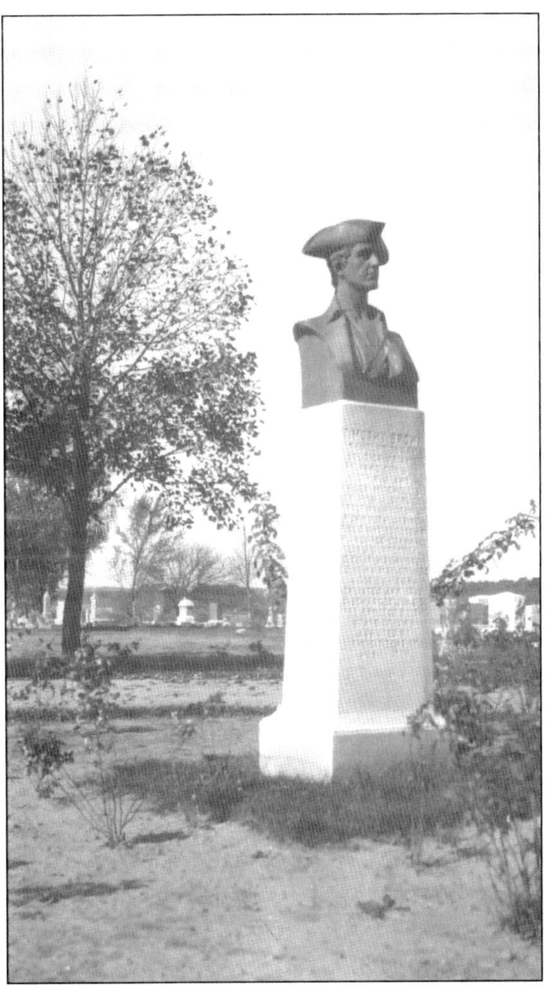

Timothy Brown is one of two Revolutionary War soldiers buried in Washington County. The other, S. Samuel Lewis, is buried in Brighton Cemetery. Brown served under George Washington at Monmouth and Springfield and witnessed the surrender of Cornwallis at Yorktown. Originally buried at the Todd Cemetery, a mile southeast of Grace Hill, in 1903 he was reinterred in the Soldiers' Circle at Elm Grove Cemetery in Washington. The state legislature provided $500 for a monument, and the local chapter of the Daughters of the American Revolution raised another $250. The monument was dedicated on May 30, 1908.

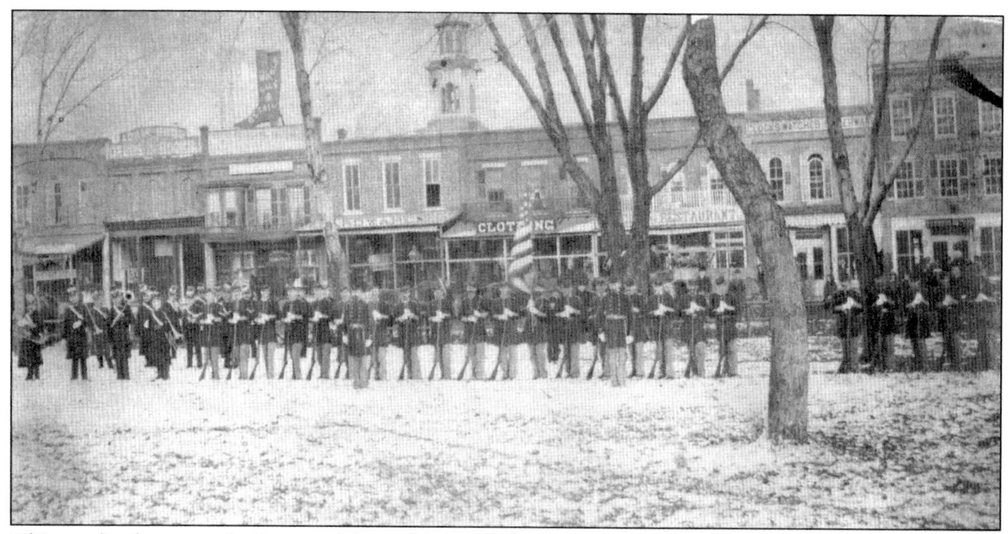

This early photograph shows soldiers, likely of the Civil War era, doing maneuvers in Central Park. The image faces the east, with the large boot-shaped sign for William's Bootery visible in the background. The cupola of the old Washington Academy building can also be seen. (Courtesy of Mike Zahs.)

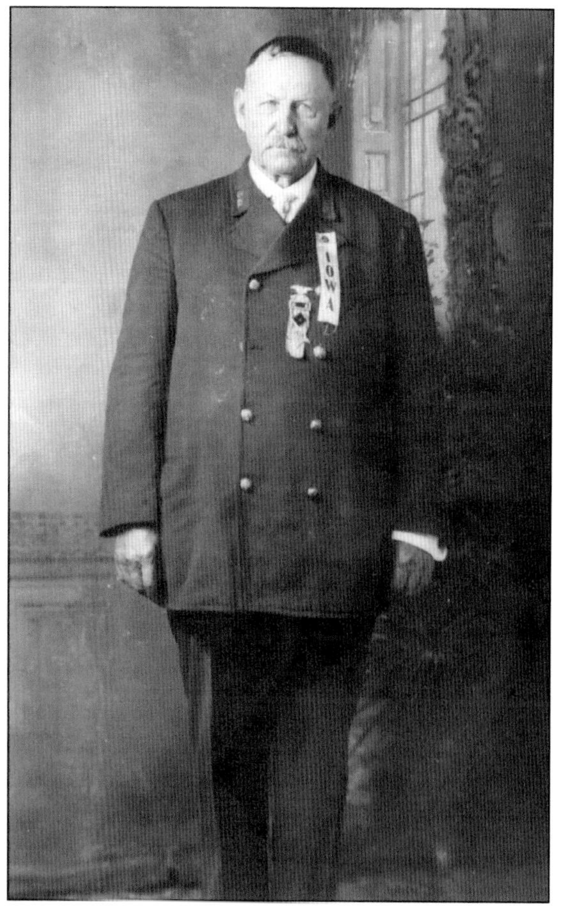

D.J. Palmer was one of Washington's outstanding Civil War soldiers. A member of Company C, 8th Iowa Infantry, he was severely injured in the Battle of Shiloh, at a location nicknamed the "Hornet's Nest," and left on the battlefield for three days. Later, he was a member of Company 4, Iowa Volunteers. He participated in the Siege of Vicksburg, the Battles of Lookout Mountain and Missionary Ridge, the Siege of Atlanta, and Sherman's March to the Sea; he was wounded two more times. After the war, he served two terms in the Iowa House of Representatives and was later appointed as a railroad commissioner. He was the national commander in chief of the Grand Army of the Republic (GAR), a major veterans' organization.

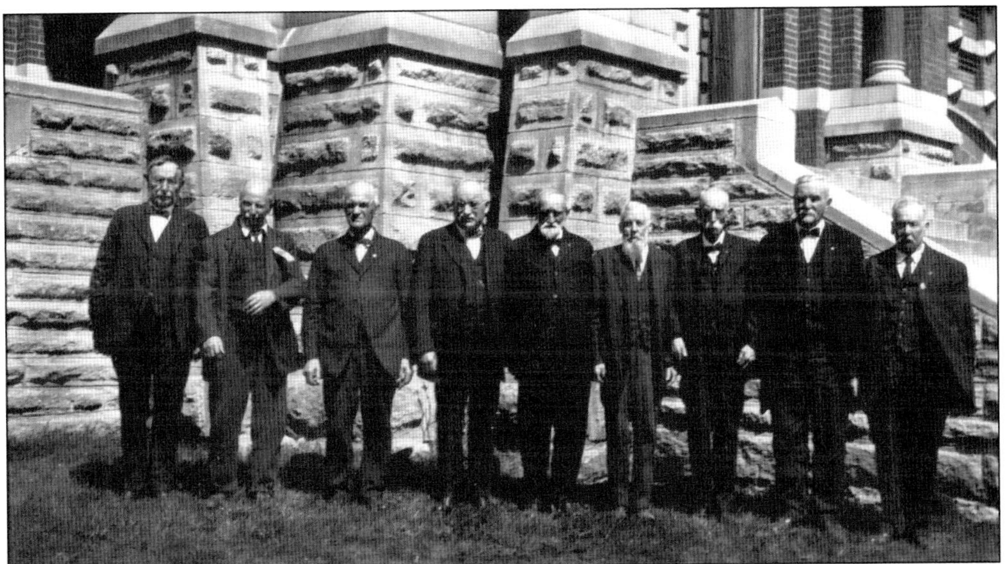

On April 4, 1921, veterans of the Battle of Shiloh gathered in front of the courthouse. Posing here are, from left to right, Jack Knause, A. Hunter, Alexander Dawson, David Gordon, R.G. McChesney, J.B. Dodds, Freeman Chelsley, Andrew Stranahan, and Col. D.J. Palmer.

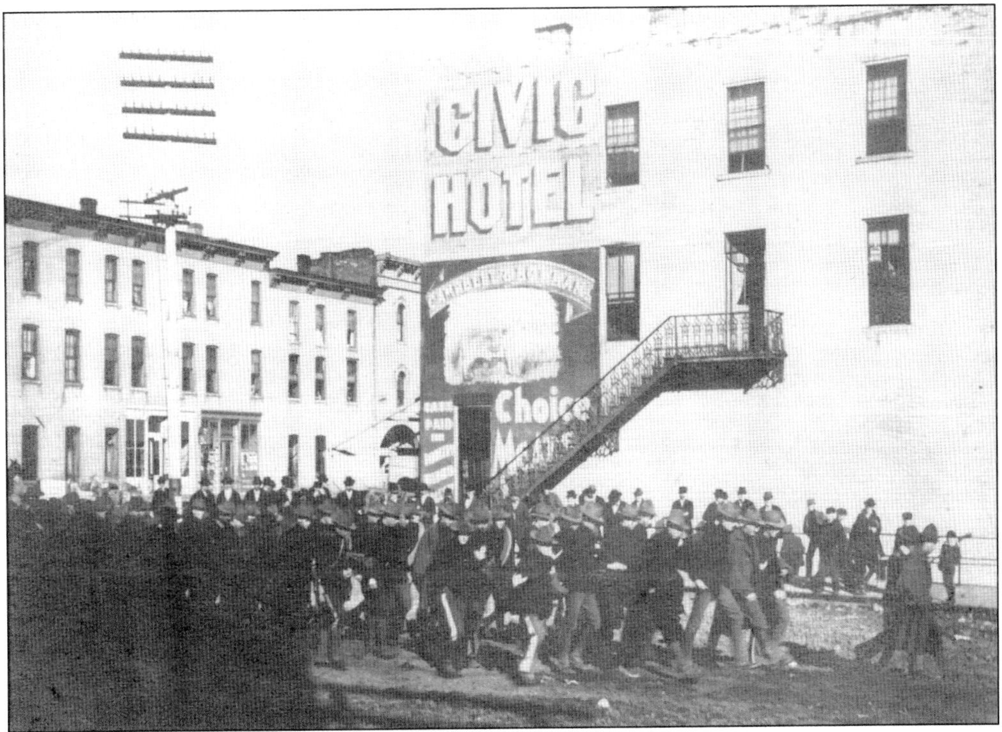

Members of Company D, 50th Iowa Infantry are shown returning home at the close of the Spanish-American War in 1898. They are marching at the intersection of East Main Street and North Iowa Avenue. In the background, on the left, is the west side of the Bryson House hotel. Above the hotel are numerous telephone lines.

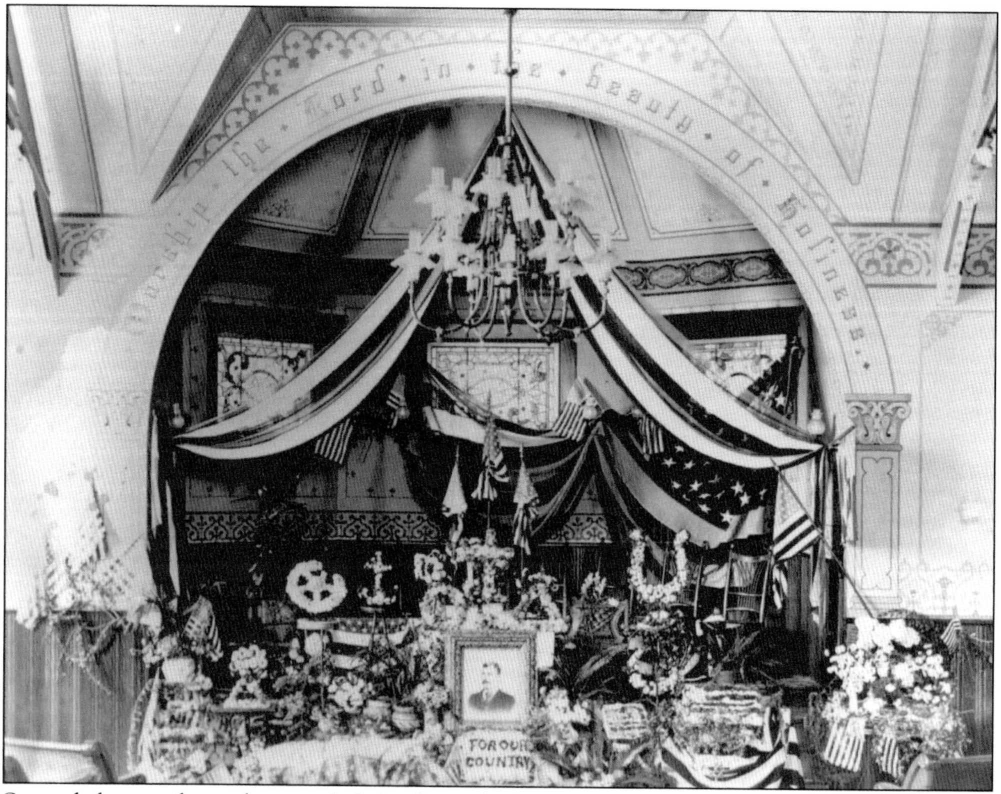

Several thousand people attended the funeral of Ralph Conger on September 4, 1891, at the Second United Presbyterian Church. A member of Company D, 50th Iowa Infantry during the Spanish-American War, Conger died of typhoid fever.

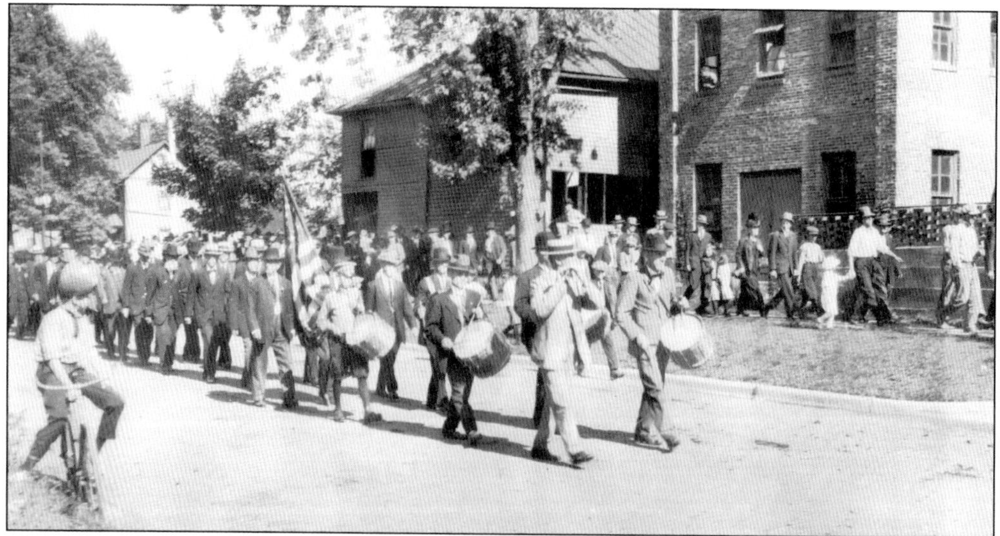

The Mexican Revolution began in 1910, and in 1916 Pancho Villa attacked the town of Columbus, New Mexico. Soldiers were recruited to defend the border under the leadership of Gen. John J. Pershing. This 1916 photograph shows Washington men leaving to serve in the border war.

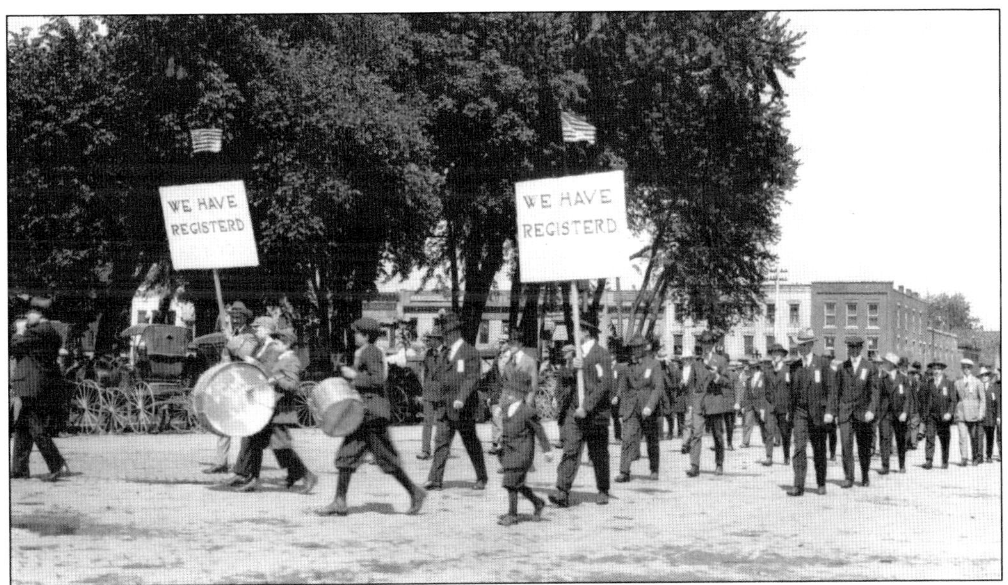

On the first registration day for World War I soldiers, June 5, 1917, a total of 1,673 men in the county signed up. The parade included several bands; groups representing the Grand Army of the Republic, the Women's Relief Corps, the Daughters of the American Revolution, and the Boy Scouts; three automobile floats carrying Red Cross nurses; and a group of newly registered men (shown here).

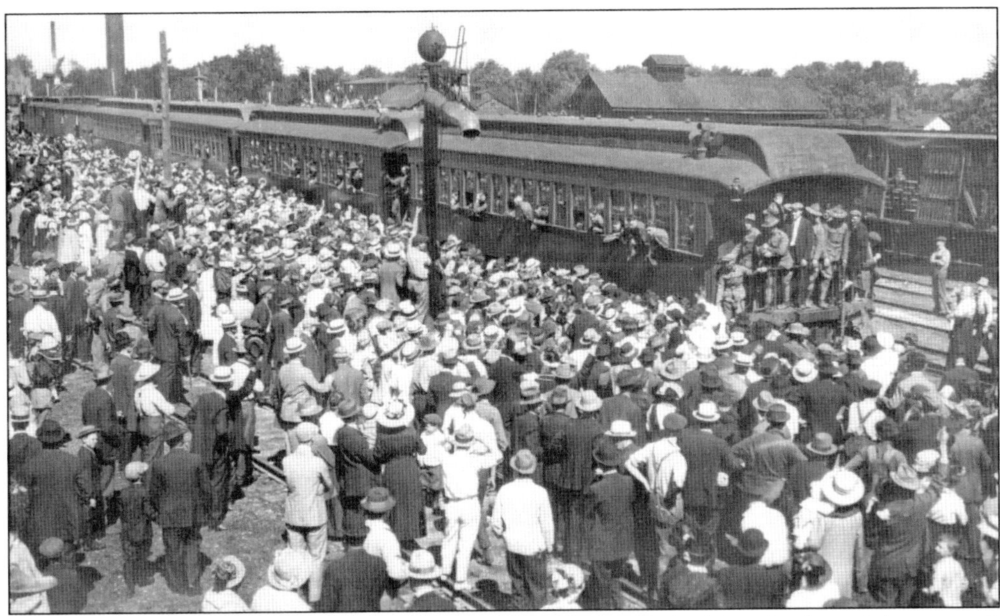
The United States declared war on Germany on April 6, 1917. By May, the first of the county's World War I troops left the Rock Island Station, heading to Fort Madison to guard the bridge crossing the river.

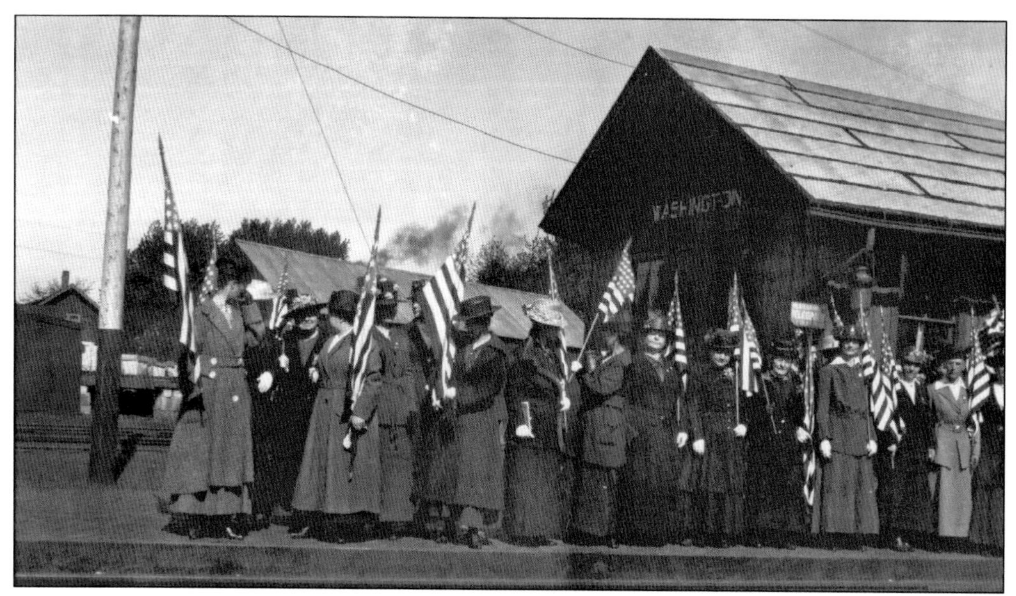

These women are seeing the last of local World War I troops off at the Chicago, Burlington & Quincy station on May 14, 1918, shortly before the end of the war on November 11.

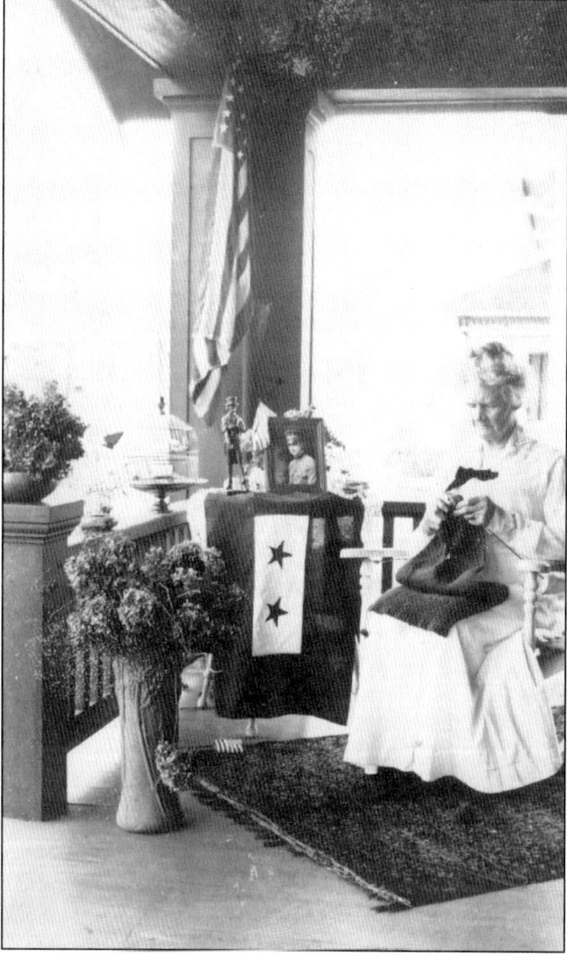

Mary Jane Buckley, who lived at 421 West Second Street, is shown doing her part for the war effort by knitting a scarf. Also pictured is a flag containing two stars, signifying that she had two sons in the service.

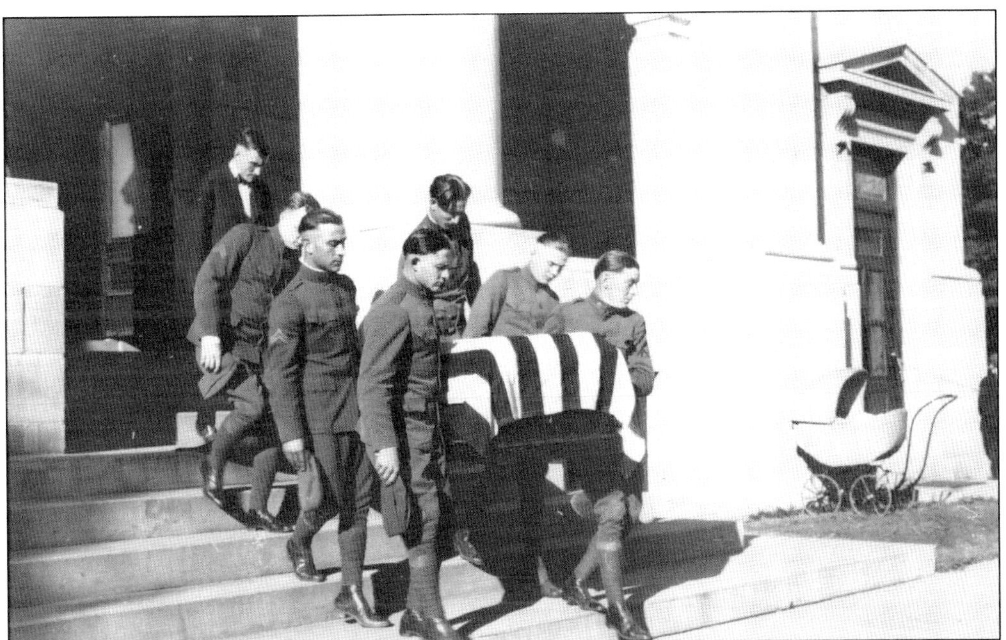

The casket of Pvt. Leon Martin Beatty is being carried down the steps of the Methodist church. Beatty was the first Washington County soldier to be killed in action during World War I, and the Washington American Legion Post, organized in 1919, was named for him.

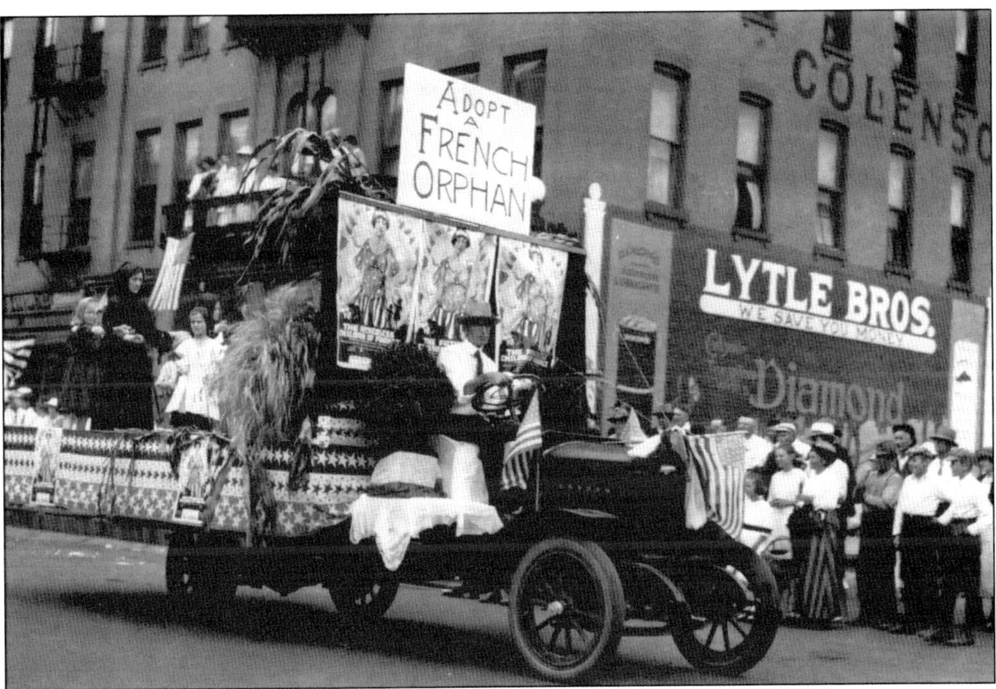

This Adopt a French Orphan float was part of a parade held during the World War I era. This photograph, taken at the corner of West Main Street and North Iowa Avenue, shows the Colenso Hotel (Previously the Bryson House) in the background. The Lytle Bros. sign advertises a grocery store located a block south at 120 South Iowa Avenue.

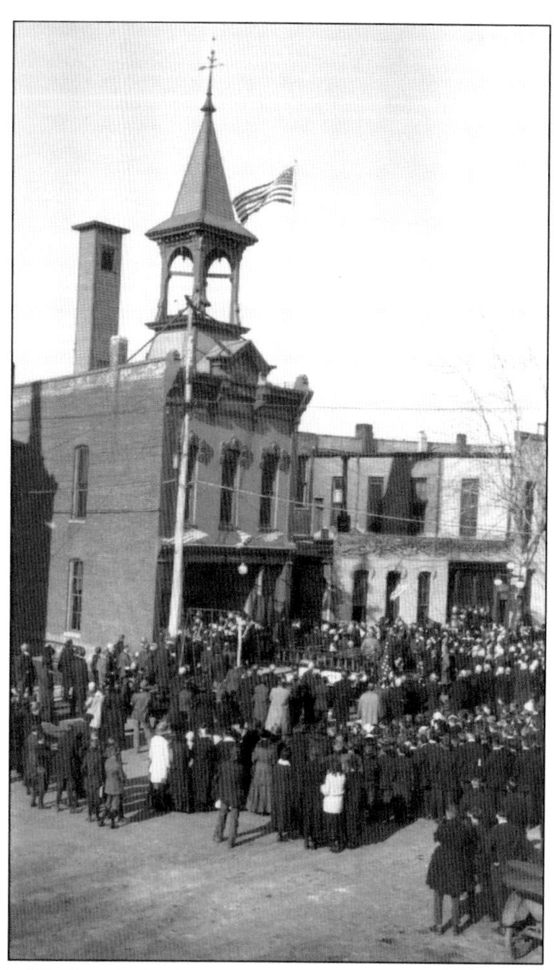

World War I Rally Day was held in front of city hall in April 1918. Located next to the courthouse, the old city hall building was later remodeled to house the Washington Loan & Trust Company. It is now home to the offices of the county assessor and county engineer.

This photograph of a World War I paper drive was taken in front of the Fox Movie Theater. The Miller Funeral Home (now Jones & Eden) is to the right, and the old *Washington Evening Journal* office is to the left.

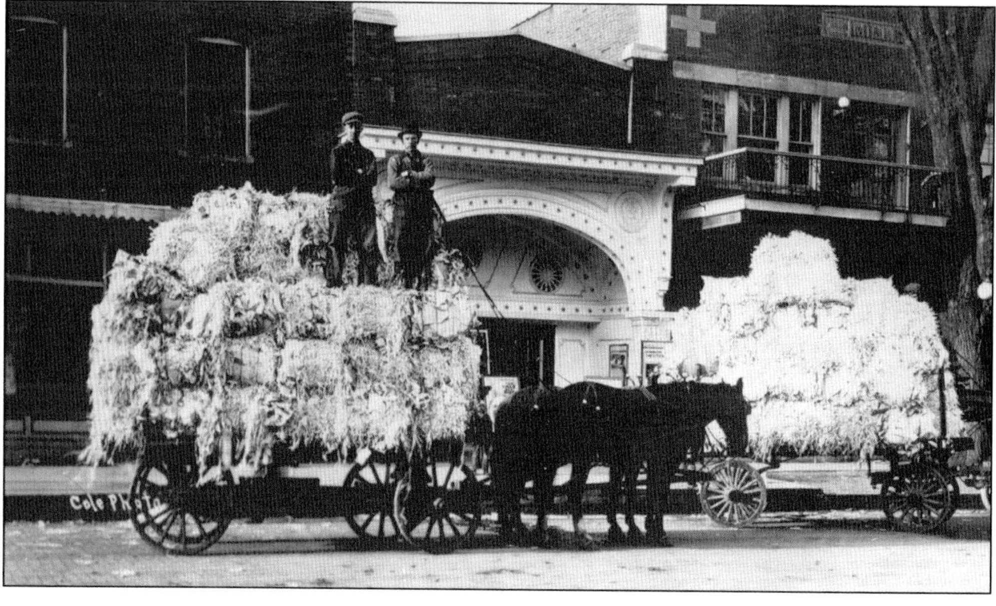

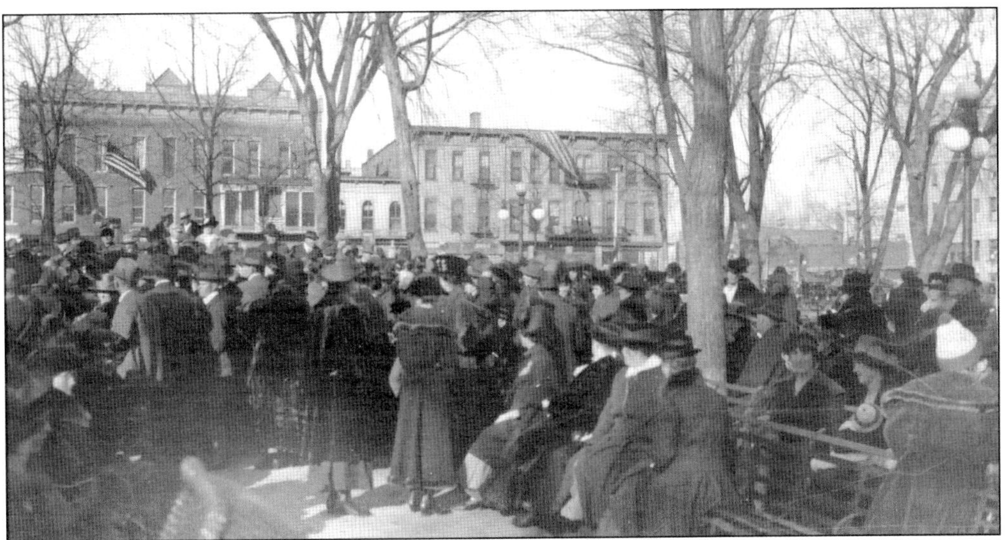

Citizens celebrated Armistice Day, November 11, 1918, in Central Park. The north side of the square is in the distance. The three-globed lights in the park had been installed only a few years earlier.

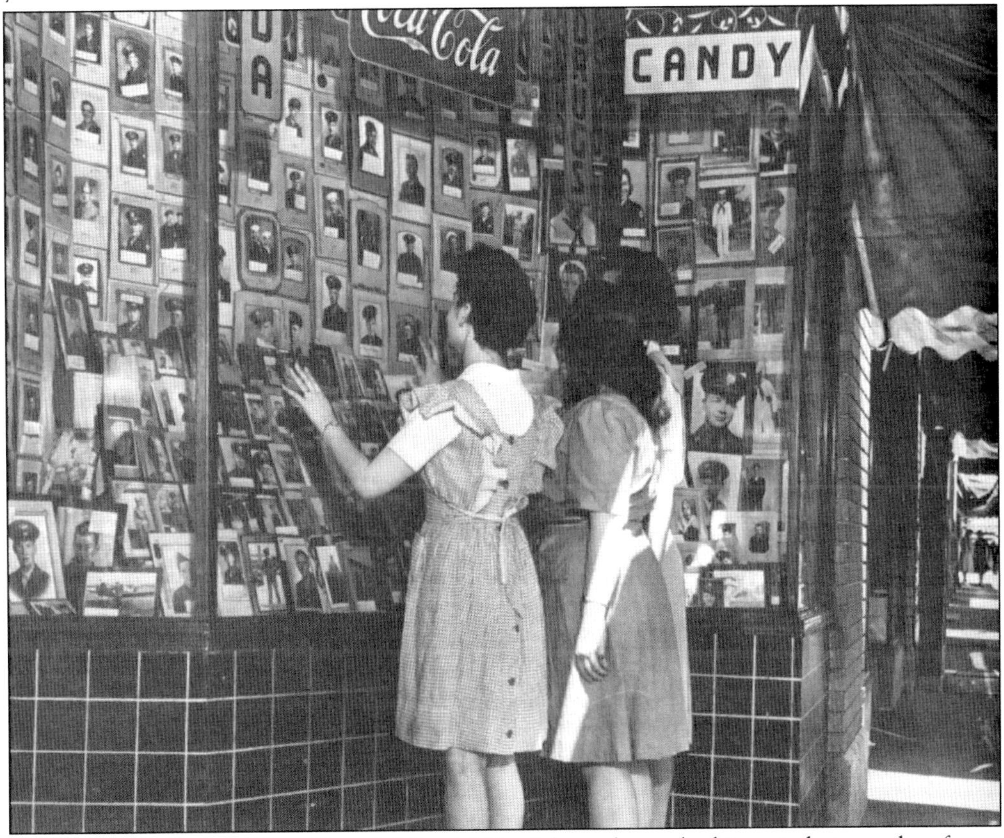

Ellen Perdock, Barbara Kessell, and Alice McDaniel are shown looking at photographs of men serving in World War II. The display was in the window of McDaniel Drug Store on the north side of the square.

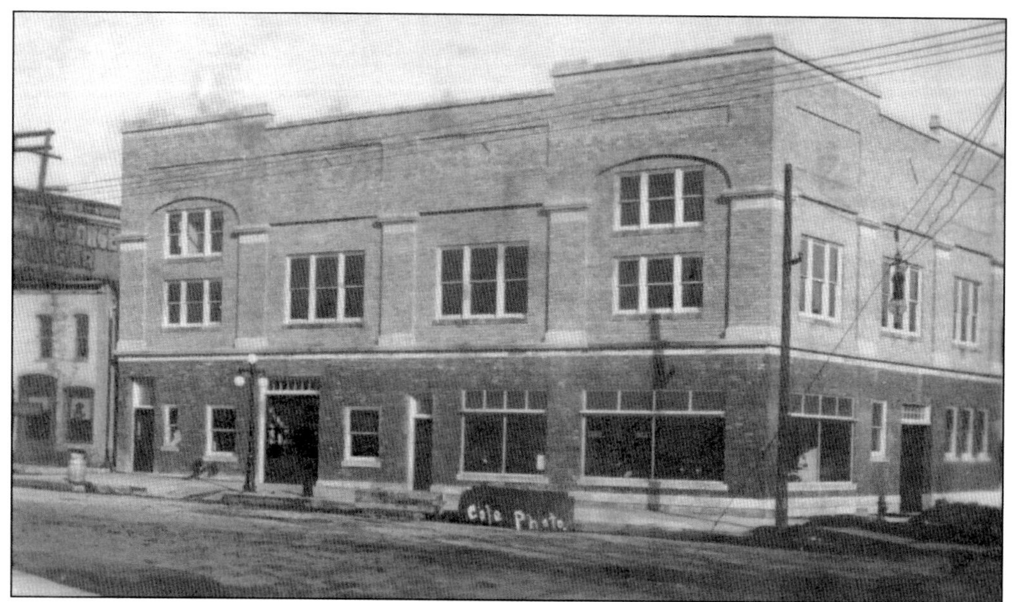

Sidney Smith had the building at 222 South Marion Avenue constructed in 1912. The first floor housed his automobile-service business, and the second floor became the armory of Company D of the Iowa National Guard from 1912 until 1928. Ross Motor Service moved into the building in 1935.

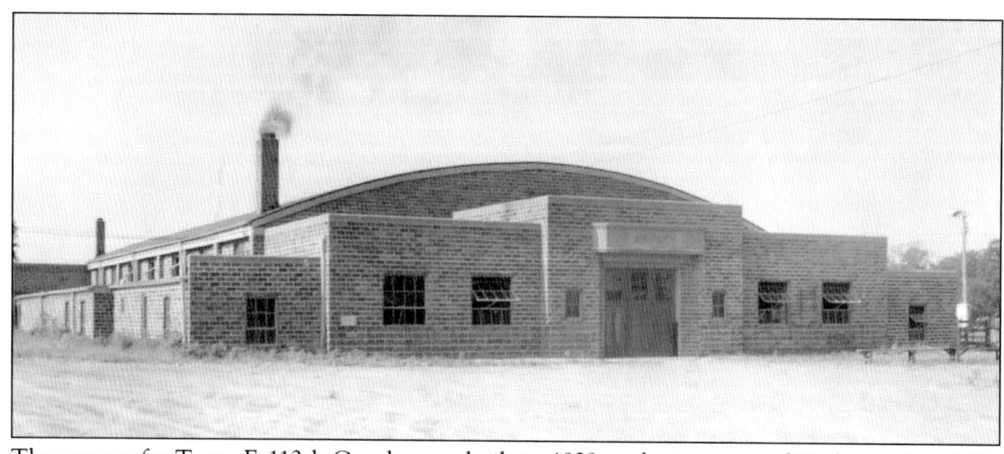

The armory for Troop F, 113th Cavalry was built in 1939 at the junction of Highways 1 and 92. It was torn down in 1984 after the completion of the current armory.

Eight

PUBLIC SERVICES

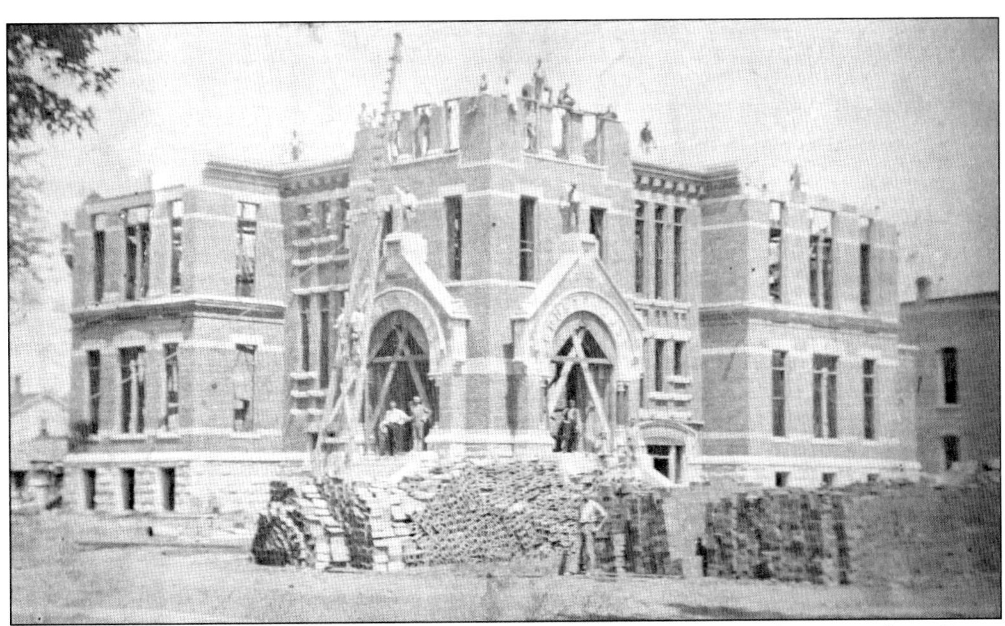

Construction of Washington County's current courthouse, designed by architects William Foster and Henry Liebbe of Des Moines, began in 1886. Foster also designed the Graham Opera House, the church (now the Christian Church) at the corner of West Second and Avenue B, and possibly also the Blair House.

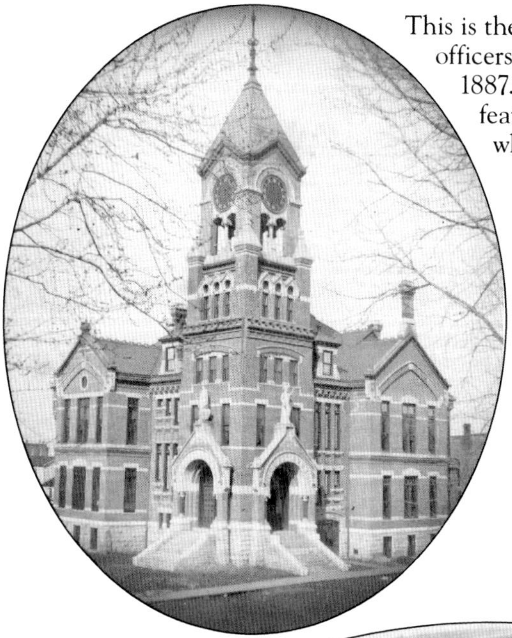

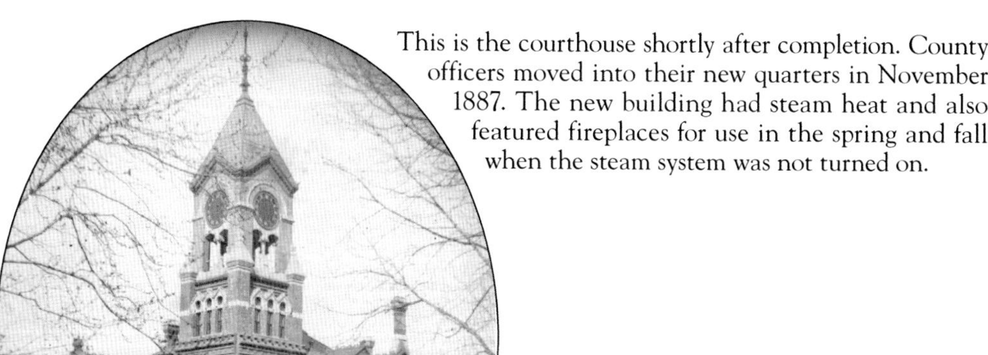

This is the courthouse shortly after completion. County officers moved into their new quarters in November 1887. The new building had steam heat and also featured fireplaces for use in the spring and fall when the steam system was not turned on.

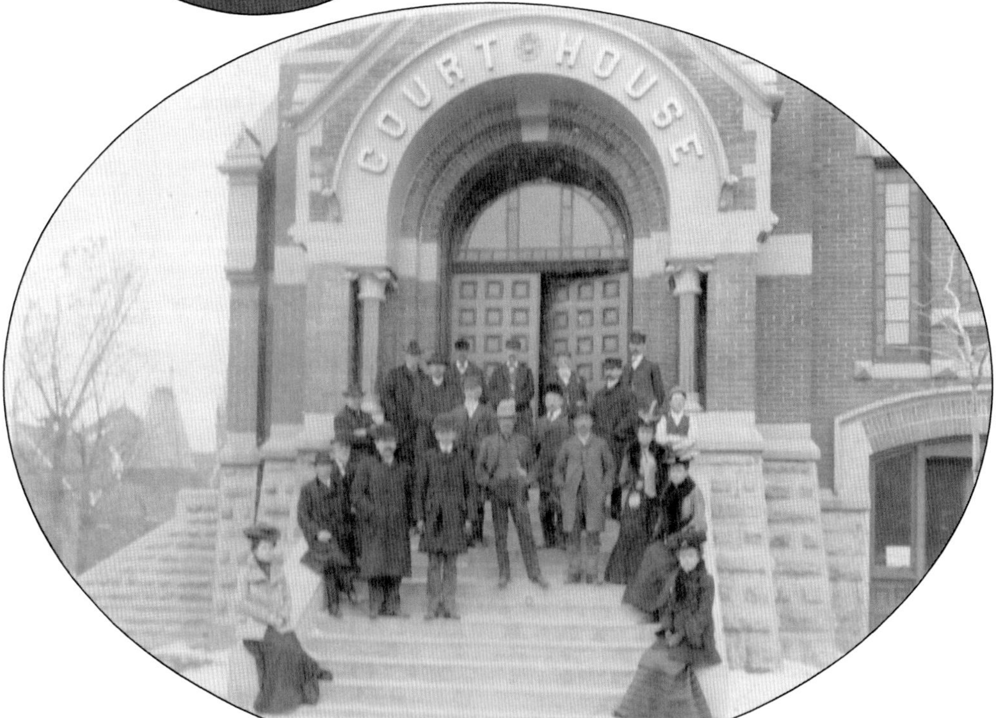

County officers and workers pose on the courthouse steps in 1901. Among them are Chauncey Meyers (top left), William Bailey (to the right of Meyers), Sheriff John Teeter (center, wearing light hat), Marsh W. Bailey (to the left of Teeter), Henry Eicher (to the left of Bailey, with black mustache), James Shearer (seated to the left of Eicher, with white beard) Col. C.J. Wilson (to the right of Teter, wearing fur cap), and janitor Billy Cunningham (far right, in shirt sleeves).

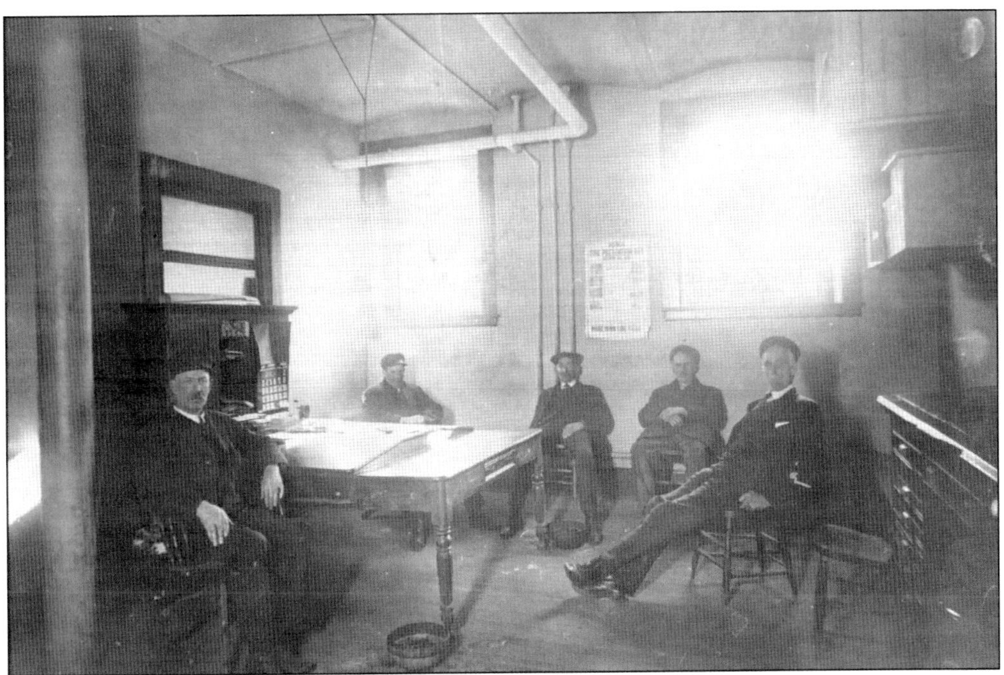

Sheriff R.H. McCarty (left) is pictured in his office in the basement of the courthouse in November 1919. The other men are G.W. Wallace, Walker Allen, James Fishburn, and D.C. Kyle.

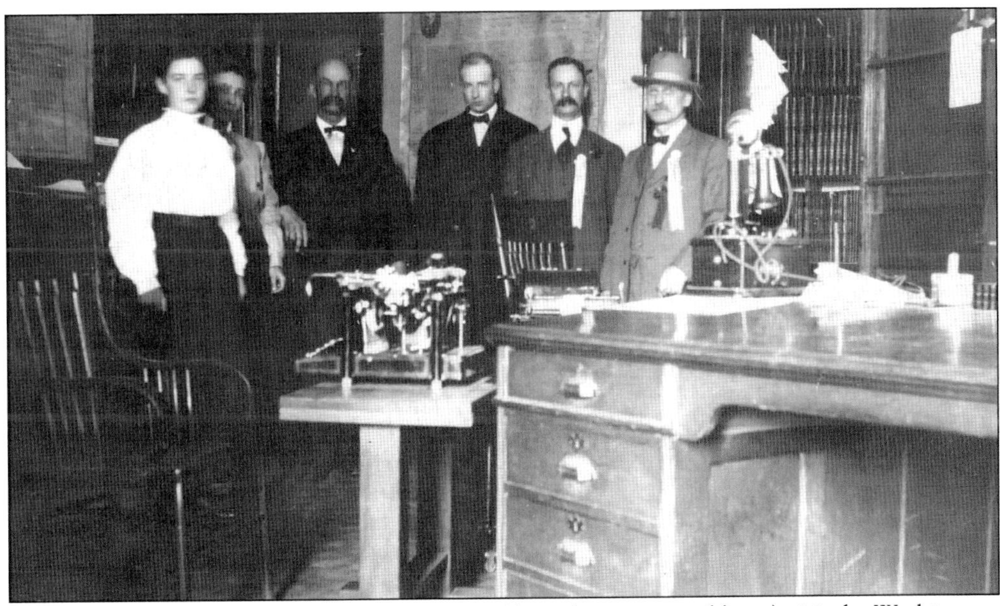

The treasurer and auditor of Muscatine County (far right, wearing ribbons) visit the Washington County treasurer's office. The others shown are Carley Dewey, J.A. McCoy, Mame Shearer, and Frances McCoy.

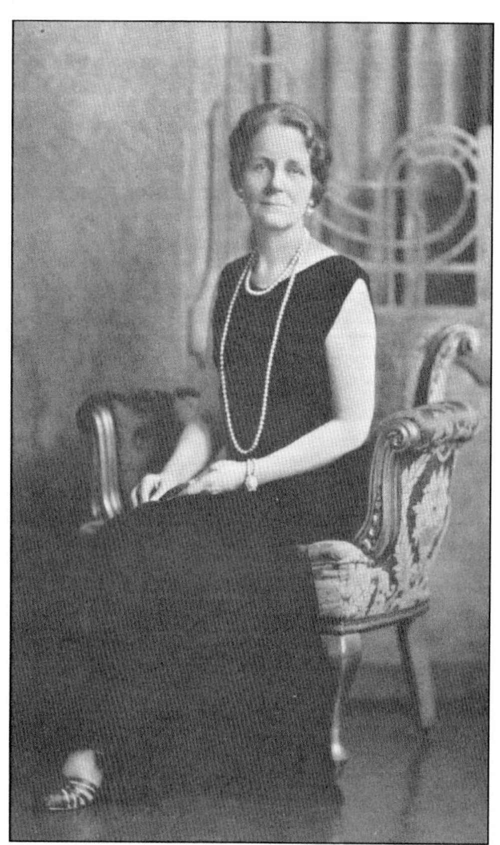

Viola Babcock Miller, the widow of Alex Miller, became Iowa's secretary of state in 1932. She was the first woman to be elected to a cabinet position in the state. During her tenure, she was instrumental in establishing the Iowa Highway Patrol. She also served as national president of the PEO Sisterhood, a woman's international service organization. In 2002, the old Iowa Historical Society building in Des Moines was rededicated and named in her honor.

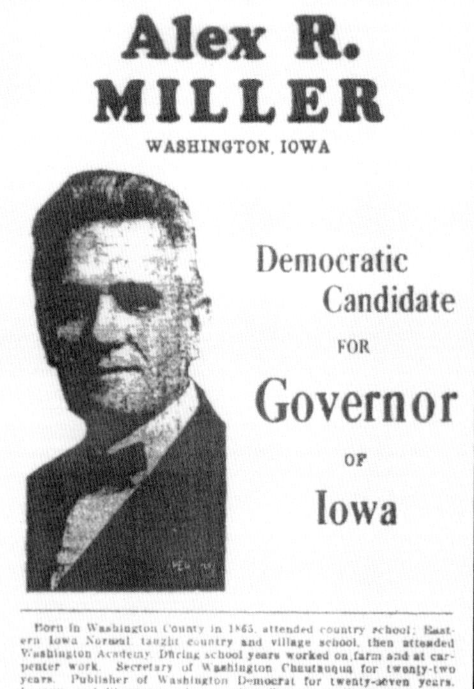

Alex Miller was the editor of the *Washington Democrat* for many years. A popular speaker, he appeared on programs for the Redpath-Horner Chautauqua circuit. In 1926, he ran for governor of Iowa on the Democratic ticket but lost to incumbent John Hammill.

Smith Wildman Brookhart (1869–1944) was born in Scotland County, Missouri. He came to Washington in 1892, began a career as a teacher while he studied law, and later entered into a law practice with two of his brothers. At the time of the Spanish-American War, he went to Florida with Company D. He was an expert rifleman and an instructor during World War I. He served in the US Senate from 1922 to 1926 and from 1927 to 1933.

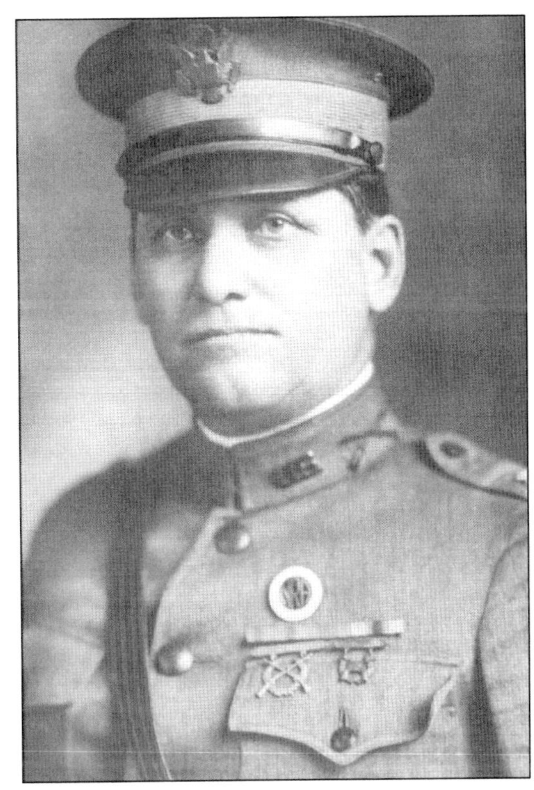

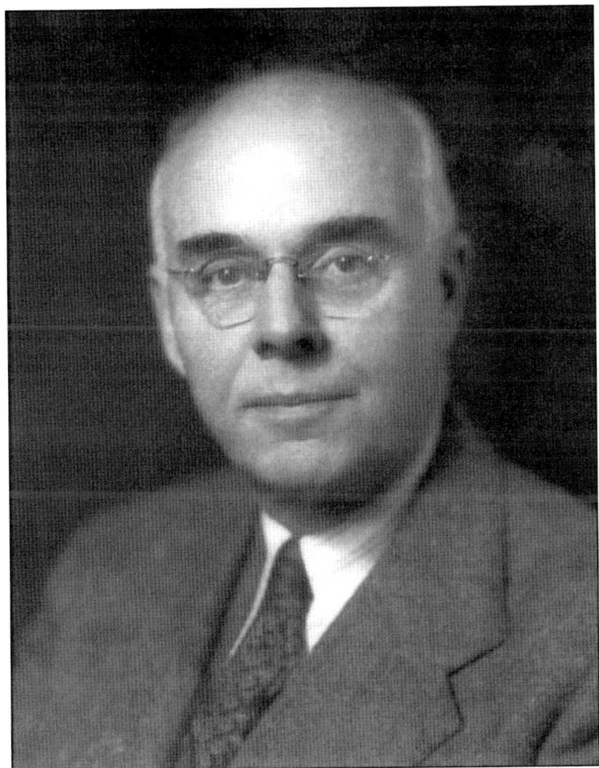

Edward Eicher (1878–1944) was the only person from Washington County to serve in the US House of Representatives. He served the Iowa 1st District from 1933 to 1938 and was later the chairman of the US Securities and Exchange Commission.

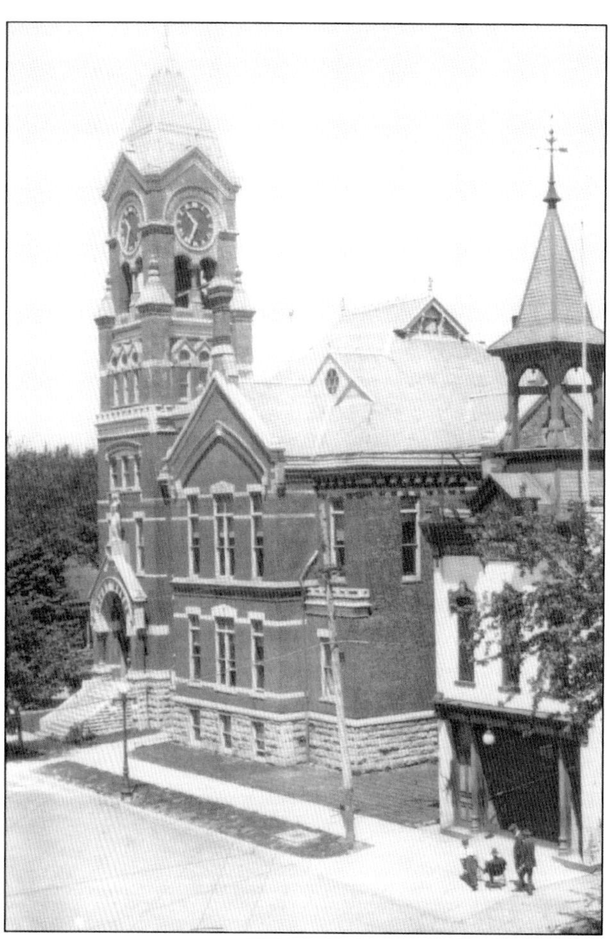

The city hall and fire station were built in 1883. The Washington Loan & Trust Company later remodeled the building. For many years, it was the office of Dr. M.L. McCreedy. It is now the courthouse annex and houses the county assessor and county engineer offices.

This 1902 image shows the city council, with Mayor C.H. Wilson (bearded) seated in the center. The woman, Bertha Curran, served as a volunteer city clerk, since females could not be elected to that position at the time.

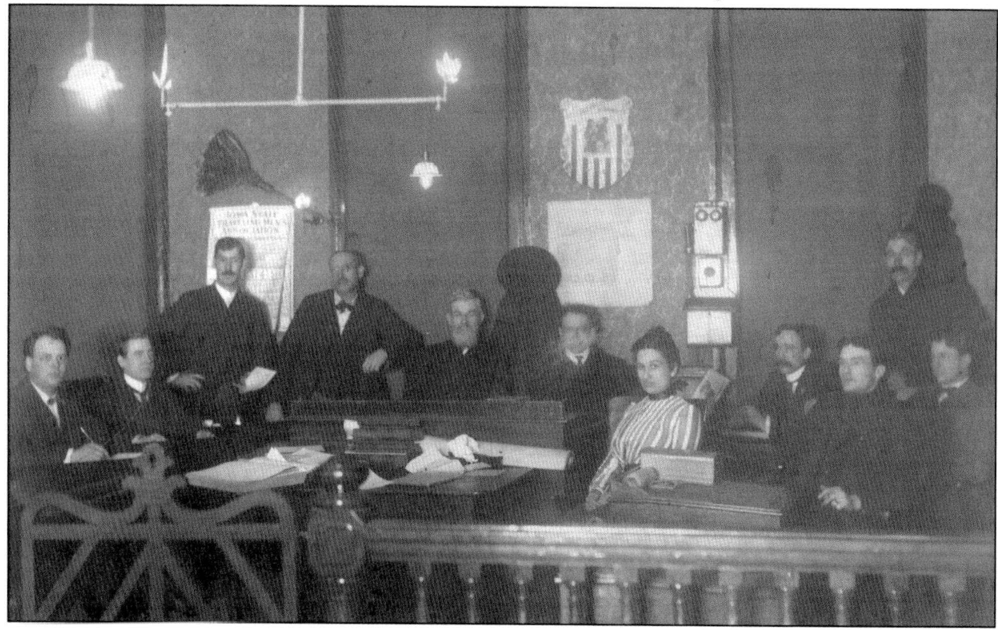

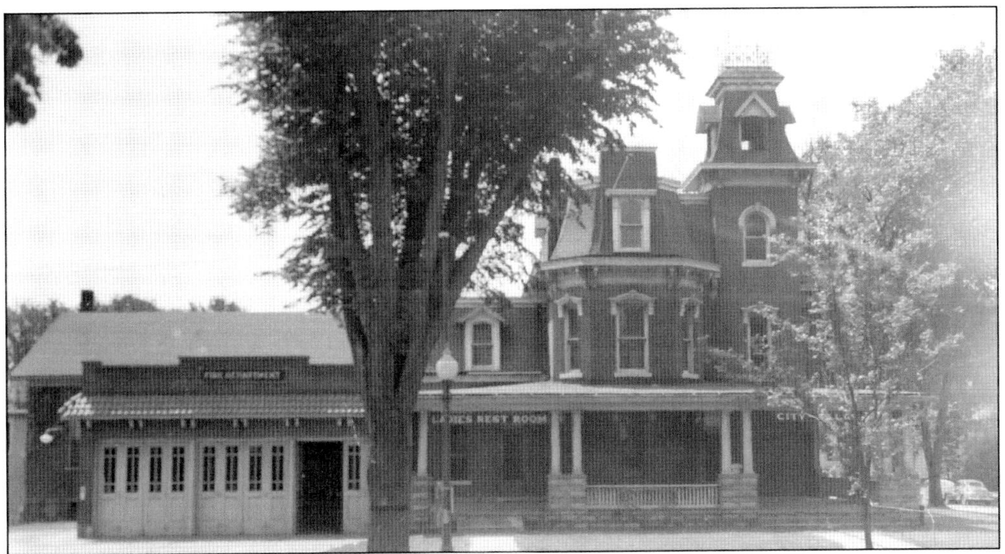

The Blair House served as the Washington City Hall. It housed a ladies restroom and lounge, primarily for use by local farm women. The large "ladies rest room" sign was prominent for many years.

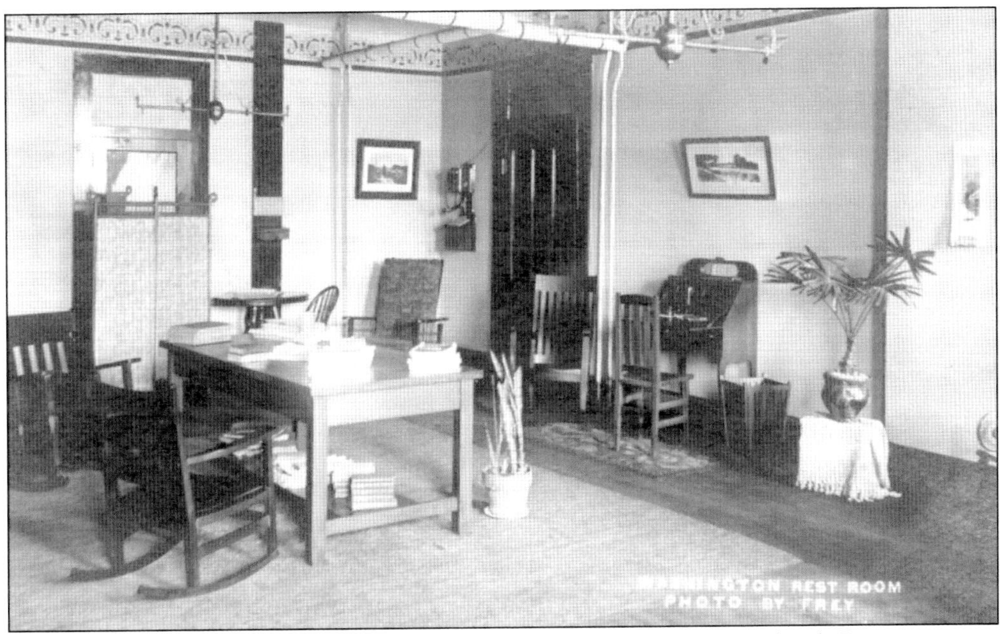

The county also provided a lounge and restroom in the courthouse (seen here). For many years, two large signs appeared on the front of the building. (Courtesy of Tom Dawson.)

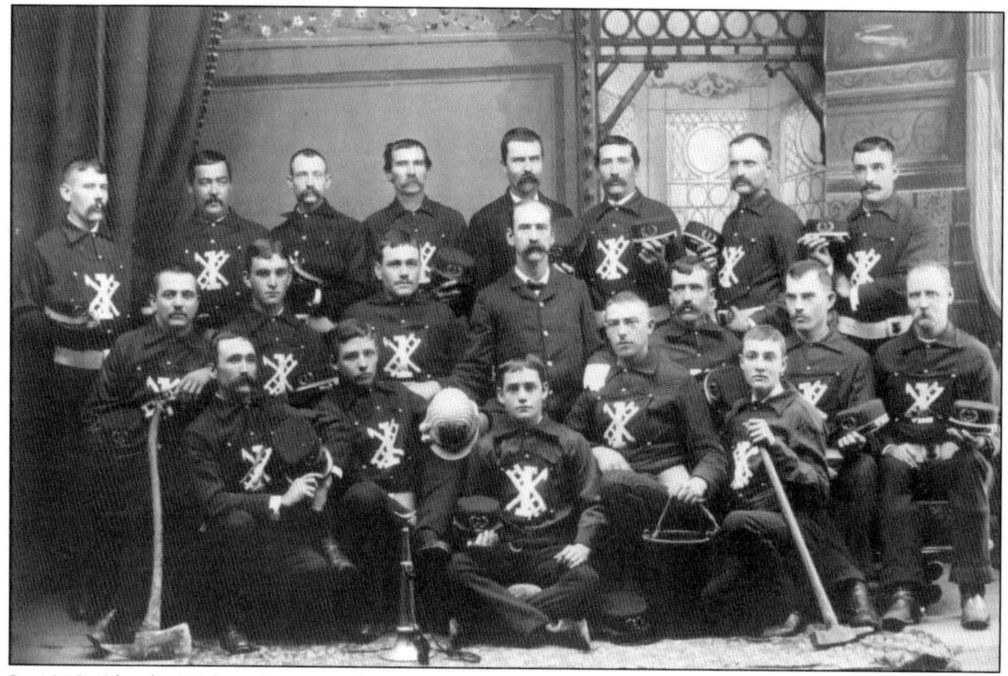

In 1883, Charles Hebner became the first chief of the city's newly organized fire department. The Washington Hook and Ladder Company is pictured here in the 1890s.

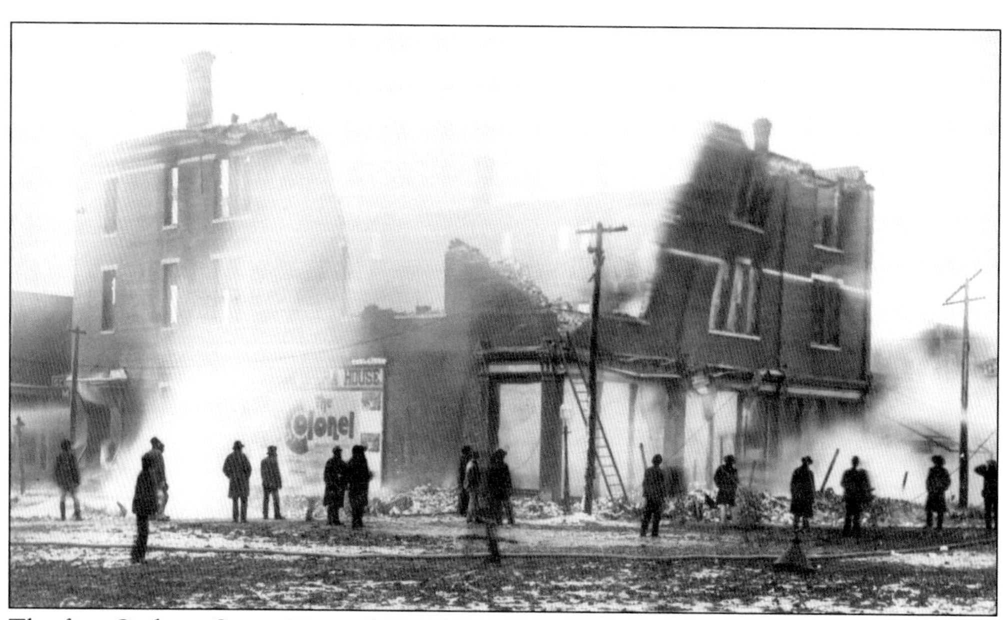

The first Graham Opera House, located on the southeast corner of the square, burned in November 1892. Its replacement, now known as the State Theater, was built at the east end of the same block.

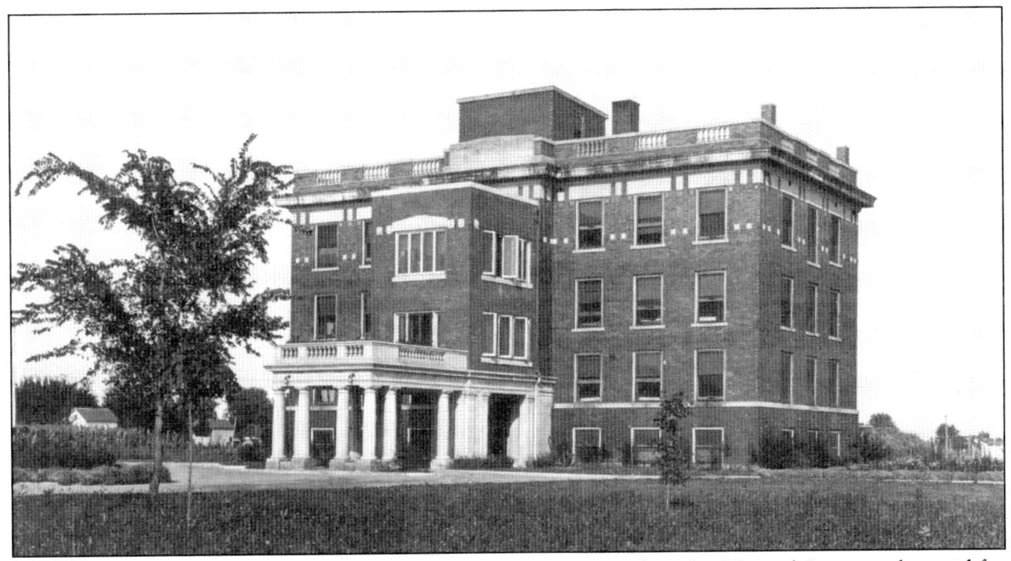

The Washington County Hospital was the first rural hospital in the United States to be paid for by tax funds. Constructed in 1912, it was later listed in the National Register of Historic Places. It was demolished in 2006.

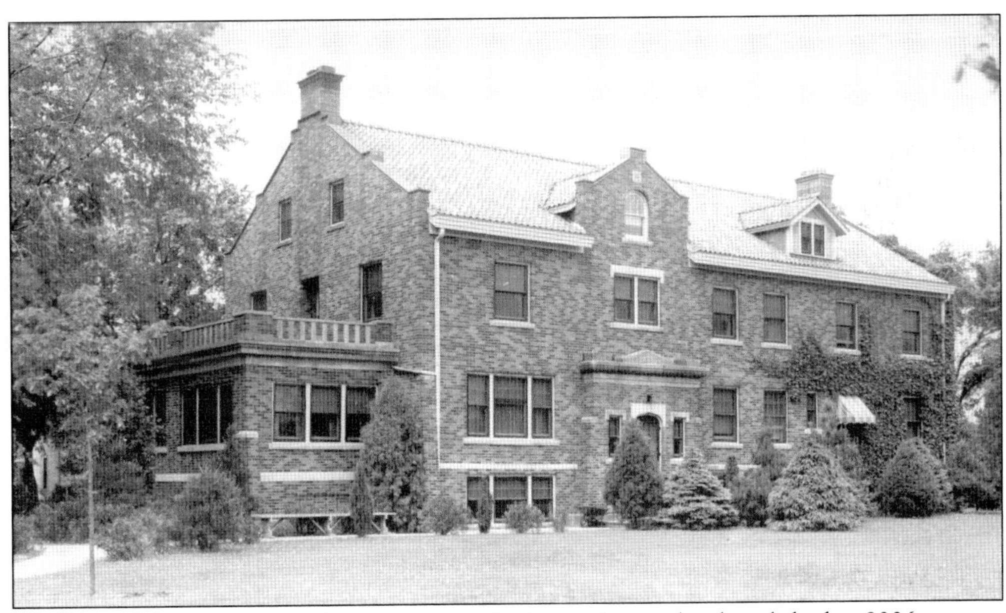

The Nurses' Home, built in 1928 just west of the hospital, was also demolished in 2006.

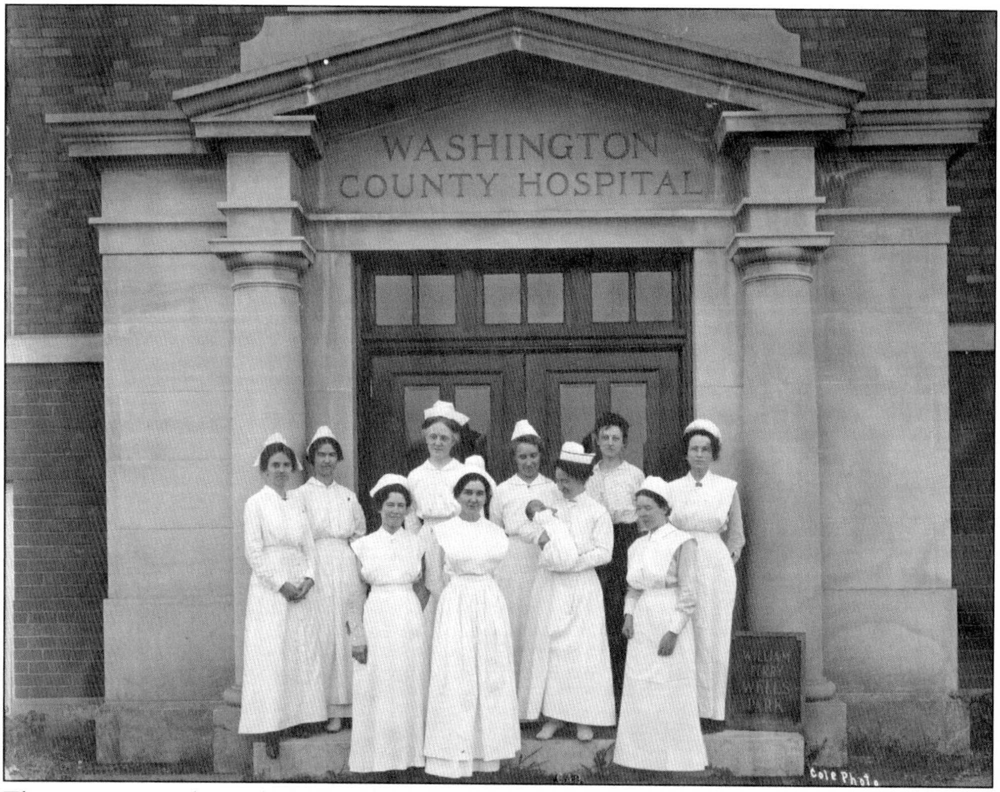

These nurses stand outside the new hospital's front entrance. Picture from left to right are (front row) Martha Porter, Alwilde Morgan, Elizabeth Finlay (holding boy), and Emily Bayliss; (back row) Grace Loveland, Blanche Stephens, Miss Thlenhorst, unidentified, Nell Hebner, and Belle Joy.

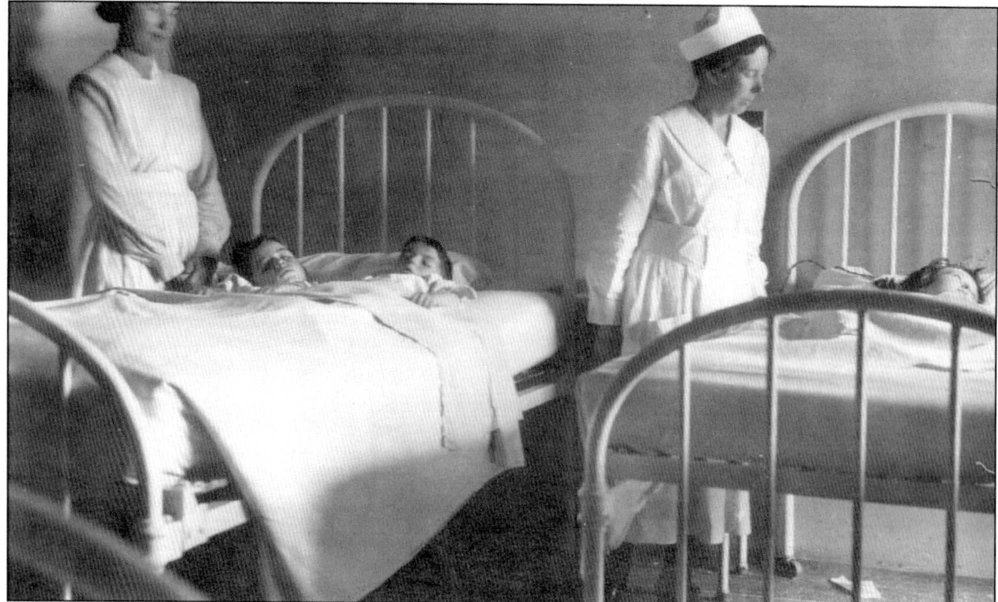

Taken shortly after the construction of the new hospital in 1912, this photograph shows nurses Martha Porter (left) and Emily Bayliss attending to children.

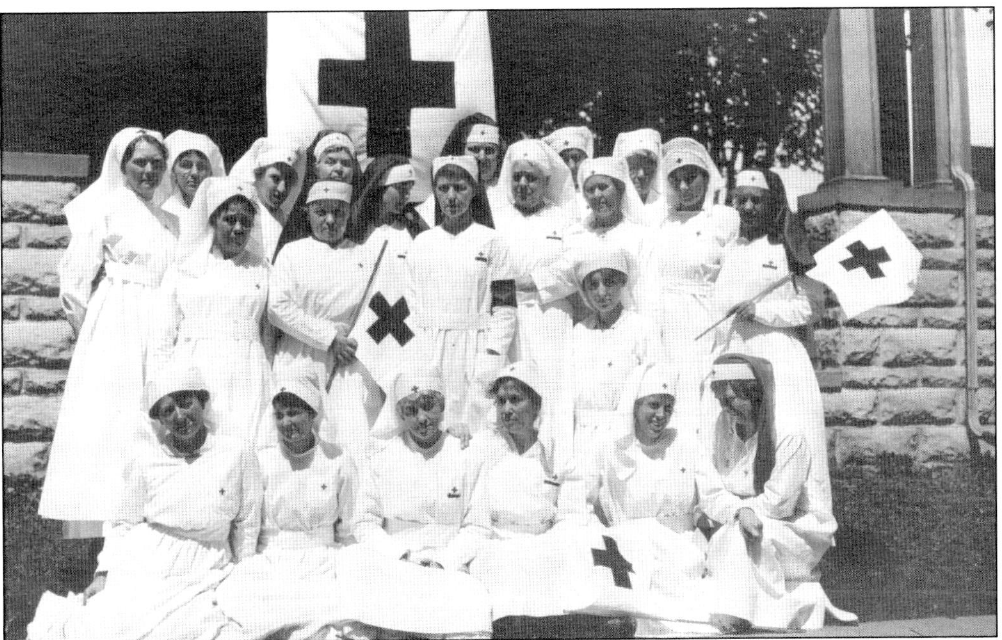

This group of Red Cross ladies is photographed shortly after the May 11, 1917, organization of the county chapter. For many years, Red Cross offices were located on the second floor of what is now the Blair House.

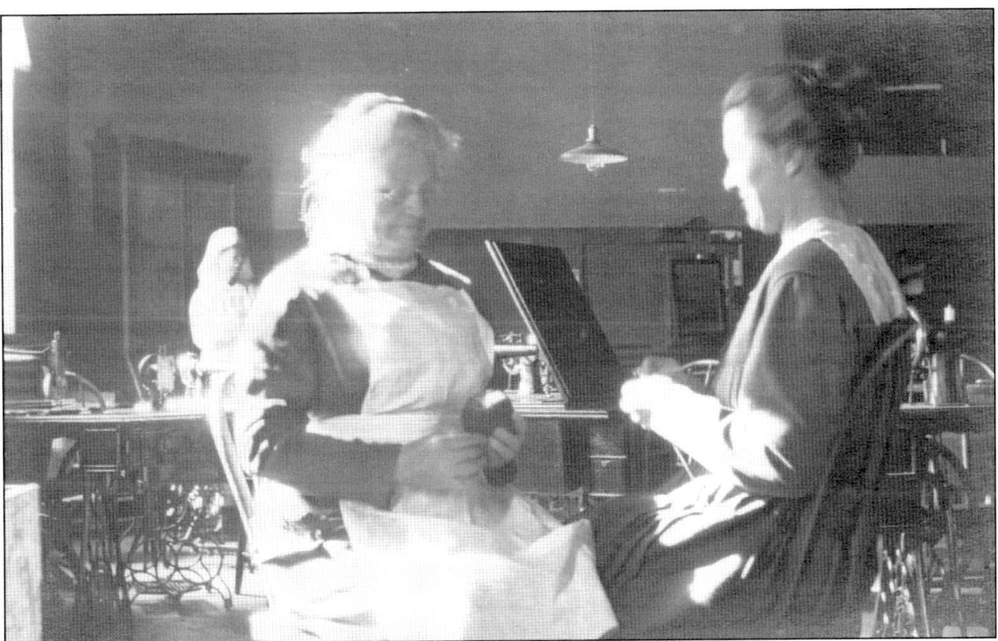

Ladies from the Red Cross knitted clothing and made hospital shirts and other articles of clothing for the war effort; they also made surgical dressings and bandages. Here, two workers are busy on the second-floor east wing of the Blair House. Julia Crail headed the organization in its early years.

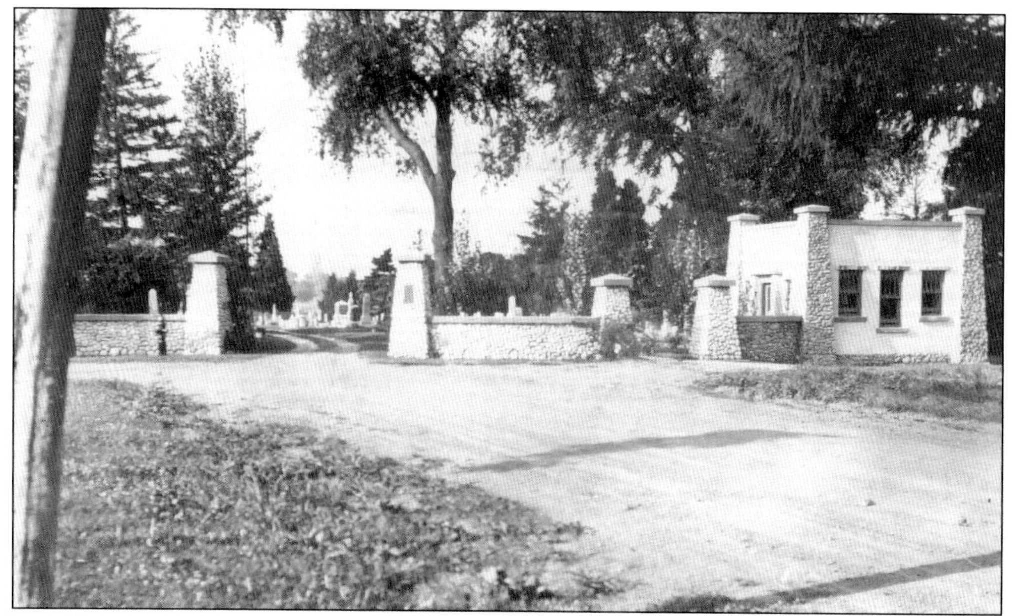

Woodlawn Cemetery was originally named City Cemetery. The first burial is believed to have been Benjamin Conley's in 1840. In 1926, the cemetery was fenced in, and these improvements—an entrance and small building housing restroom facilities—were built.

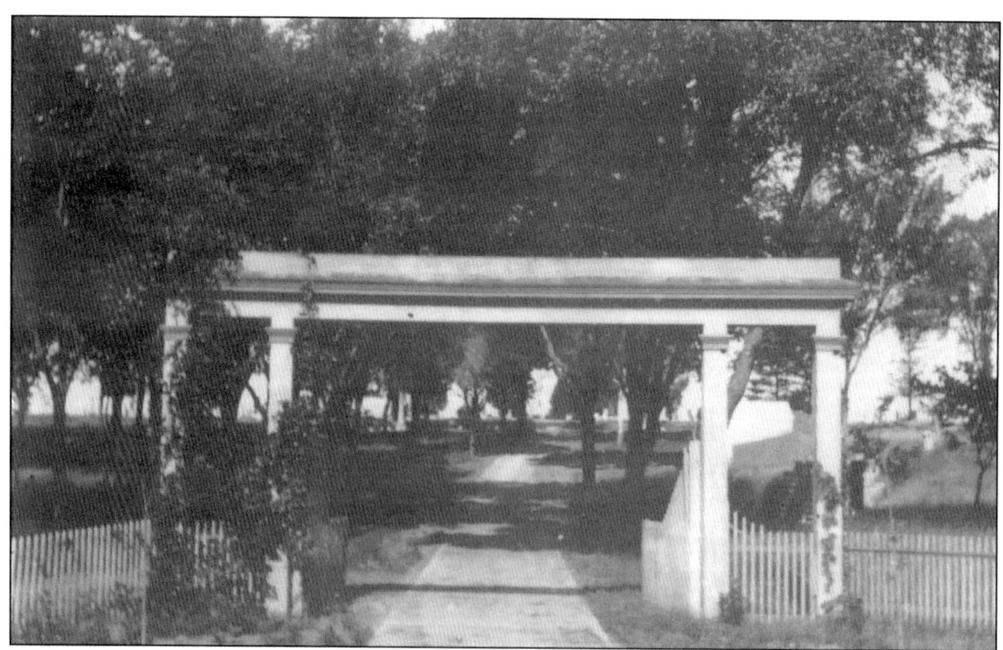

Elm Grove Cemetery was established in 1887 when Woodlawn Cemetery was running out of room. Elm Grove originally contained just over 30 acres and was initially maintained by a private corporation. The cemetery was turned over to the city in 1961.

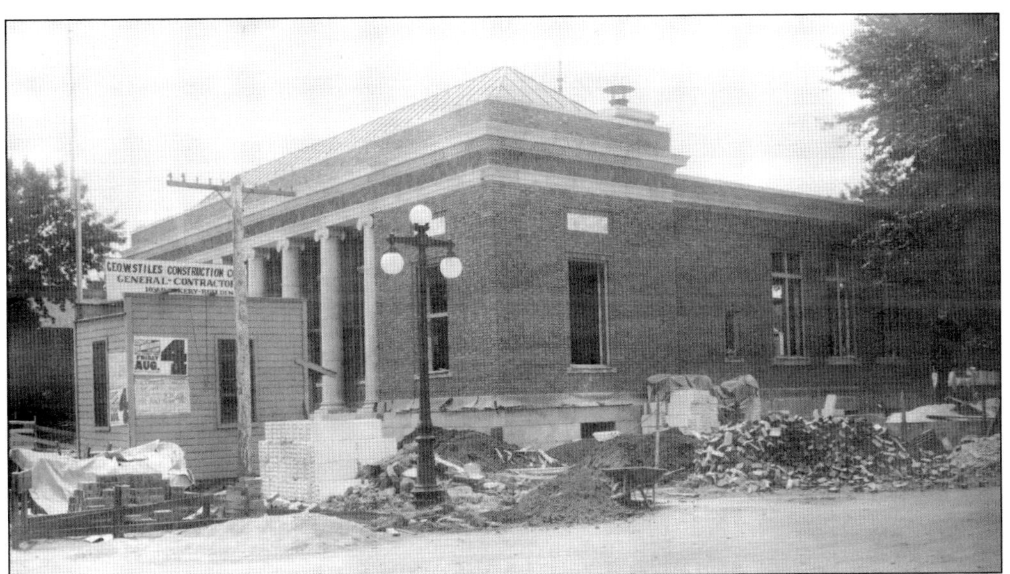

A large celebration was held on May 26, 1916, for the laying of the cornerstone for the new post office. The building is shown under construction in July of that year.

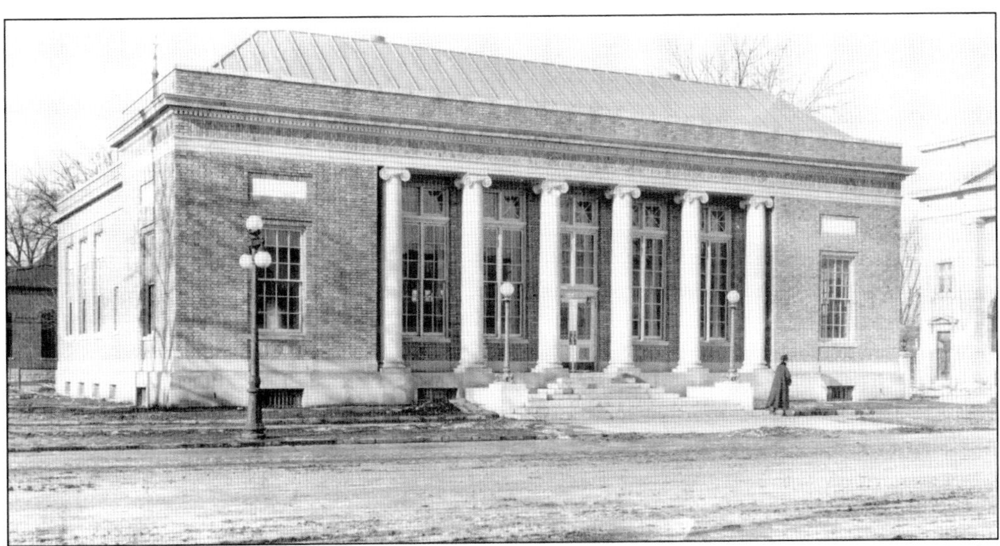
The newly completed post office, pictured here, opened on February 5, 1917, even though the lighting fixtures had not arrived.

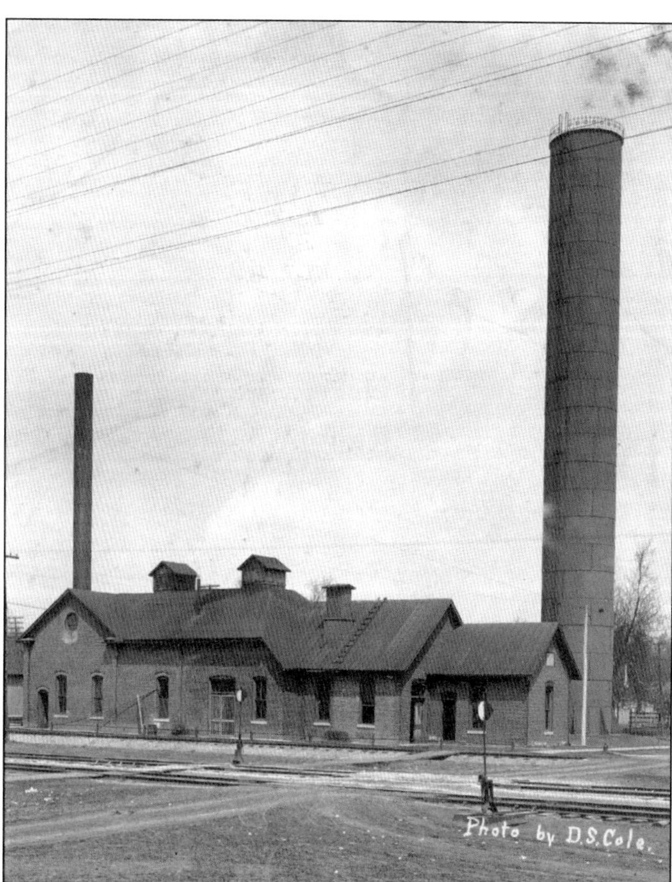

The city's waterworks was completed in 1891, and the 110-foot-tall standpipe dominated the skyline for many years.

Beginning in 1893, before the streets were paved, this water wagon was used to help control dust. The wagon was originally privately owned, but the city took over street cleaning in 1917.

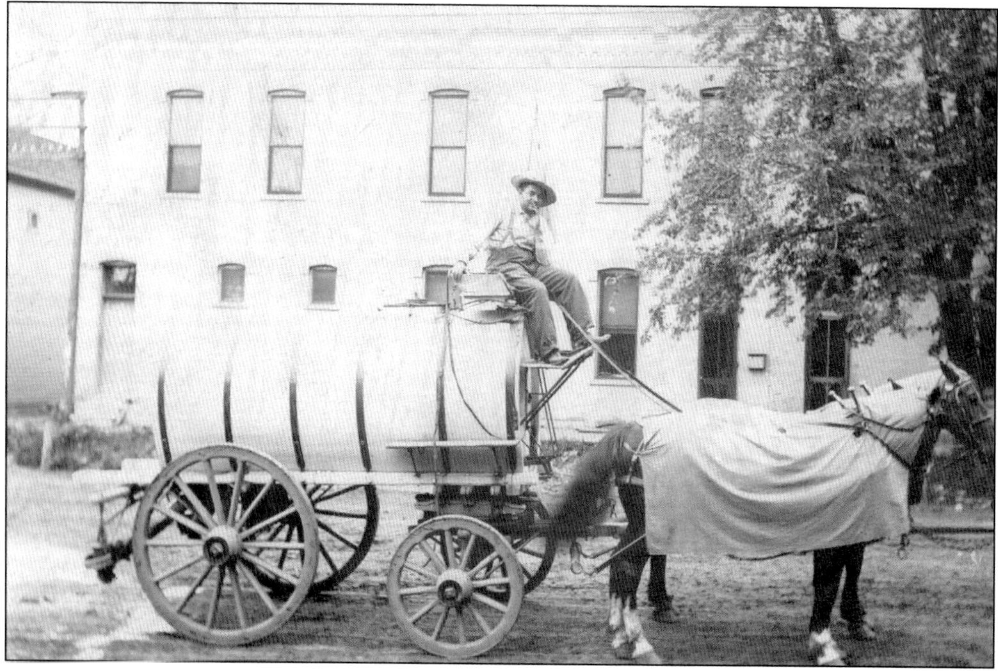

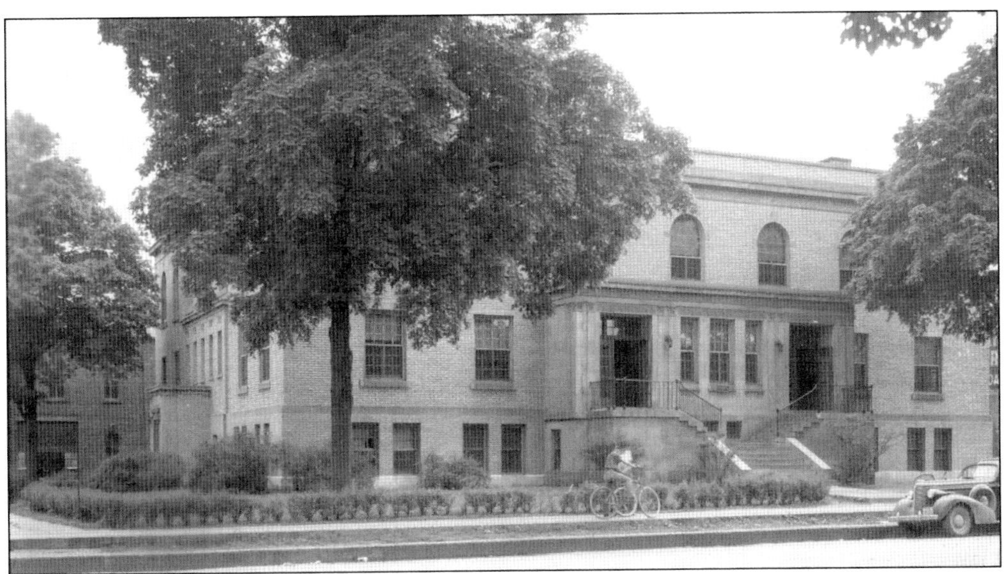

The cornerstone of the YMCA building was laid on May 31, 1924. The structure was later remodeled with additions between 1965 and 1966. Washington is one of the nation's smallest communities to have its own YMCA.

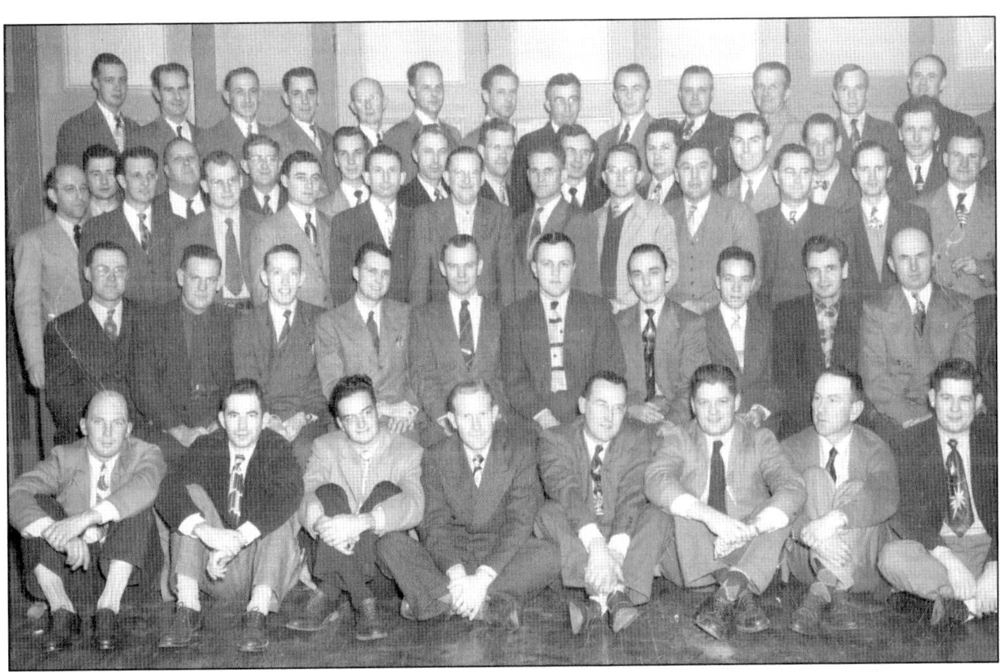

This is a meeting of the Y's Men's Club, which was founded in 1926 to help promote and raise money to support the YMCA. For many years, it produced an annual play. (Courtesy of Lori Bauer.)

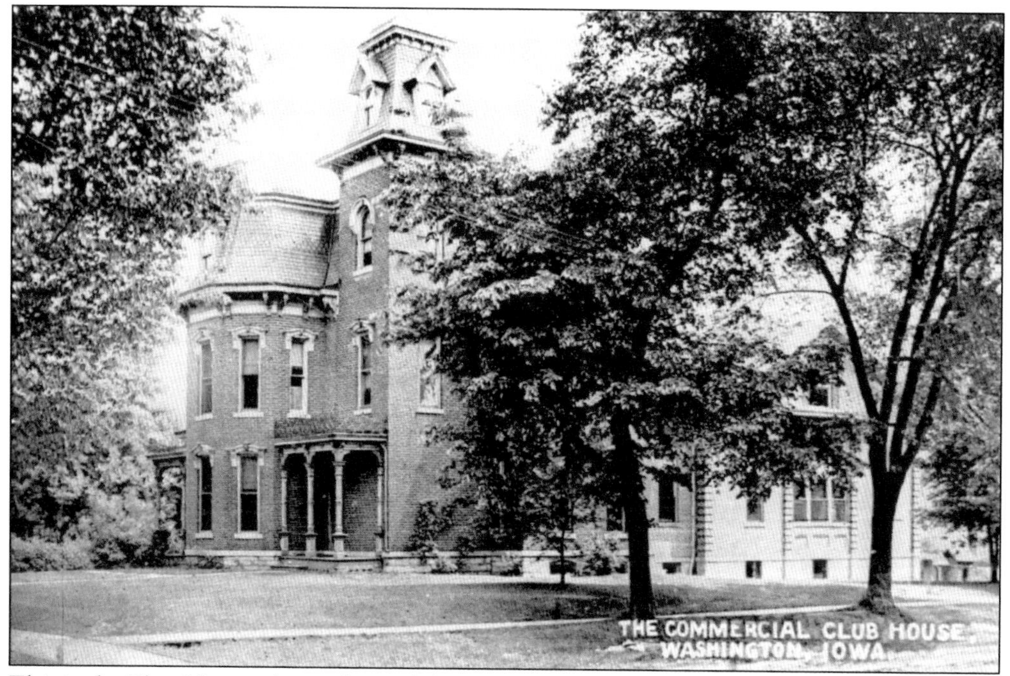

This is the Blair House when it housed the Commercial Club, a forerunner of the Washington Chamber of Commerce. The building also housed a bowling alley and a meeting room.

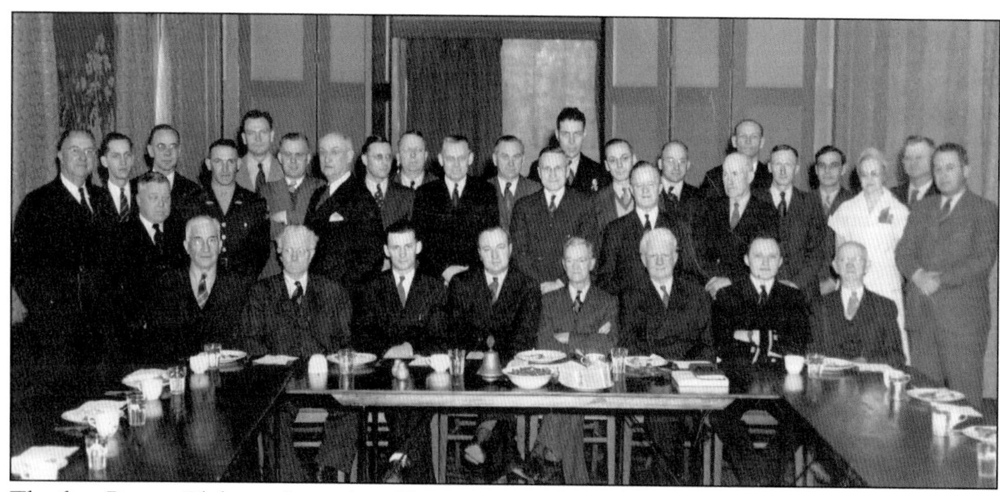

The first Rotary Club was formed in Chicago in 1905. Washington's chapter is pictured here in the meeting room of the YMCA on February 6, 1944. The woman in the photograph was the YMCA cook, not a member. The organization would eventually vote to admit women in 1986.

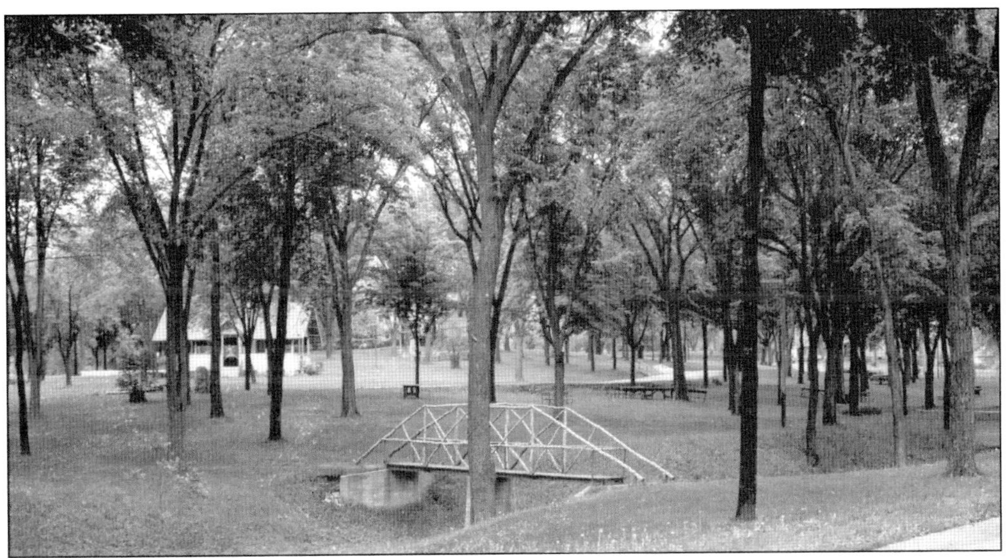

Frank Stewart was the moving force behind the formal establishment of Sunset Park in 1904. This is an early view of the park.

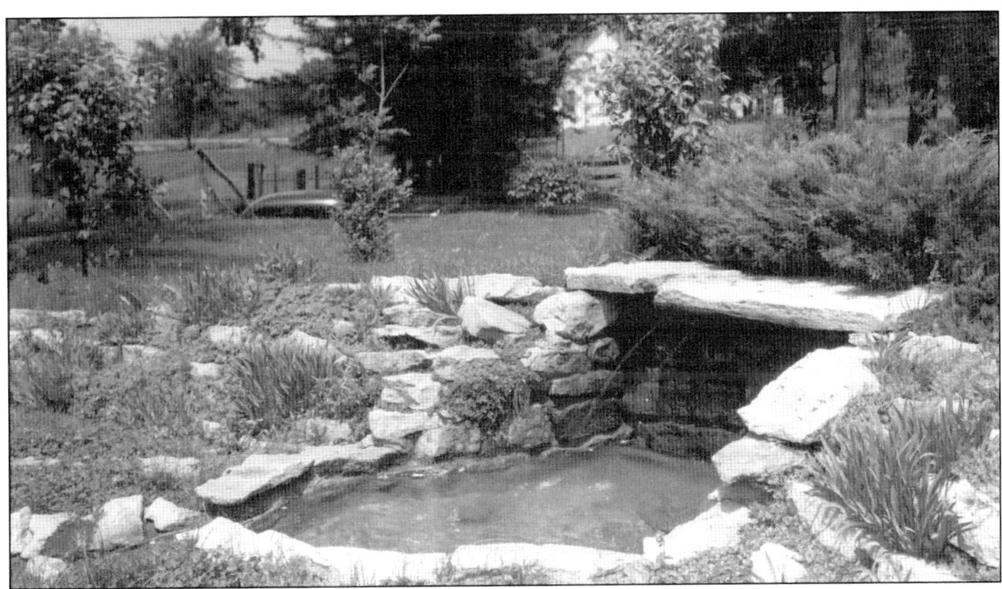

Frank Stewart also did most of the landscape planning of Sunset Park, including this water feature. He donated his time and often bought trees and plants with his own money.

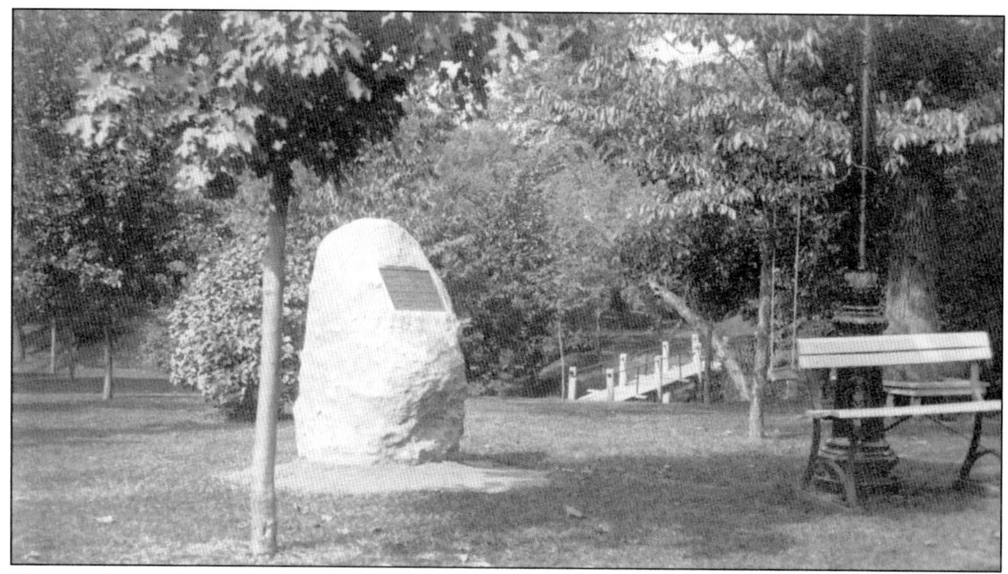

This marker in Sunset Park is dedicated to Abijah Savage, who purchased and donated the land for the establishment of the park. Additional land was acquired for the park through the years, and it is now approximately 60 acres.

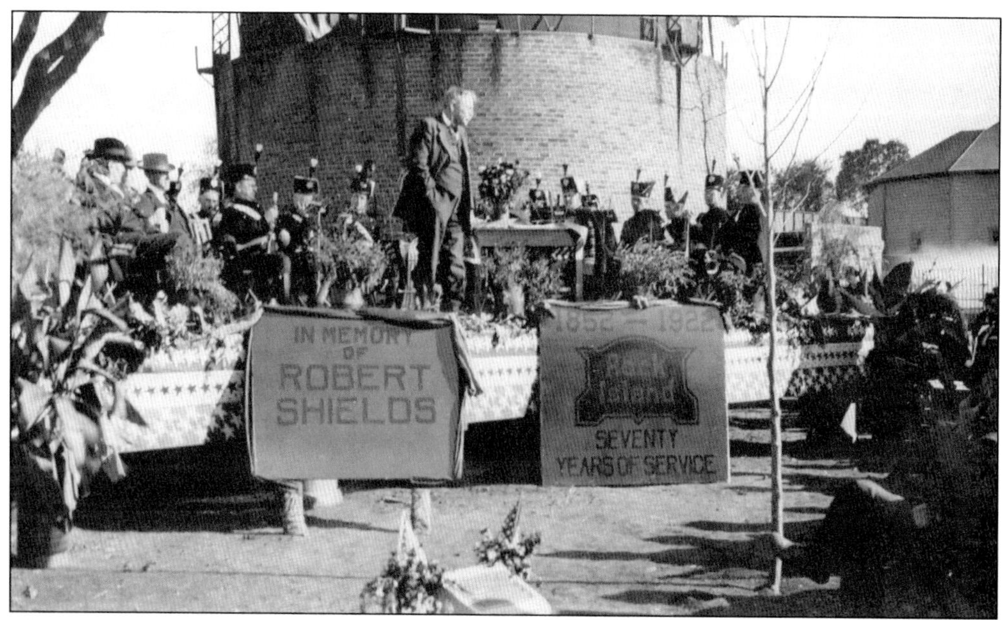

The dedication of Robert Shields Park, seen here around 1922, featured Col. D.J. Palmer as the speaker. The gas plant is in the background.

Nine

Entertainment

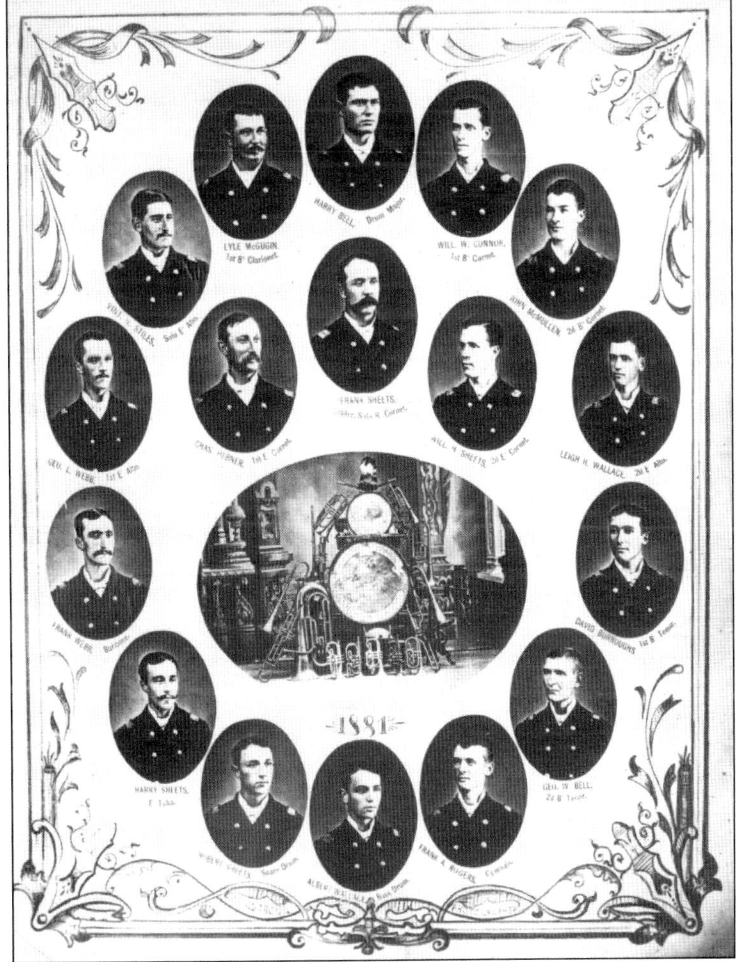

The Washington Junior Cornet Band was organized in 1866. The 1881 members were, clockwise from the top, (outer circle) drum major Harry Bell, Will W. Connor, John McMullen, Leigh H. Wallace, David Burroughs, George W. Bell, Frank A. Rogers, Albert Wallace, Robert Sheets, Harry Sheets, Frank Webb, George L. Webb, Vincent H. Stiles, and Lyle M. Guy; from left to right, (in the center) Charles Hebner, Frank Sheets, and William H. Sheets.

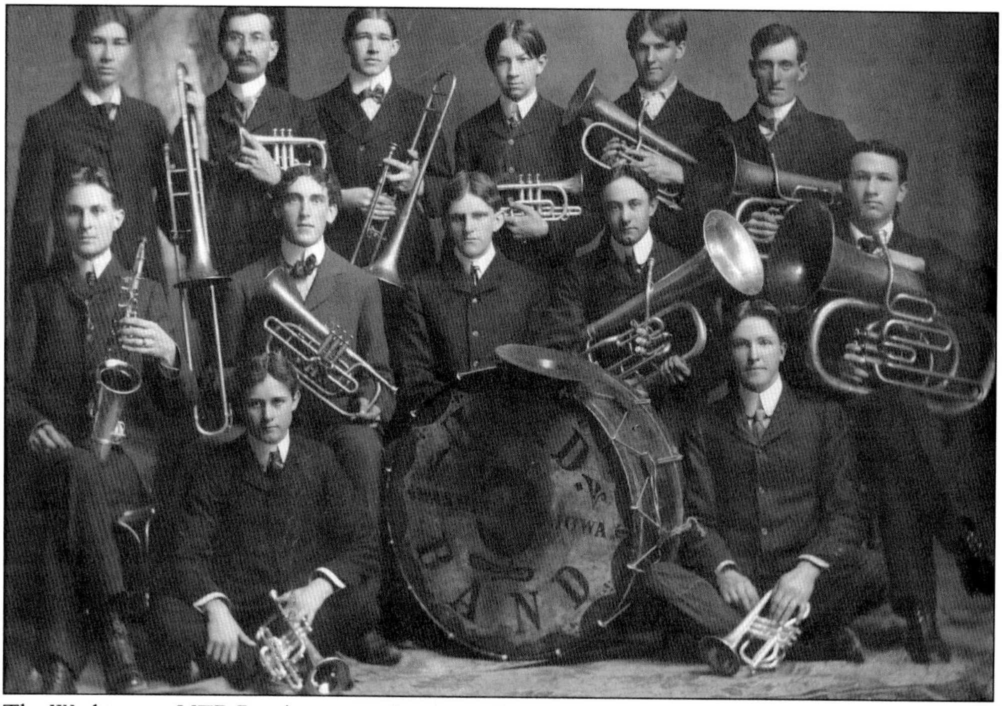

The Washington UTD Band is pictured at the end of the 19th century. Unfortunately, the members are not identified, and very little is known about the history of the organization.

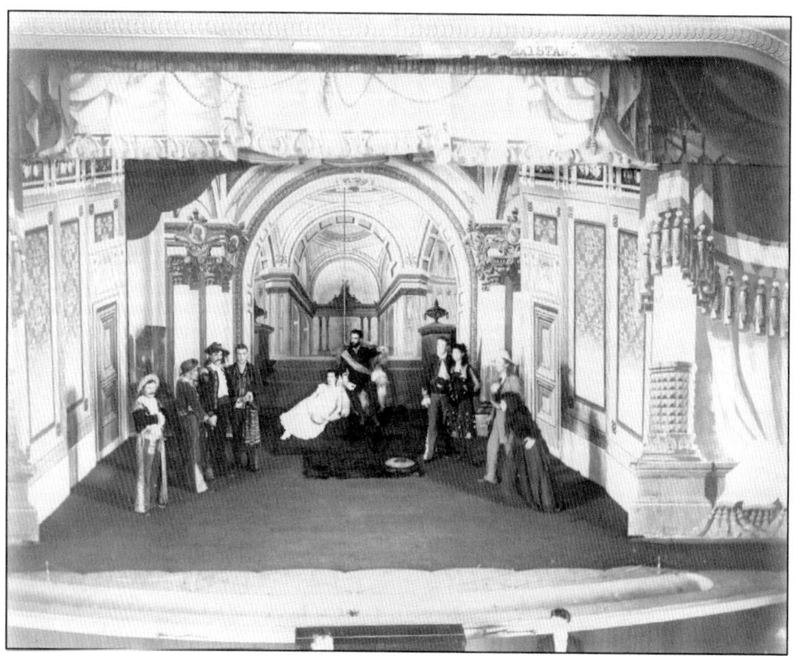

This is the interior of first Graham Opera House. On stage is the Spooner Company, which performed a week's repertoire of plays in the opera house four times during the 1890s. The building was destroyed by a spectacular fire on November 23, 1892. (Courtesy of the Theatre Museum, Mount Pleasant, Iowa.)

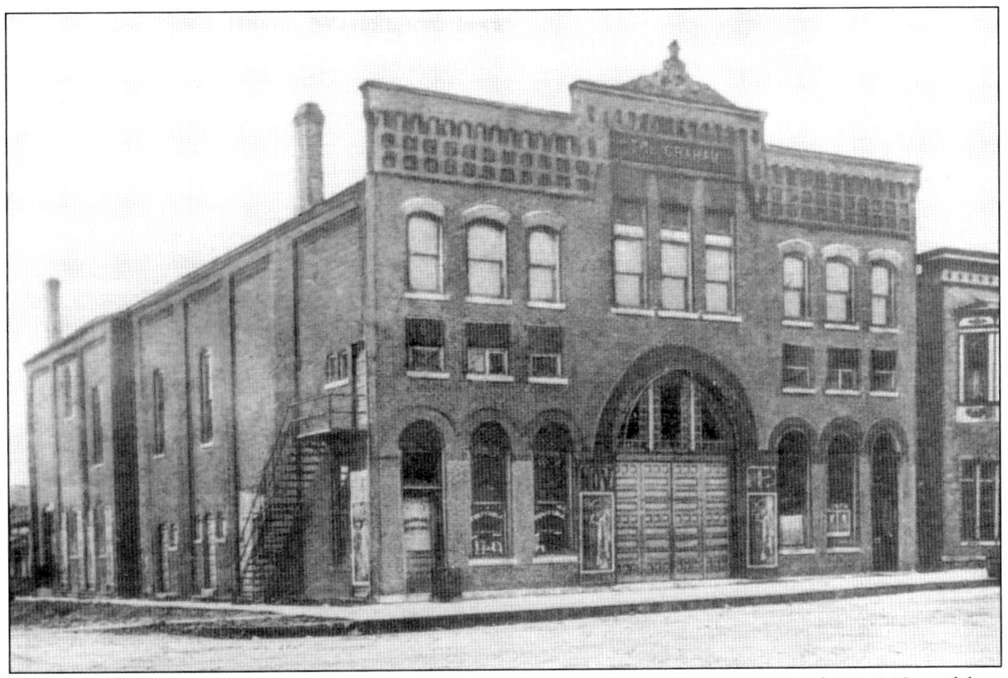

The second Graham Opera House (now the State Theater) was constructed in 1893 and has housed a variety of entertainments ever since. The first motion picture was shown here in 1894, and it continues to show movies today.

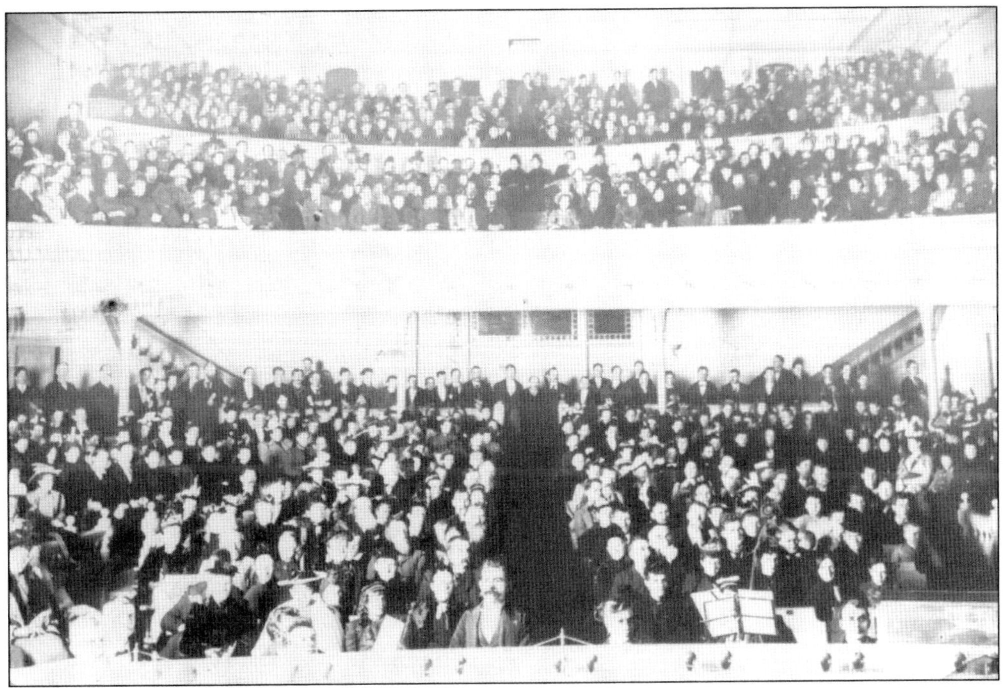

Here is an early audience in the second Graham Opera House; the conductor can also be seen at the bottom of the picture. The balconies were remodeled extensively in the 1940s.

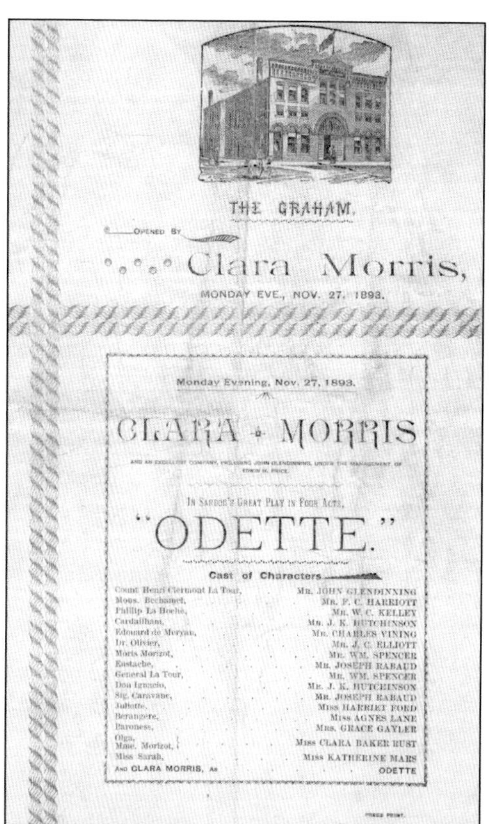

THE GRAHAM.

OPENED BY

Clara Morris,

MONDAY EVE., NOV. 27, 1893.

Monday Evening, Nov. 27, 1893.

CLARA MORRIS

IN SARDOU'S GREAT PLAY IN FOUR ACTS,

"ODETTE."

Cast of Characters

Count Henri Clermont La Tour,	MR. JOHN GLENDINNING
Mous. Bechamel,	MR. F. C. HARRIOTT
Phillip La Roche,	MR. W. C. KELLEY
Cardaillhan,	MR. J. K. HUTCHINSON
Edouard de Meryan,	MR. CHARLES VINING
Dr. Olivier,	MR. J. C. ELLIOTT
Moris Morizot,	MR. WM. SPENCER
Eustache,	MR. JOSEPH RABAUD
General La Tour,	MR. WM. SPENCER
Don Ignacio,	MR. J. K. HUTCHINSON
Sig. Caravane,	MR. JOSEPH RABAUD
Juliette,	MISS HARRIET FORD
Berangere,	MISS AGNES LANE
Baroness,	MRS. GRACE GAYLER
Olga, Mme. Morizot,	MISS CLARA BAKER RUST
Miss Sarah,	MISS KATHERINE MARS
AND CLARA MORRIS, AS	ODETTE

This is the opening-night program of the second Graham Opera House, dated November 27, 1893. The play *Odette* featured nationally noted actress Clara Morris.

This 1929 home-talent production of *Way Down East*, a popular melodrama of the time, was a benefit for the city band. Note the live chickens on stage, adding to the realism of the play.

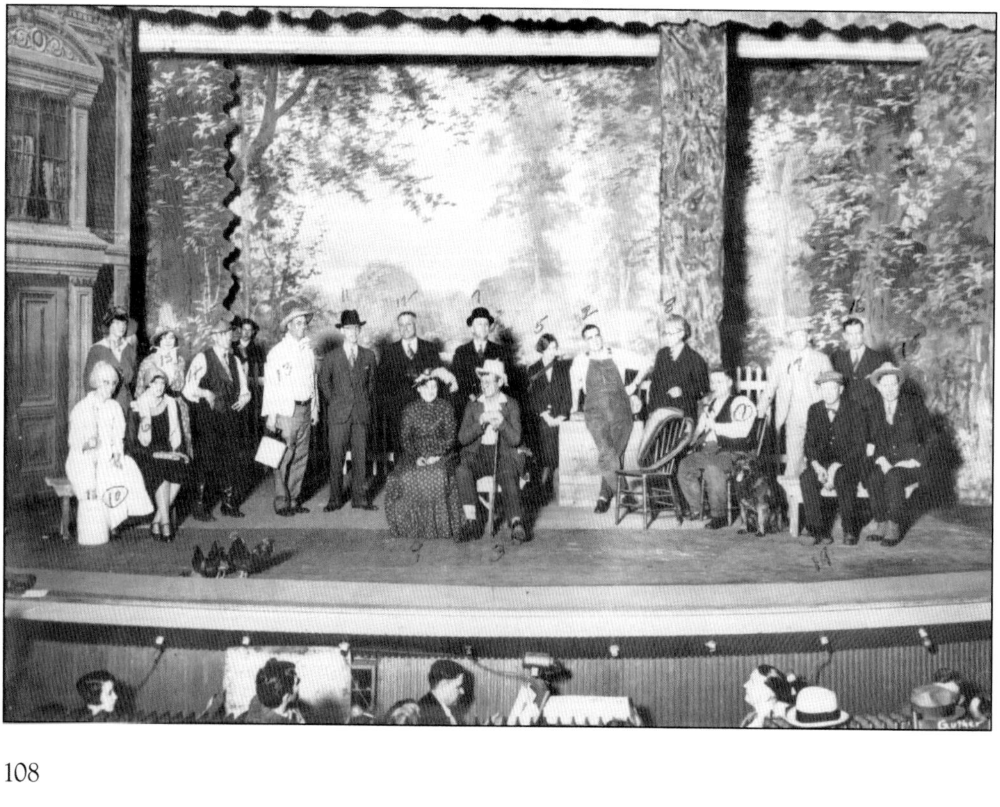

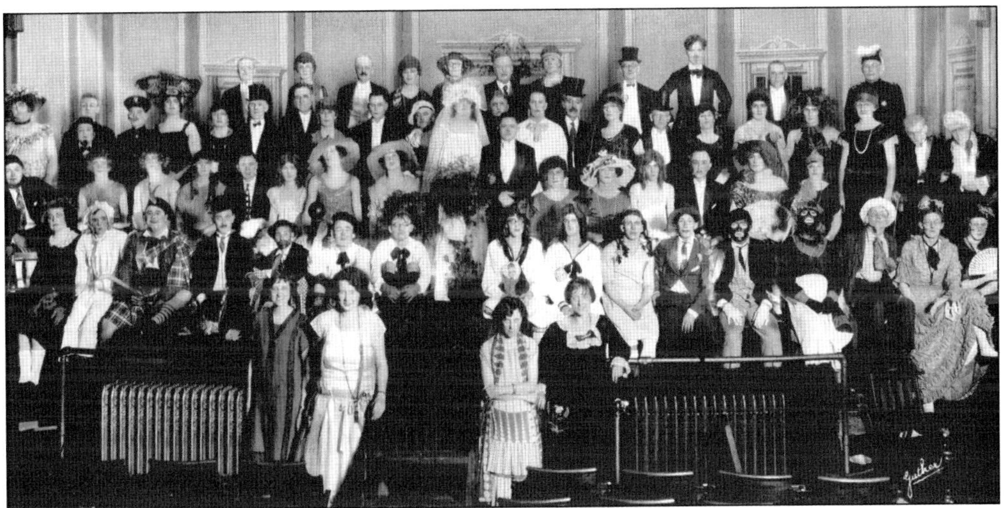

The Womanless Wedding was a popular play for amateur productions. This Washington production, performed in the fall of 1925, featured Ralph Livingston, owner of the *Washington Press* newspaper, as the bride.

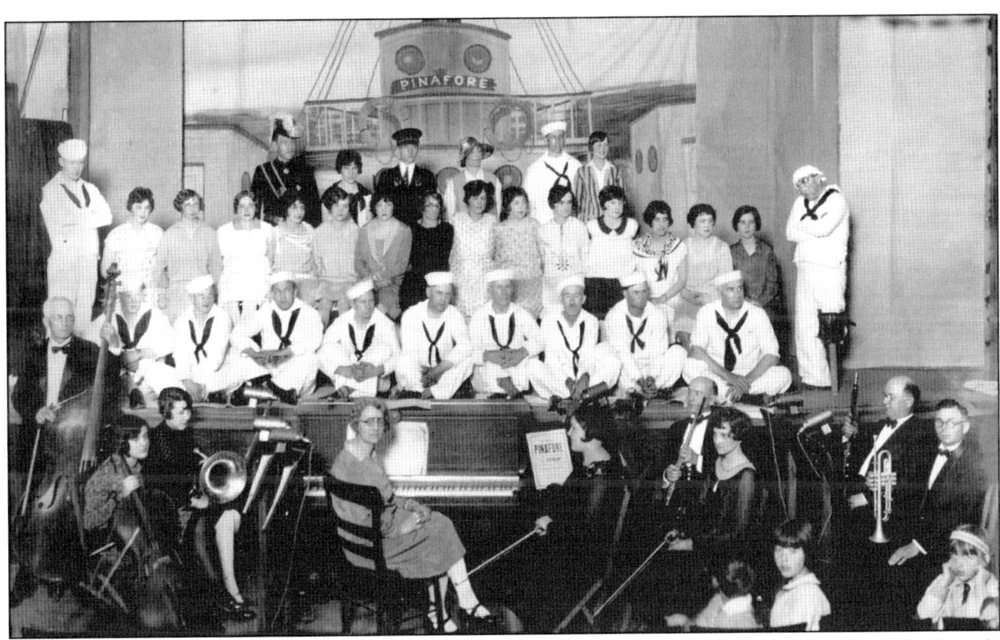

The Methodist church choir performed a home-talent production of Gilbert and Sullivan's *H.M.S. Pinafore* in the high school auditorium on May 29, 1928. The principal performers included H.N. Schuster, Ray Fitch, Everett Griffith, Carlton Haven, Winfield Allen, Andy Christian, Gladys William, and Lewis Warren.

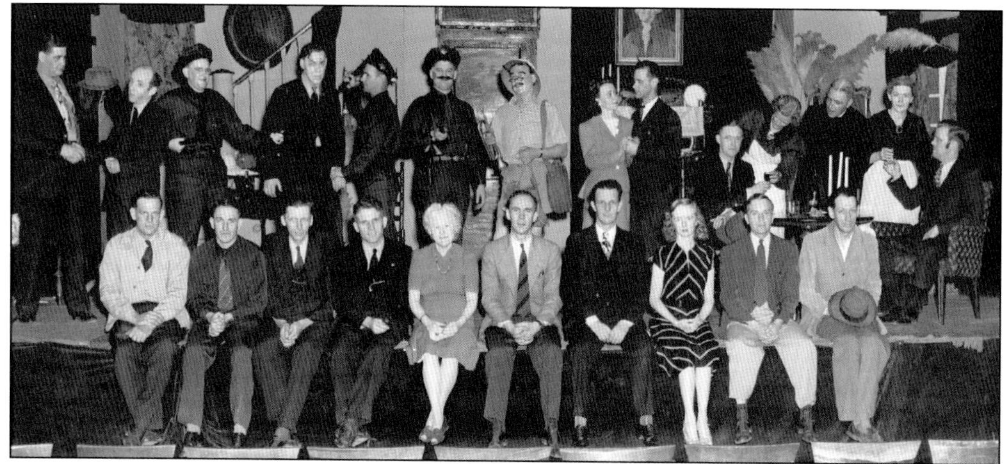

Each year, beginning in 1930, the Y's Men's Club performed a home-talent play to raise money in support of the local YMCA. Shown here are the cast and crew of a 1947 production of *Arsenic and Old Lace*.

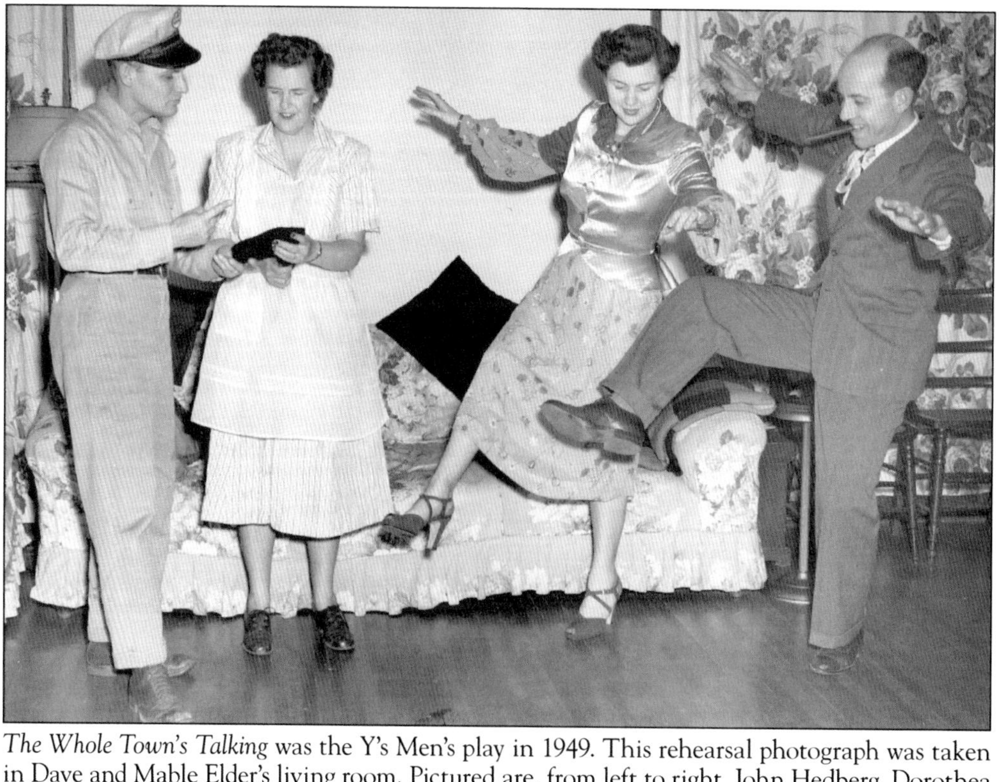

The Whole Town's Talking was the Y's Men's play in 1949. This rehearsal photograph was taken in Dave and Mable Elder's living room. Pictured are, from left to right, John Hedberg, Dorothea Brindley, Mary Lynn Wehr, and Dave Elder.

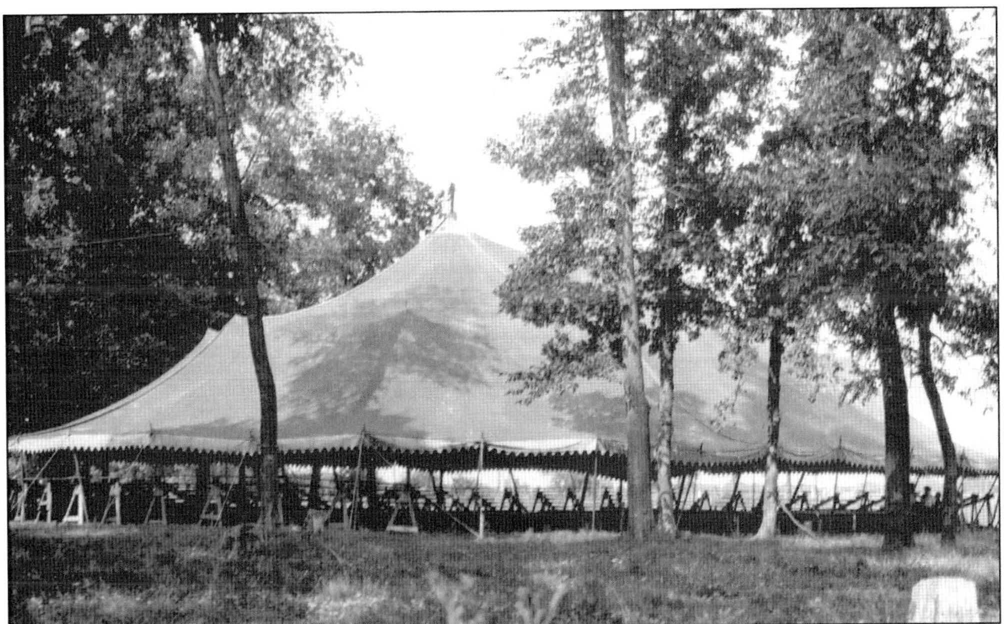

Chautauquas were traveling programs that created a family religious and educational movement in the late 19th and early 20th centuries. They brought entertainment and culture to many rural communities. This is the main Chautauqua tent in Washington; the Chautauqua grounds are now the county fairgrounds.

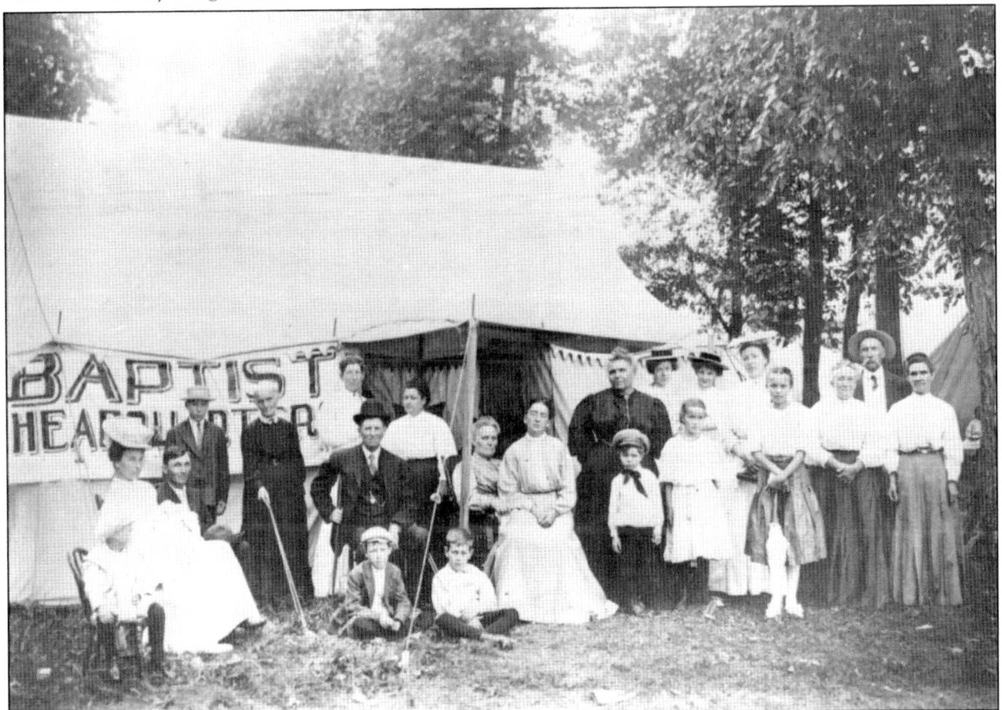

This photograph shows a group outside the Baptist headquarters tent on the Chautauqua grounds in 1906. Many of the Chautauqua programs had religious themes, and many of the various church denominations participated.

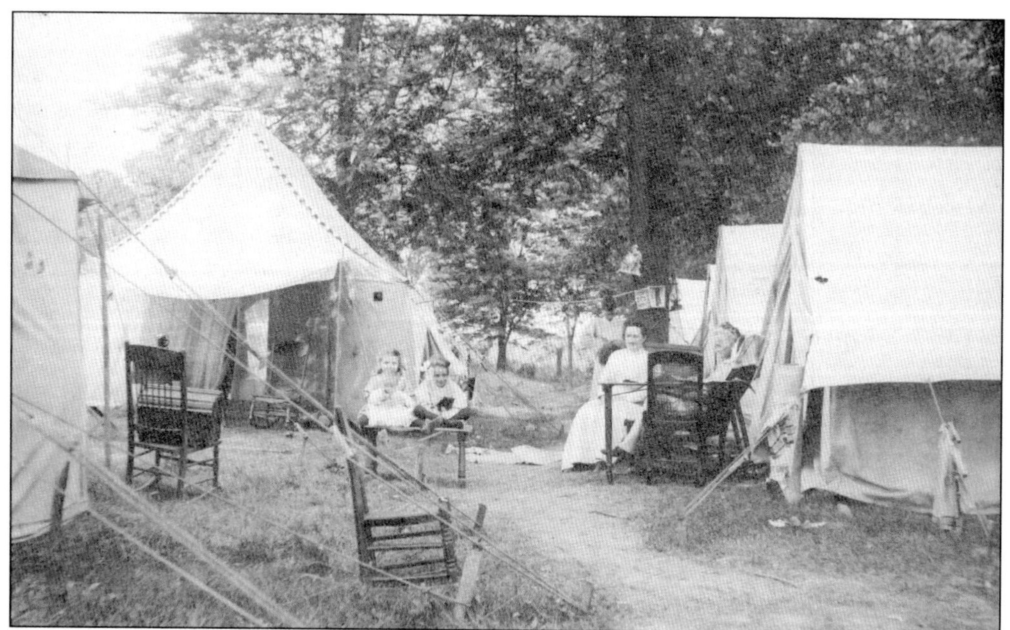

The north end of the Chautauqua grounds was reserved for family tents. Family vacations were often taken during the Chautauqua, and many families owned or rented tents so they could camp out during the entire week.

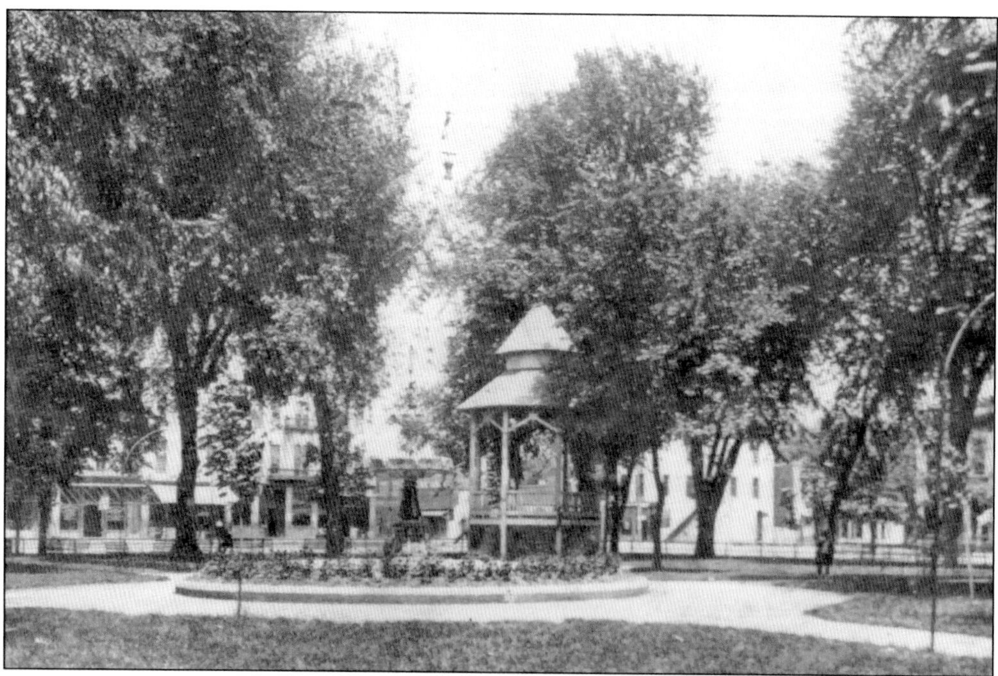

The first bandstand in Central Park was likely built after 1869, when the old courthouse was demolished. This is its second bandstand, located in the park's northeast corner. It is unclear when the bandstand was built, but it remained in Central Park until February 1916, when it was moved to Sunset Park.

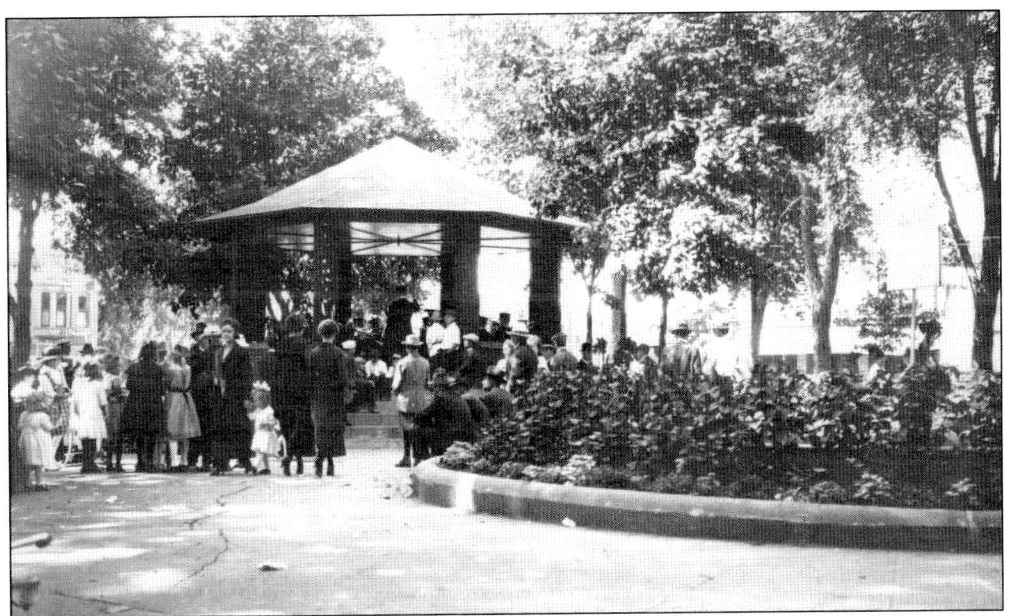

The third bandstand in Central Park stood just southwest of the park's center. It was constructed of brick and concrete in 1916 and was the first to have electric lighting. It was eventually replaced by the Ralph Smith Memorial Bandstand, constructed in 1952.

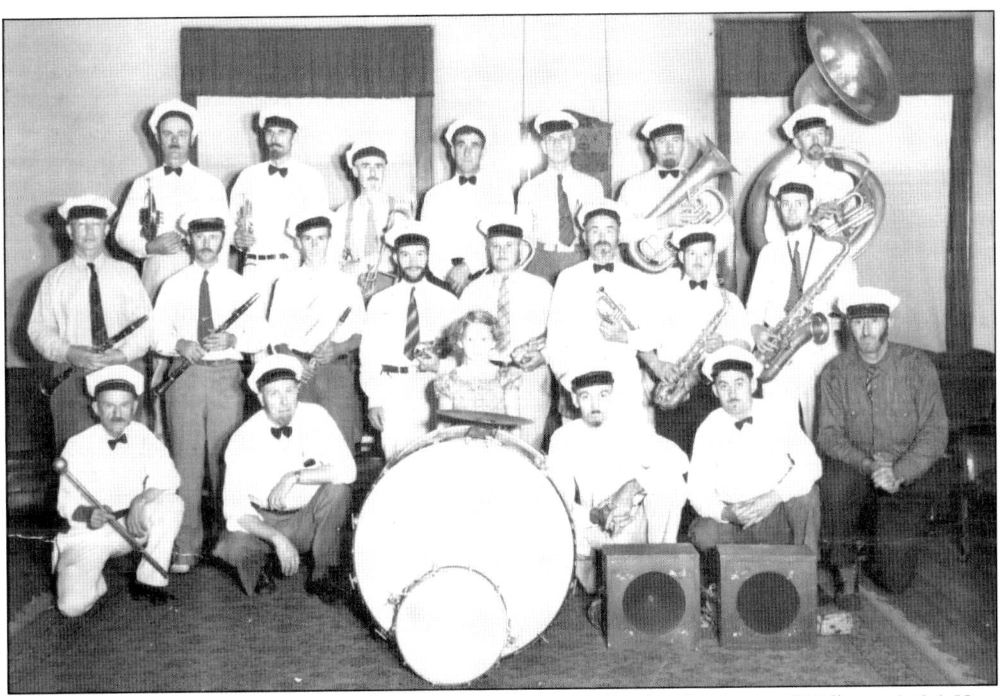

The Washington Municipal Band was founded in 1933 under the direction of Milburn A. McKay. In its first year, it performed 24 concerts, appearing on Saturdays in Central Park and on Sunday afternoons in Sunset Park. In this 1939 photograph, several of the members have beards grown for the city's centennial celebration.

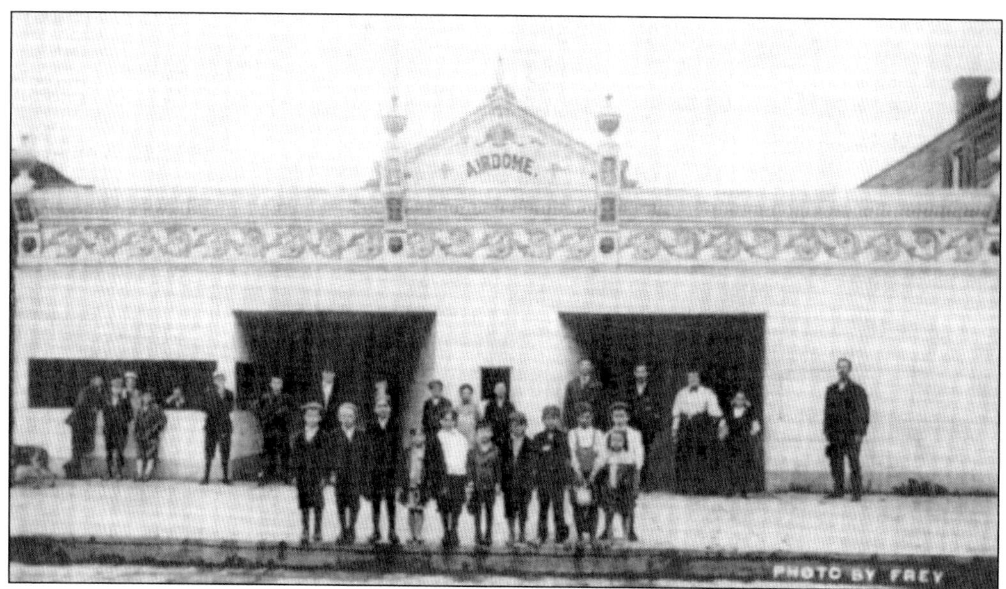

The Airdome, operated by F.W. Brinton and opened on July 9, 1908, was located on the northeast corner of South Iowa Avenue and East Jefferson Street. It was an open-air theater and took advantage of the natural slope of the lot for audience seating. The Airdome featured moving pictures and vaudeville acts and was particularly popular in the summer months in the years before the Opera House installed air-conditioning. (Courtesy of Mike Zahs.)

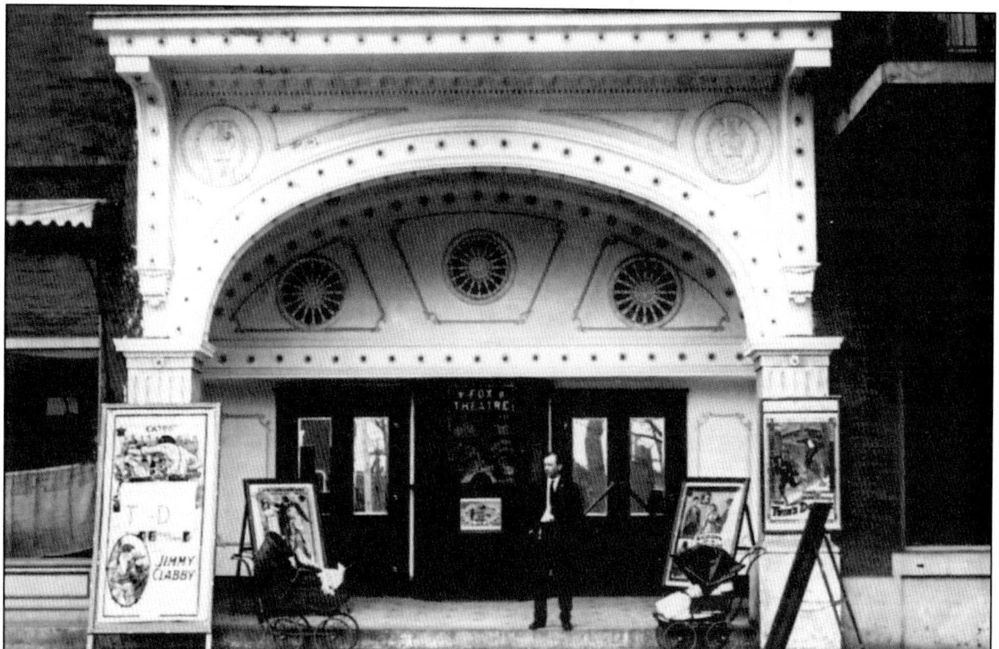

The Fox Movie Theater's opening night (January 10, 1914) featured several one-reel films, with musical performances by the Hinkle Trio between reels. The theater closed in 1953 and, having been greatly remodeled, is now the annex of the Jones Funeral Home.

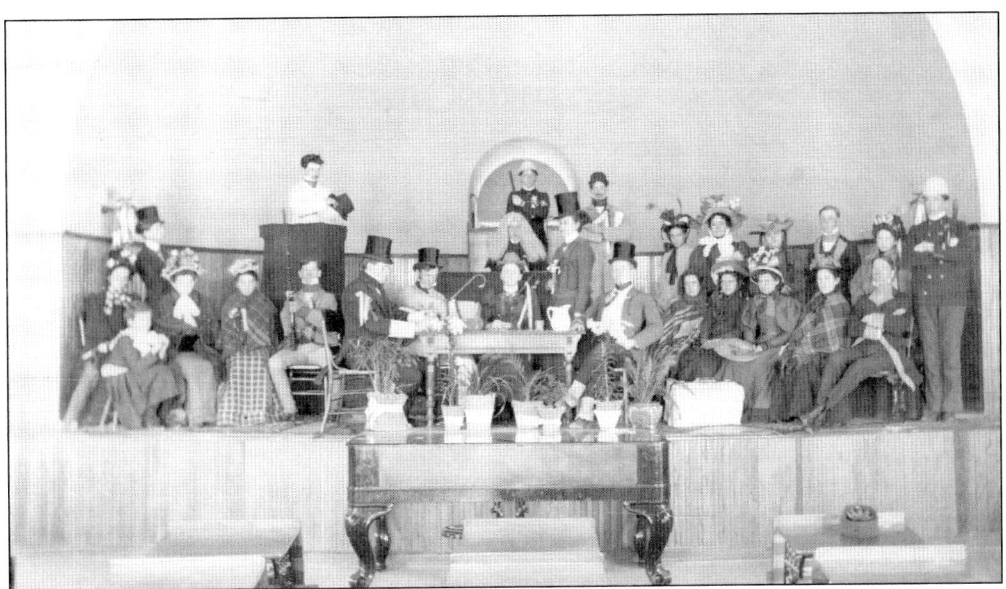

The cast of the 1901 high school play is shown in the school's auditorium. John Fisher (center) played a judge, and jury members (at right) included Bess Dayton, Lillie Minick, Will Kerr, ? Moothart, Blanch Patterson, Birdie McElroy, Nora Crone, Will Harwood, and Marion Stewart. Other cast members included Dick Montgomery, Leland Clapper, Dwinnie Ranken, Kate Buckley, Elma Sickles, Henry Shields, Clara Bickford, Mable Morton, Percy Wallace, Charles Davis, and Ralph Junkin.

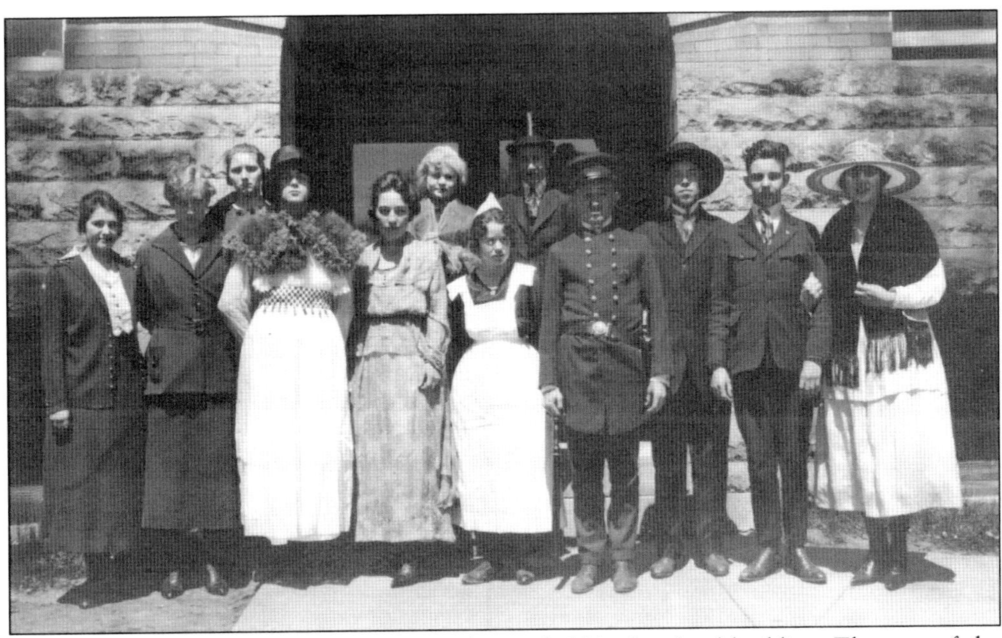

The cast of the high school play poses in front of old high school building. The year of the photograph is uncertain, but it predates 1918.

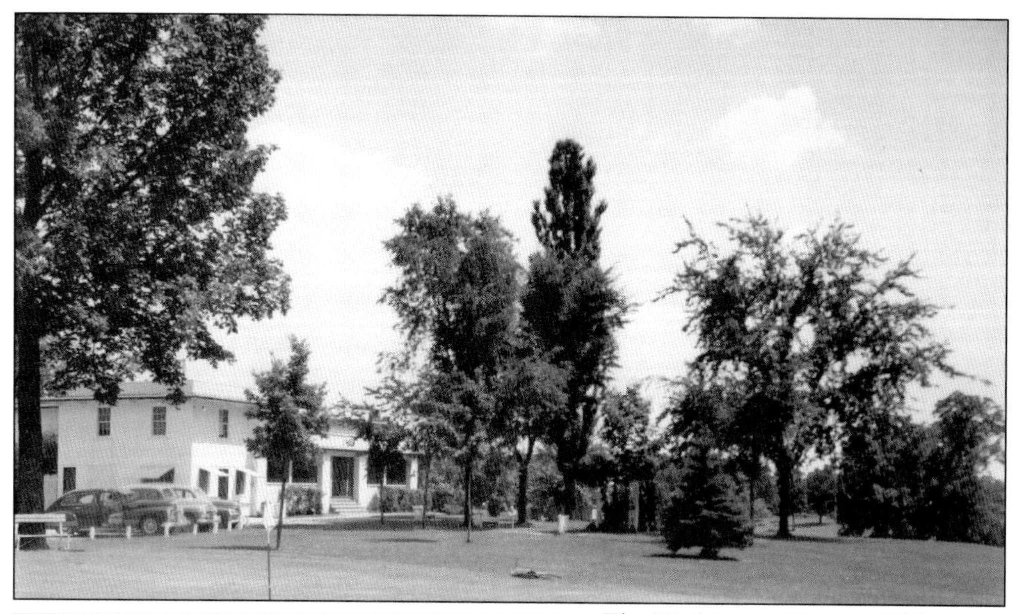

The Washington Country Club was founded on a 60-acre wooded tract south of town in 1924. It is shown here in the 1940s.

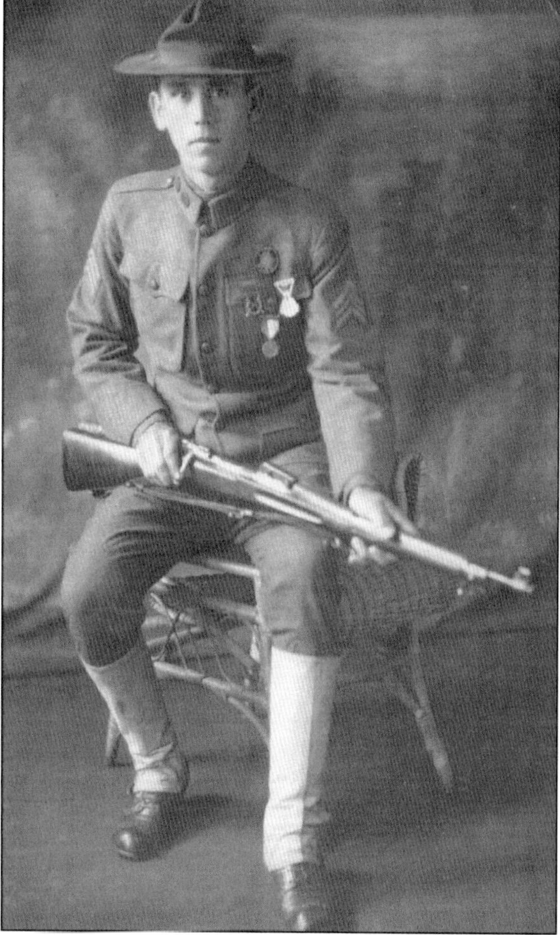

John E. Jackson of Washington was one of three Iowans to participate in the 1912 Olympic Games in Stockholm, Sweden. He competed on the US rifle team, winning the gold medal in the team military rifle competition and the bronze medal in the 600-meter free rifle event.

Ten

CELEBRATIONS

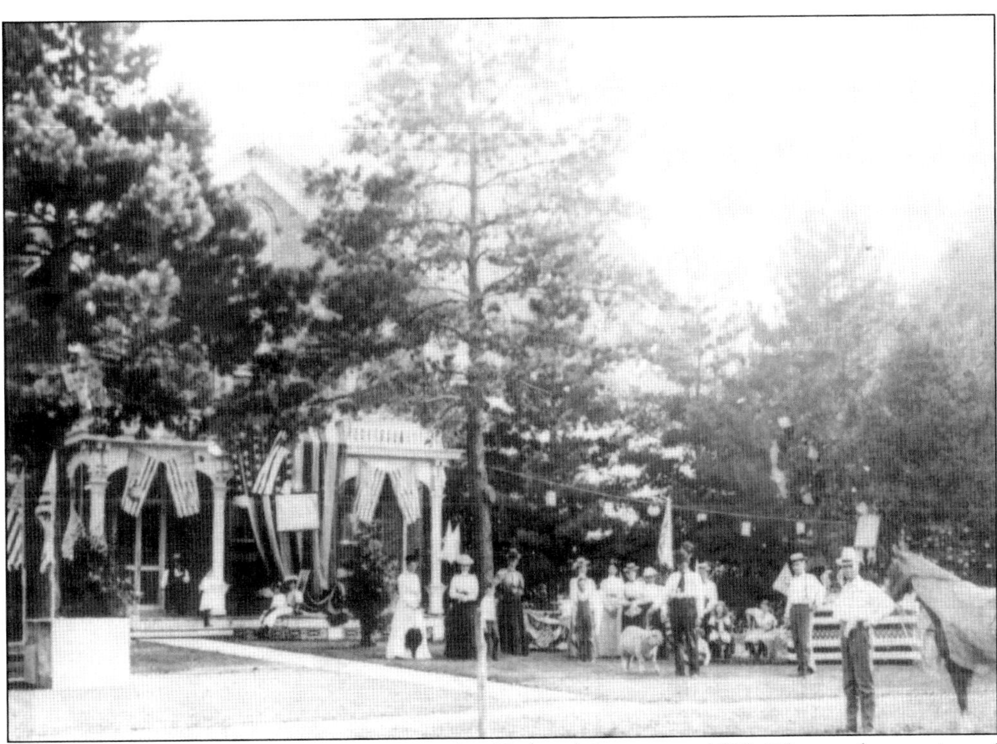

The Conger House is decorated for a Fourth of July celebration in 1898. The southeast wing of the house dates back to 1847, when Thomas Ritchey, one of two men who founded Washington, owned the house and 77 acres. Jonathan and Jane Conger bought the property in 1855 and enlarged the house, finishing it in 1868. The home was later owned by Col. C.J. Wilson and his wife, Clara (daughter of Jonathan and Jane Conger). It later functioned as a supper club and eventually became a nursing home. The property, currently maintained as a museum by the Washington County Historical Society, is listed in the National Register of Historic Places.

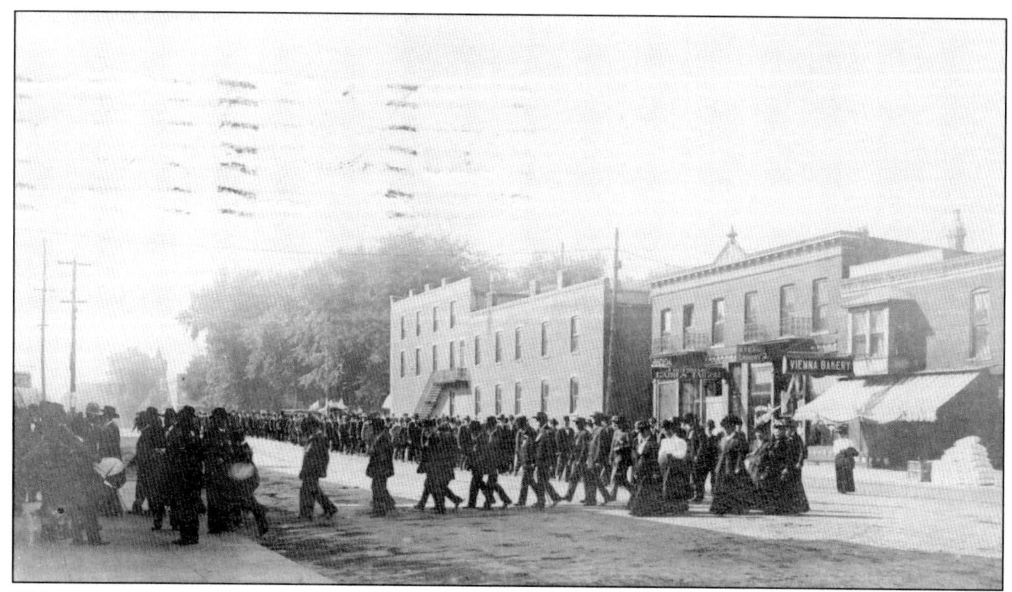

This postcard, with a cancellation date of 1910, shows a parade honoring a Grand Army of the Republic reunion of old soldiers. The participants are heading for a program at the Graham Opera House.

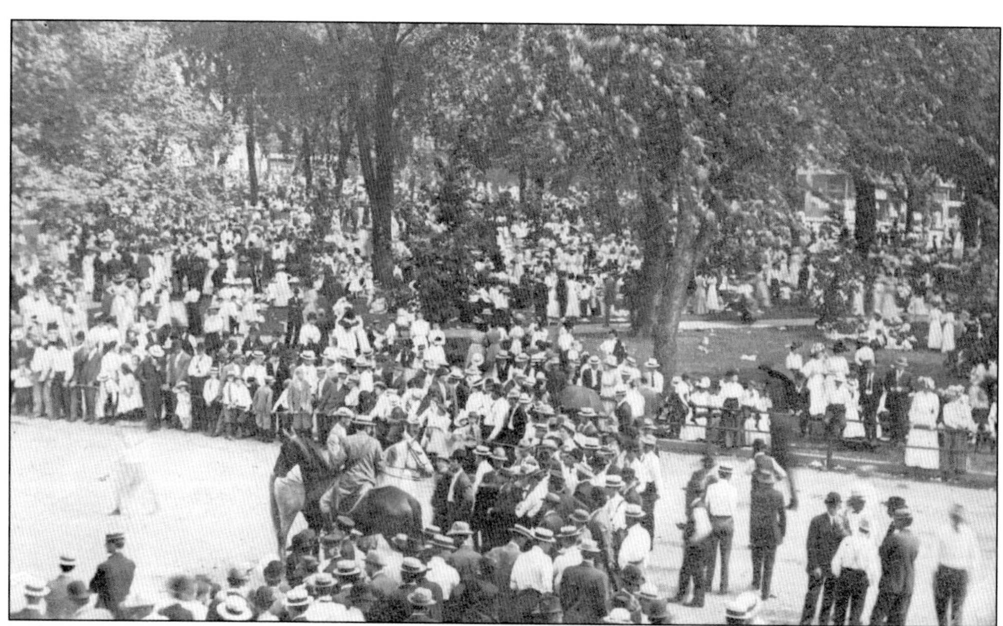

A large crowd is shown around 1890 gathering in Central Park for what is likely a Fourth of July celebration.

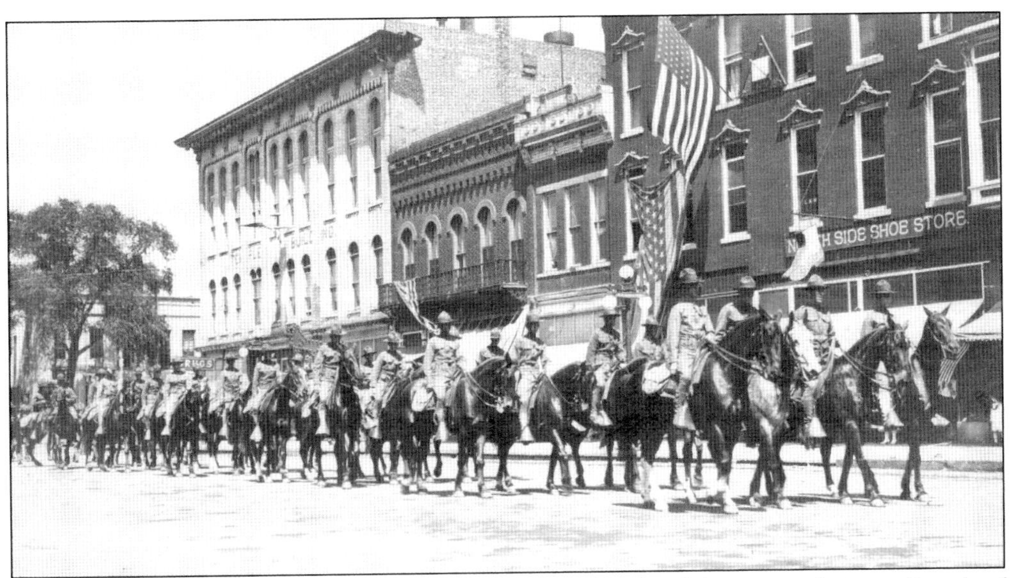

Troop F, 113th Cavalry Regiment is shown on the north side of the square during a Fourth of July parade.

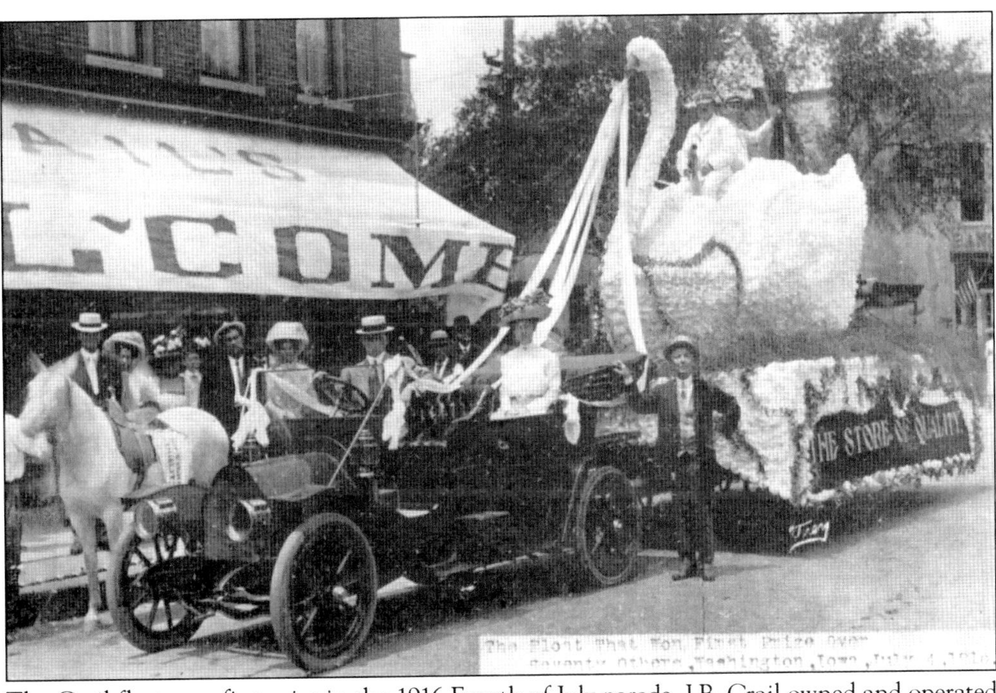

The Crail float won first prize in the 1916 Fourth of July parade. J.B. Crail owned and operated a dry-goods store for many years at 101 South Marion Avenue. It was replaced in the 1920s by a J.C. Penney store.

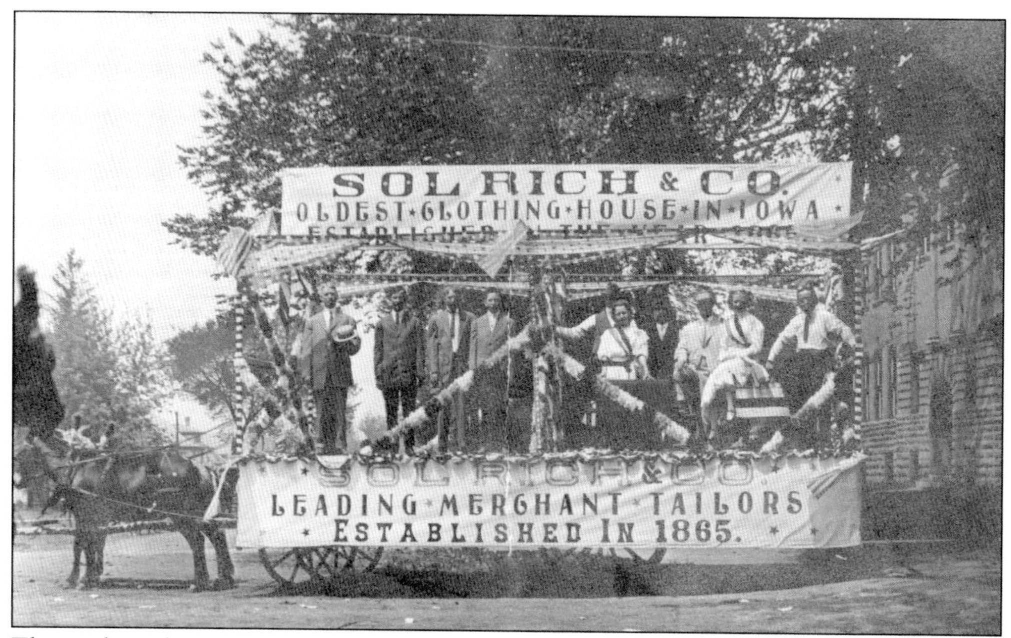

This is the Sol Rich float in the 1910 Fourth of July parade. Sol Rich men's clothing store, established in 1864, operated for many years at 112 South Iowa Avenue. Note the float's claim that it was the oldest clothing store in Iowa.

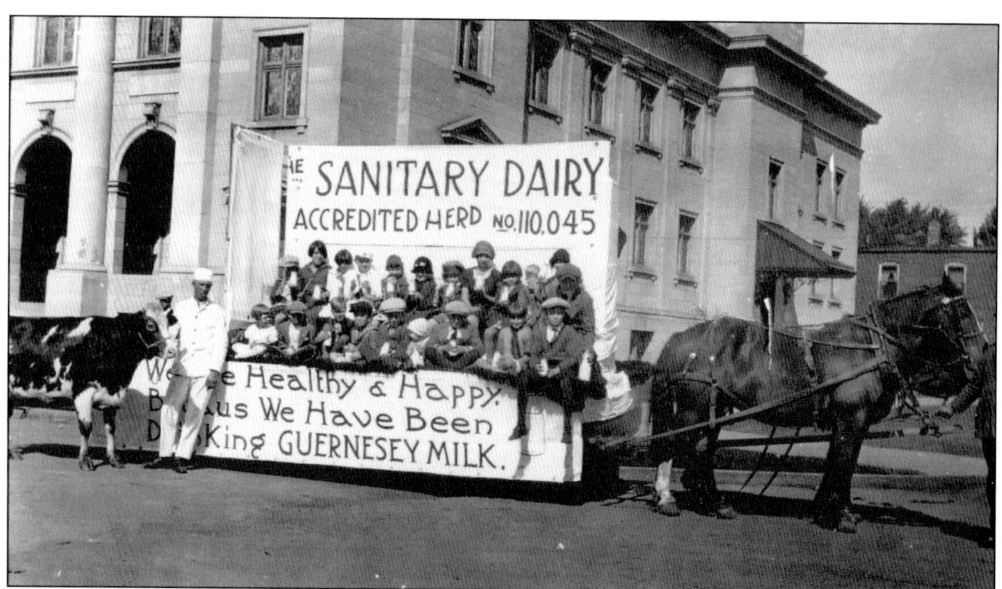

The Sanitary Dairy float, seen here in front of the Methodist church, was led by a horse and followed by a Guernsey cow.

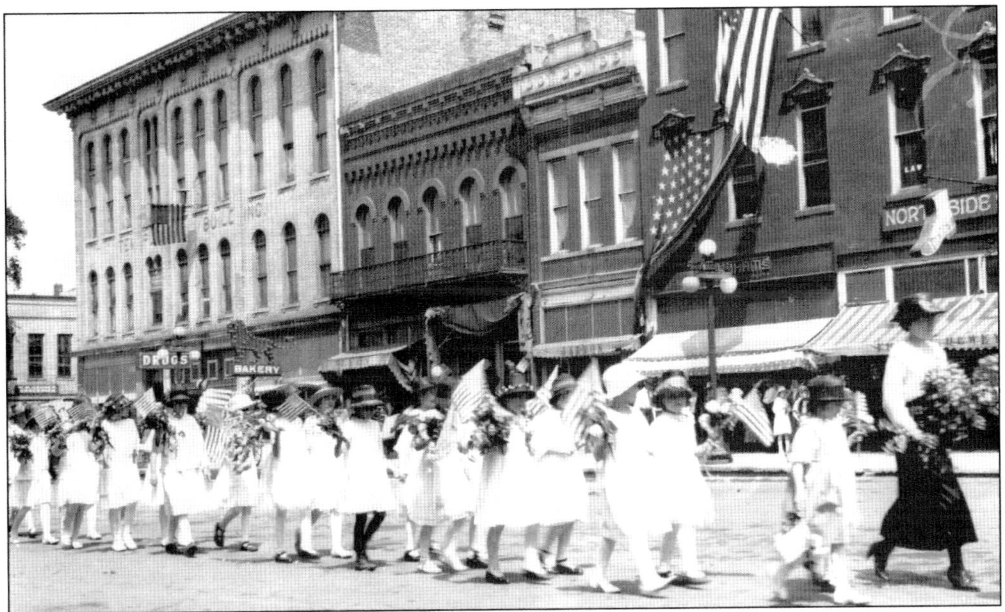

A group of young girls participated in the Welcome Home parade on September 11, 1919, celebrating the return of local soldiers at the end of World War I. The north side of the square is in the background.

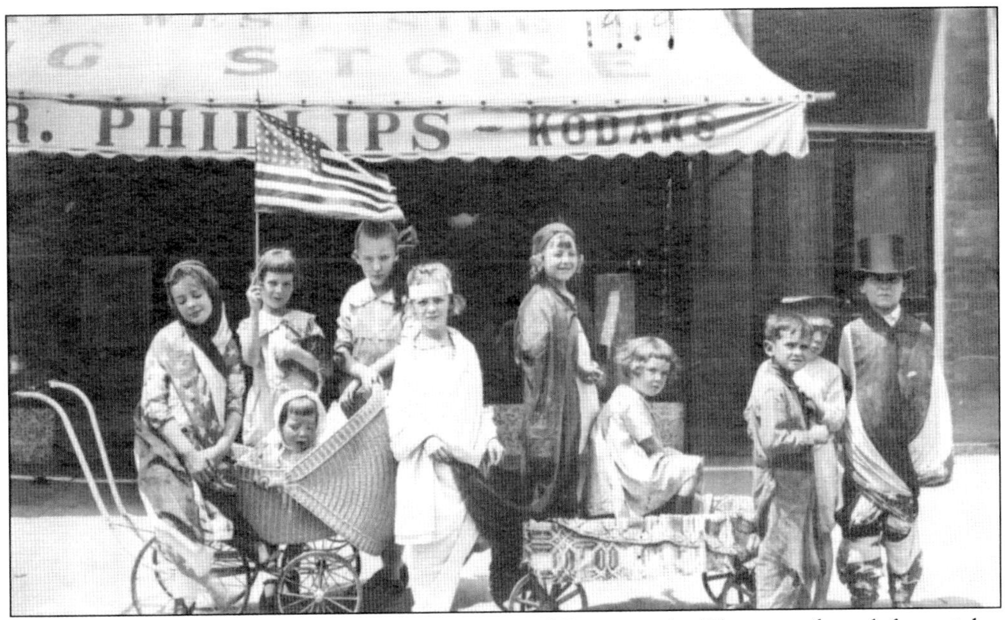

These children participated in the 1919 Memorial Day parade. They are, from left to right, Margaret Stewart, Maxine Barden, Joan Keeley (in buggy), Evelyn Gibson, Lucille Schmoeller, Patricia Keeley, Loa Jean Stewart, Tom Stewart, unidentified, and Bob Lytle.

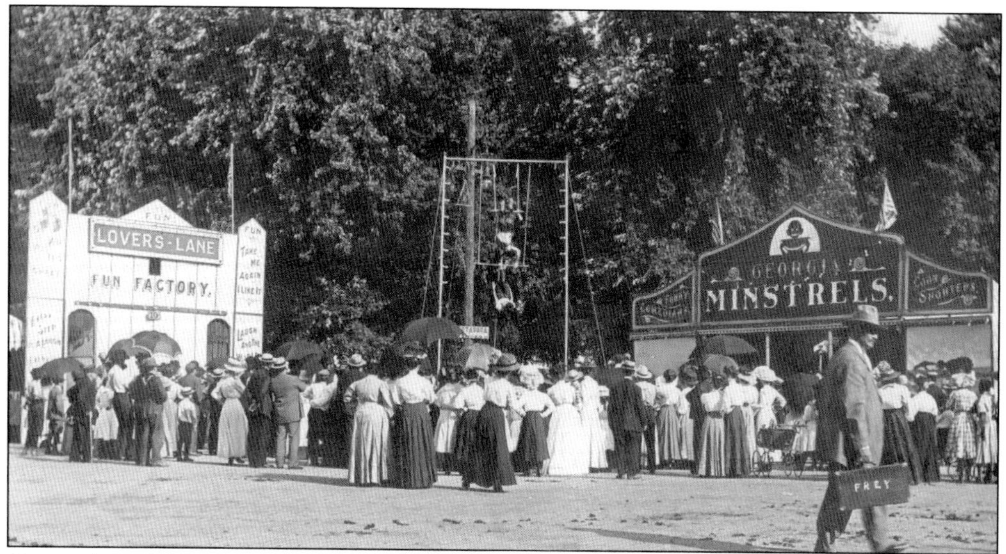

Carnivals and circuses were popular forms of entertainment every summer. The first circus to come to town is thought to have been John Robinson's Circus, which set up in 1852 on a West Main Street lot just a block from the square. This photograph shows a carnival, complete with a minstrel show, set up on the edge of the square in 1909.

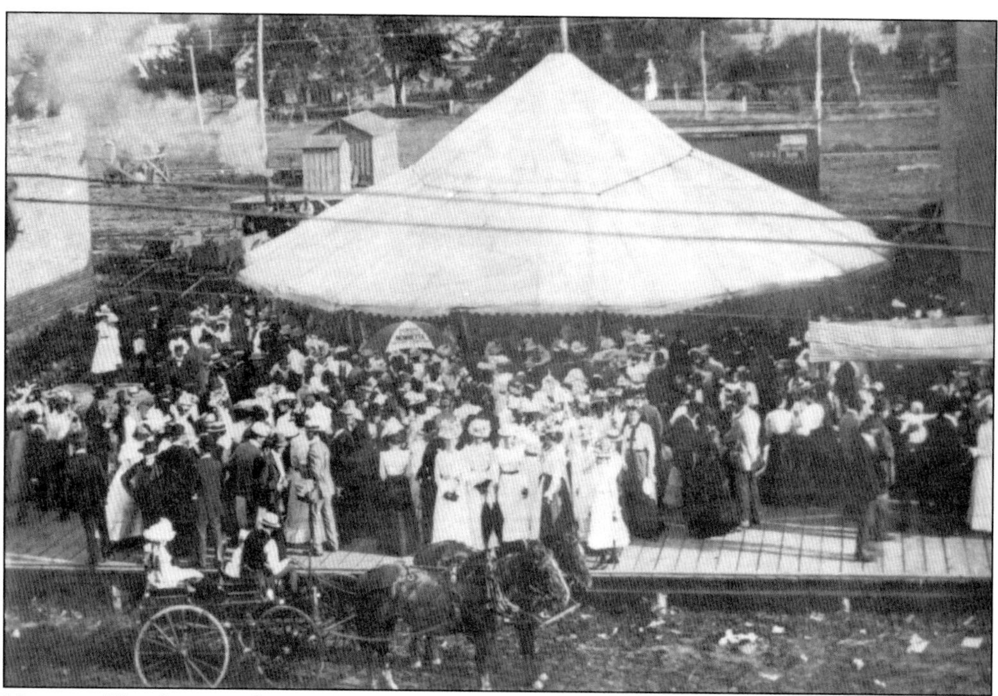

Harrison Allender arrived in Washington County with his parents in the 1850s. He began operating a horse-powered merry-go-round—perhaps the first in the state—in the 1880s. He purchased a steam-powered one in 1892, and it was featured in almost all of the county's celebrations until Allender sold it in 1916.

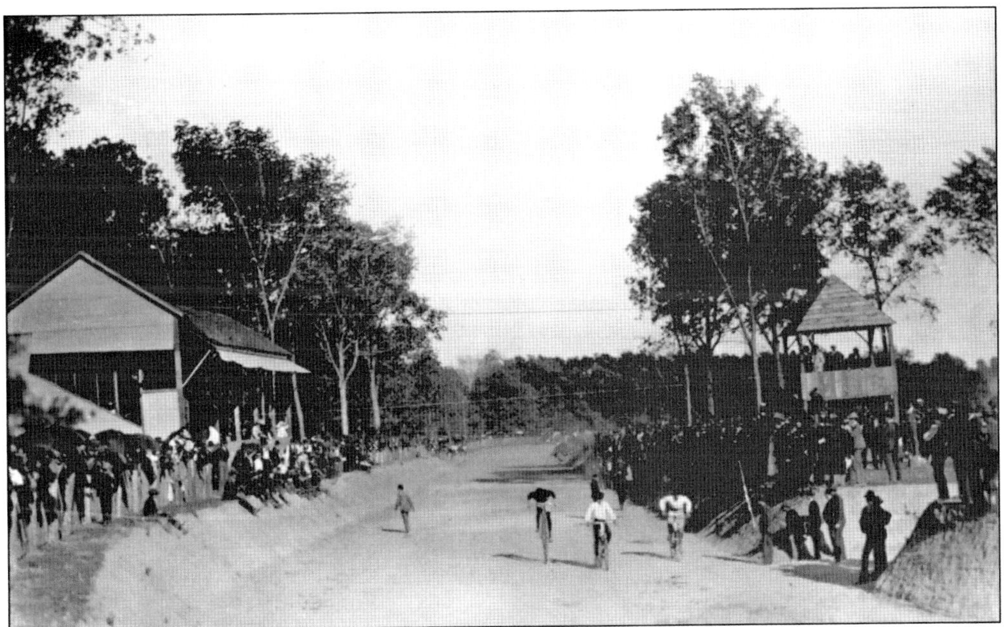

The Washington County Agricultural Society organized in 1853 to sponsor the first Washington County Fair. The first several fairs were held on the south edge of town, growing each year until, by 1866, the event was moved to its new grounds on the west edge of town. This photograph shows bicycle races at the fairgrounds around 1897.

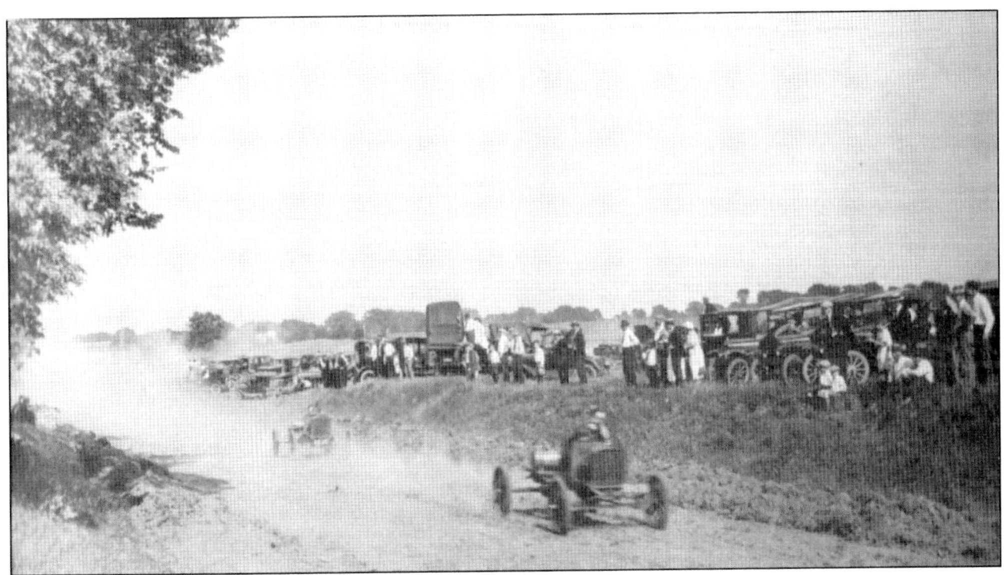

Automobile races replaced bicycle races at the fairgrounds by the 1920s. This c. 1922 photograph shows a race in progress.

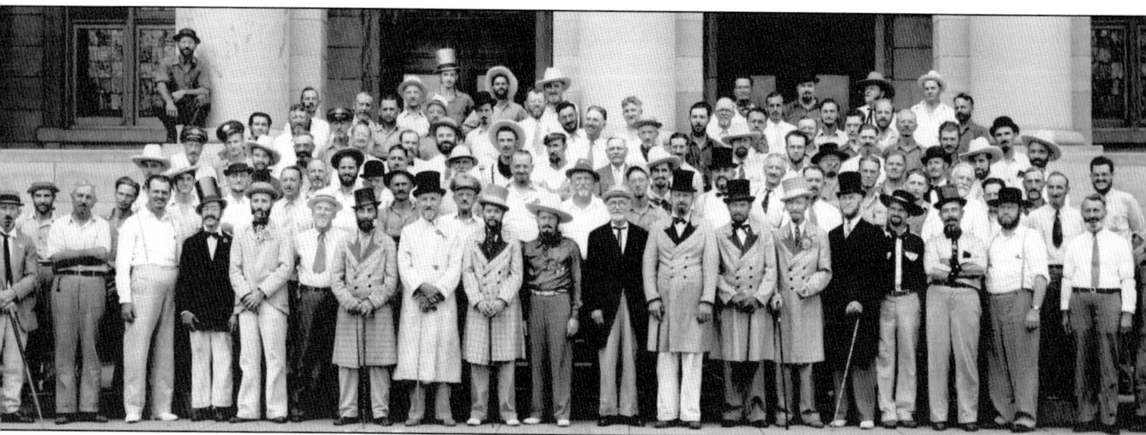

In honor of the city's centennial celebration in 1939, many of Washington's men grew beards. This photograph, taken on the steps of the Methodist church, shows members of the unofficial Washington Whisker Club.

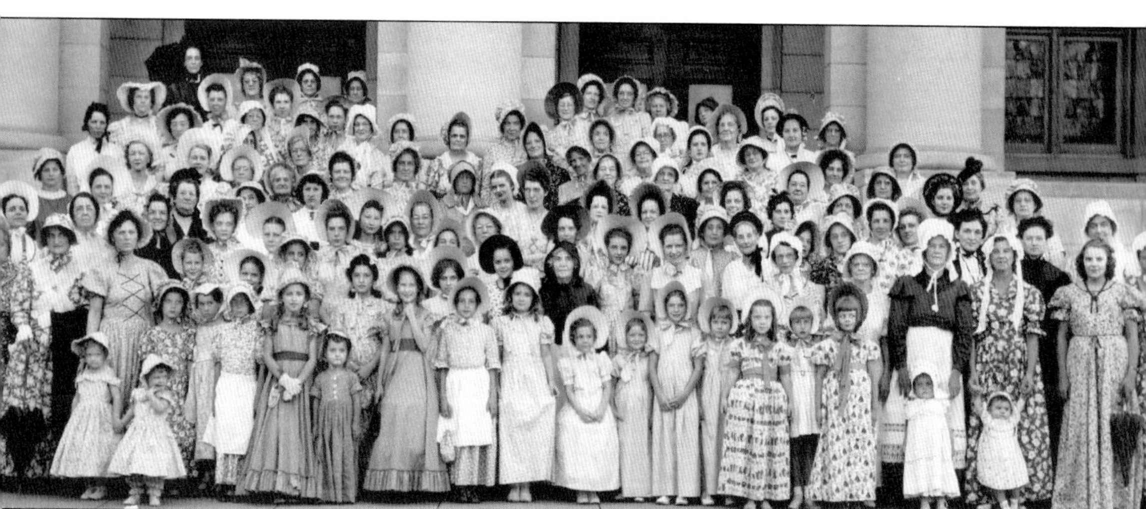

A women's organization formed to celebrate the city's centennial as a companion group to the men's Washington Whisker Club. The Sunbonnet Club, as it was called, was also photographed on the steps of the Methodist church.

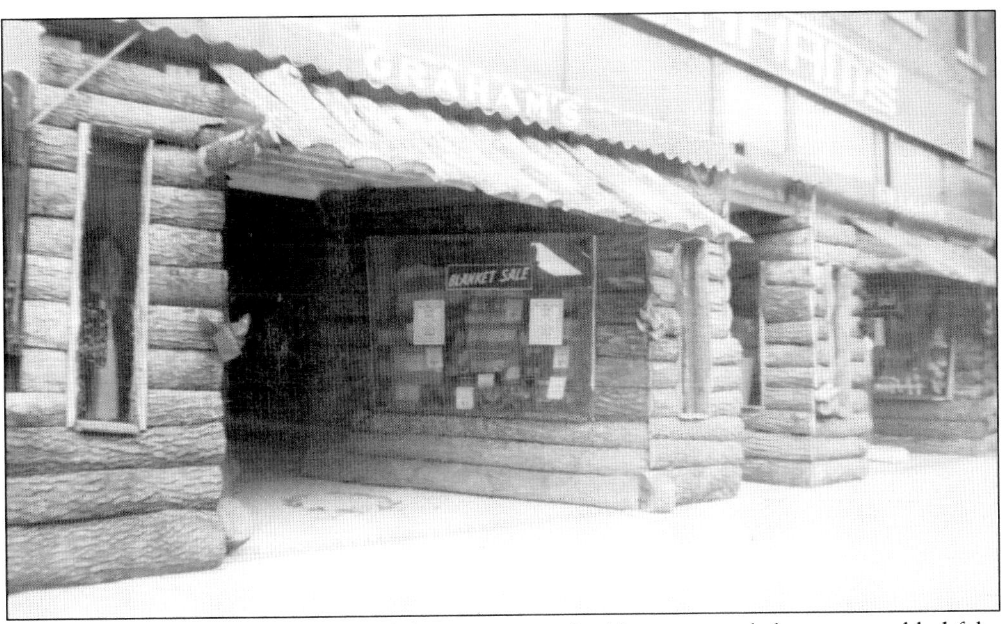

During the 1939 city centennial celebration, many buildings around the square added fake log facades. This is Graham's Department Store, which opened in the early 1920s at 112 West Main Street.

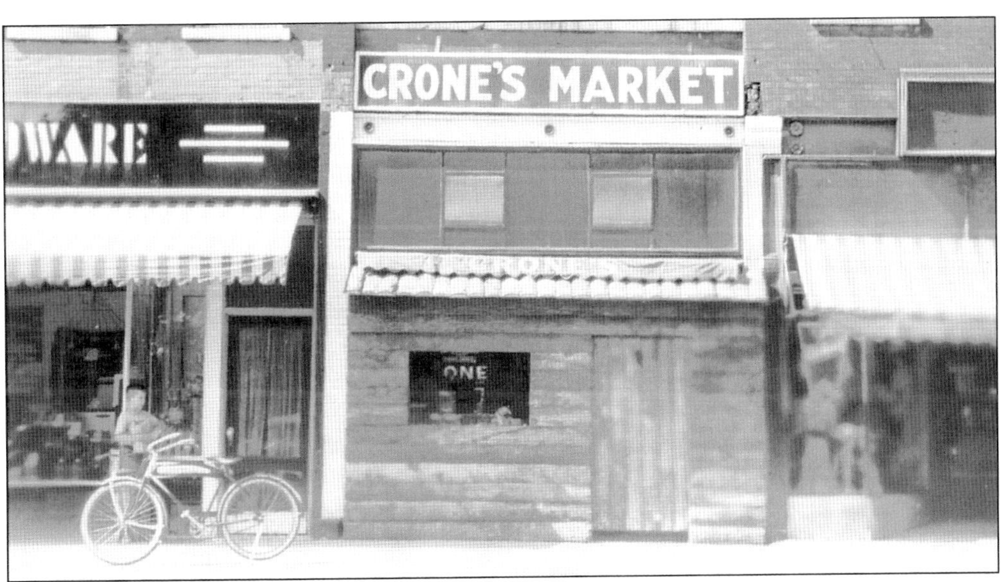

Crone's Market, at 114 West Main Street, is shown here during the centennial celebration. Crone's began in the early 1900s and continued in the grocery business until the mid-1960s. For many years, it was part of the Jack Sprat grocery chain.

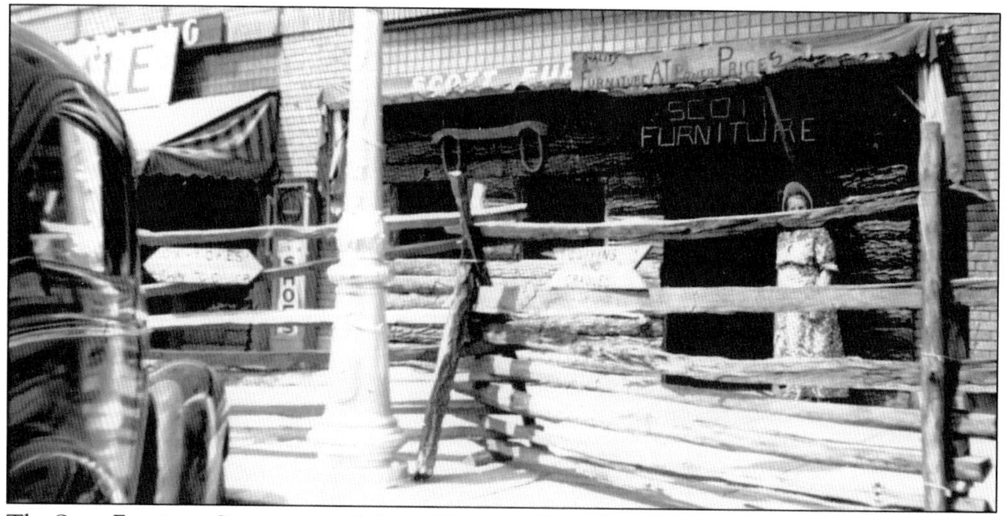

The Scott Furniture Store occupied the old Everson Block (Masonic Building) on the north side of the square when it burned in January 1930. The store reopened in the new Masonic Building. Here, it is decorated for the city's 1939 centennial, with split rail fence added for the celebration.

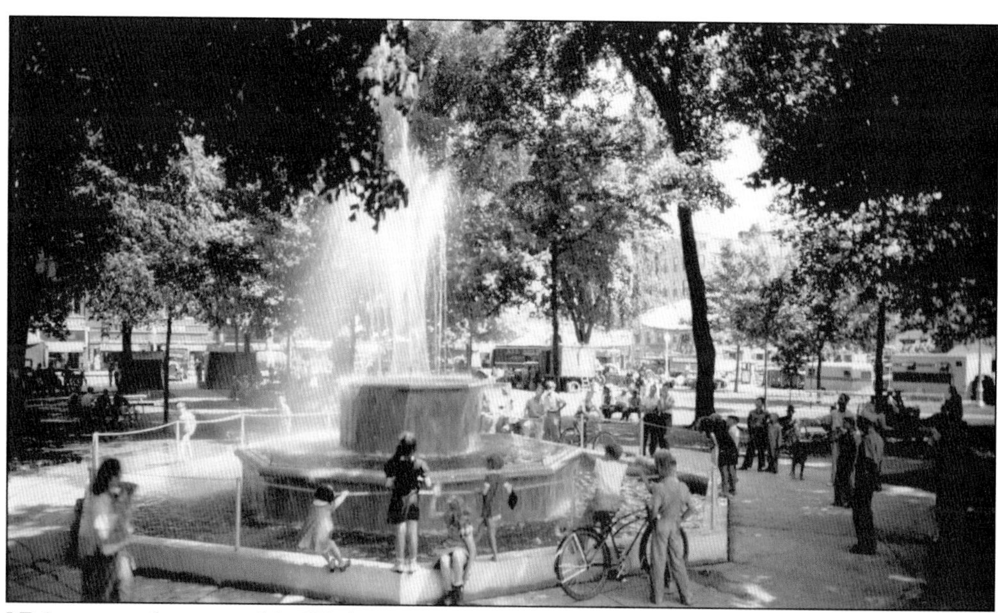

J.E. Lemmon, chairman of the Washington Park Board, got the idea for a fountain while vacationing in the Missouri Ozarks. The board had some money for the project, but a public fundraising campaign brought in the remaining $2,000 that was needed. The Centennial Fountain, in the middle of Central Park, was dedicated on August 7, 1939, as part of Washington's centennial celebrations.

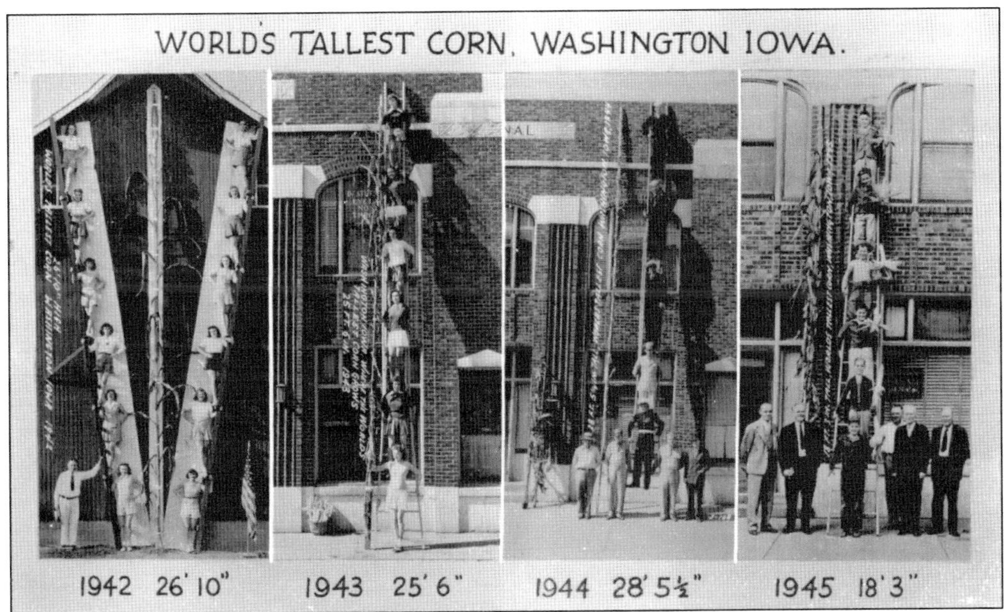

The *Washington Evening Journal* began a "tall-corn" contest in 1938. Don Radda won the competition for several years. This postcard shows the winning stalks from 1942 to 1945. The ladies in the 1942 photograph are arranged in a V for victory in World War II. Radda established a world record in 1946 with a stalk that measured 31 feet and seven-eighths of an inch.

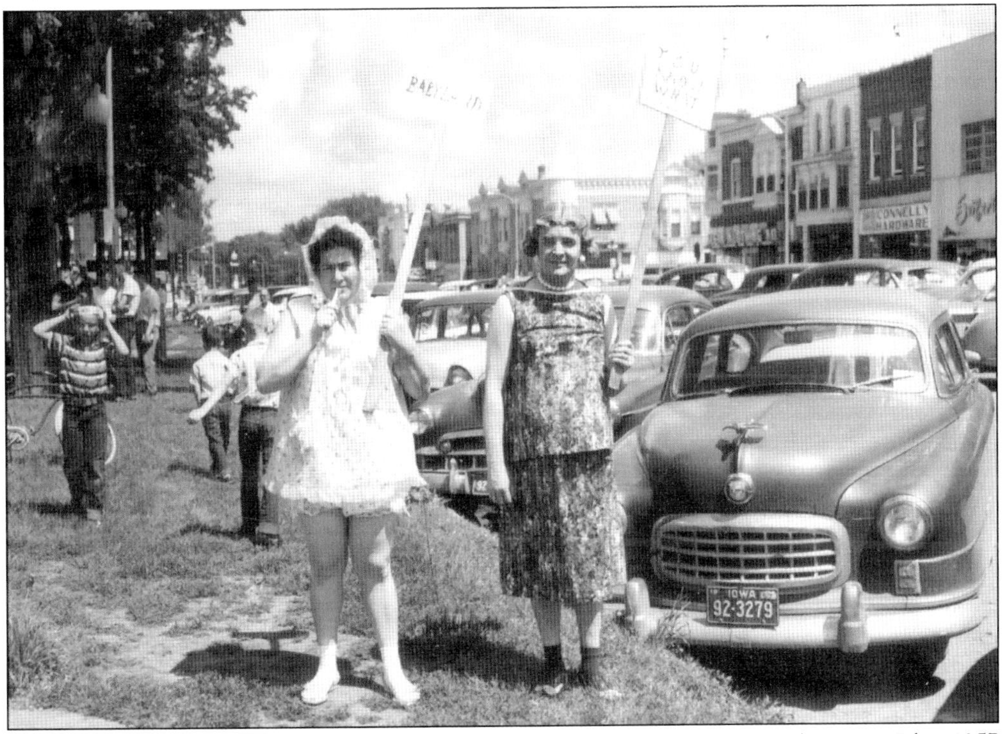

Begun in 1947, Ridiculous Days is an annual event to promote downtown shopping. This 1957 photograph shows Cathleen Godfrey (left) and Tom Duncan, winners of the first and second prizes for best individual costume.

Consistent with our mission to preserve history on a local level, this book was printed in South Carolina on American-made paper and manufactured entirely in the United States. Products carrying the accredited Forest Stewardship Council (FSC) label are printed on 100 percent FSC-certified paper.

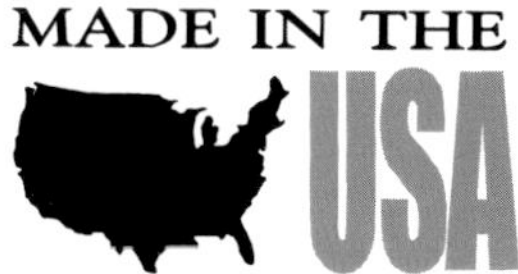